Multiculturalism in East Asia

Asian Cultural Studies:
Transnational and Dialogic Approaches

The series advances transnational intellectual dialogue over diverse issues that are shared in various Asian countries and cities.

Series Editor

Koichi Iwabuchi, Professor of Media and Cultural Studies and Director of Monash Asia Institute, Monash University, Australia

Editorial Collective

Ien Ang (University of Western Sydney)
Chris Berry (King's College London)
John Erni (Hong Kong Baptist University)
Daniel Goh (National University of Singapore)
Ariel Heryanto (Australian National University)
Hyun Mee Kim (Yonsei University)

Titles in the Series

Multiculturalism in East Asia

A Transnational Exploration of Japan, South Korea and Taiwan

Edited by
Koichi Iwabuchi, Hyun Mee Kim
and Hsiao-Chuan Hsia

ROWMAN & LITTLEFIELD
INTERNATIONAL

London • New York

Published by Rowman & Littlefield International, Ltd.
Unit A, Whitacre Mews, 26-34 Stannary Street, London SE11 4AB
www.rowmaninternational.com

Rowman & Littlefield International, Ltd. is an affiliate of Rowman & Littlefield
4501 Forbes Boulevard, Suite 200, Lanham, Maryland 20706, USA
With additional offices in Boulder, New York, Toronto (Canada), and Plymouth (UK)
www.rowman.com

British Library Cataloguing in Publication Data
A catalogue record for this book is available from the British Library

ISBN: HB 978-1-7834-8497-3
     PB 978-1-7834-8498-0

Library of Congress Cataloging-in-Publication Data
Names: Iwabuchi, Koichi, 1960- editor of compilation. | Kim, Hyun Mee, editor of
   compilation. | Hsia, Hsiao-Chuan, editor of compilation.
Title: Multiculturalism in East Asia : a transnational exploration of Japan, South Korea
   and Taiwan / edited by Koichi Iwabuchi, Hyun Mee Kim, and Hsiao-Chuan Hsia.
Description: London ; New York : Rowman & Littlefield International, [2016]
   | Series: Asian cultural studies : transnational and dialogic approaches |
   Includes bibliographical references and index.
Identifiers: LCCN 2016033423 (print) | LCCN 2016034326 (ebook) |
   ISBN 9781783484973 (cloth : alkaline paper) | ISBN 9781783484980
   (paperback : alkaline paper) | ISBN 9781783484997 (Electronic)
Subjects: LCSH: Multiculturalism—East Asia. | Multiculturalism—Japan. |
   Multiculturalism—Korea (South) | Multiculturalism—Taiwan. | Transnationalism—
   Social aspects—East Asia. | Minorities—Government policy—East Asia. |
   East Asia—Ethnic relations—Government policy. | Japan—Ethnic relations—
   Government policy. | Korea (South)—Ethnic relations—Government policy. |
   Taiwan—Ethnic relations—Government policy.
Classification: LCC DS509.5.A1 M85 2016 (print) | LCC DS509.5.A1 (ebook) |
   DDC 320.56/1—dc23 LC record available at https://lccn.loc.gov/2016033423

∞™ The paper used in this publication meets the minimum requirements of American
National Standard for Information Sciences—Permanence of Paper for Printed Library
Materials, ANSI/NISO Z39.48-1992.

Printed in the United States of America

Contents

Chapter 1

Rethinking Multiculturalism from a Trans-East-Asian Perspective

Koichi Iwabuchi, Hyun Mee Kim and Hsiao-Chuan Hsia

The first decade of the twenty-first century has witnessed the profusion of multicultural policies and discourses in East Asian countries, including in Japan, South Korea, and Taiwan, which have been historically identified as more "ethnically homogenous" than most other countries in the world (Castles and Davision 2000). While these three countries have not yet developed a comprehensive, consistent policy on migration and multiculturalism, the increasing number of migrants they have accepted and the intensifying cultural diversity that accompanies have already posed vital social issues they are faced with in this new century. This edited volume examines the growing multicultural encounters, the accompanying policy discussions and racialized discourses on cultural diversity, as well as the processes of political and cultural negotiation that the marginalized newcomers and old-comers are drawn into. In addition to a problematic legacy of the Japanese imperial project, Japan, South Korea, and Taiwan share an experience of inter-Asian migration in the process of ethno-cultural globalization since the late 1980s. In these three countries—in addition to their own indigenous or long-term racial and ethnic minorities—the number of foreign-national residents, migrants, and people of mixed heritage has risen notably in the last two to three decades. Although none of the governments welcomed migrants with open arms, the influx of laborers and international marriage migrants has been observed, primarily from China and Southeast Asia. More recently, due to the sharply declining birth rate and the rapidly aging population, with a strong push from domestic industrial sectors, governments in Japan, South Korea, and Taiwan have begun to discuss under what conditions migrants should be accepted and what policies should be implemented. In this context, there has been a growing focus on increased multicultural interactions within their borders and the impacts of cultural diversity on the fabric of their nations in the three countries.

This book adds to the emerging scholarly literature on multiculturalism in East Asia (e.g., Kymlicka and He 2005; Parreñas and Kim 2011; Eng, Collins & Yeoh 2013; Nagy 2014; Kim 2014) and takes a unique trans-East-Asian comparative and collaborative approach to examining emergent multicultural situations in Japan, South Korea, and Taiwan. In addition to contextualizing the situation in each of the countries represented, the contributors to this volume have been asked to consciously reference and compare domestic situations with other East Asian cases as well as to situate their cases in a wider, transnational context. Our intention was to add relevant voices from East Asia to our understanding of multiculturalism as a set of policies, discourses and practices that manage, negotiate with, and embrace growing human mobility and accompanied cultural diversity—a field that has developed primarily in Euro-American and Australian contexts. Our book also aims to denationalize the discussion of multiculturalism as a policy for managing cultural diversity within the nation-state. A trans-East-Asian perspective is significant as it elucidates the shared-ness and the "similarity-in-difference" when examining multicultural issues in Japan, South Korea, and Taiwan, as it endows us with fresh insights into the multicultural issues in a more transnationally informed sense. A full understanding of both the possibilities and limitations of multicultural policies, discourses, and practices as they have been addressed by national policy makers, local communities, NGOs, NPOs, civic organizations, and the migrant subjects themselves in the three societies will contribute to a renewed discussion of how one might advance a more multicultural future in domestic contexts as well as through transnational cooperation, dialogue, and mutual empowerment. In the following, we will offer our rationale for the consideration of trans-East-Asian multiculturalism by discussing in more detail the socio-historical backgrounds and the key issues that the three countries share.

CRISIS OF SOCIAL REPRODUCTION AND THE MIGRATION "BOOM"

We have been observing the growing impact of globalization and neoliberalism resulting in domestic and interregional migrations, which in turn has generated a wide range of changes that have deepened interdependency among and mobilities across nation-states in this new "age of migration" (Castles and Davidson 2000). East Asian countries are not exceptions to this trend, though they were latecomers in accepting migrants. Unlike the United States and European countries that encouraged family migration when faced with labor shortages after the 1960s, the three nations of East Asia—Japan, South Korea, and Taiwan—managed to achieve rapid economic development relying on their own ample domestic labor and, thus, did not actively accept migrants. However, these nation-states have been facing a demographic crisis of considerable proportion since the 1980s due to low fertility rates, a rapidly aging population, and a decline in able-bodied workers. In 2013, the birth rates in Japan, South Korea, and Taiwan were 1.39, 1.24, and 1.11 respectively. According to the United Nation's International Migration 2014, the percentage of the population over 65 years in Japan stood at 24.8%, South Korea at 12.3%, and Taiwan at 11.6%.[1] In Japan, the number of foreign-national residents (except short-time visitors) as of 2015 was 2,232,189 according to the Japanese Ministry of Justice, which is nearly 1.8% of the total registered population.[2] In South Korea, at the end of 2014, there were 1,797,618 foreign residents, who accounted for 3.1% of the total registered population of 51,141,463. That means that 1 out of 32 persons is a foreign resident.[3] In Taiwan, as of February 2016, the number of foreign-national residents was 642,991 (excluding those who were married to Taiwanese nationals and who entered with temporary visas)[4] and the population of non-Taiwanese married to Taiwanese nationals (including those who are already naturalized) was 511,623, which is 4.9% of the total registered population.[5] Of these foreign residents, 53.0%, 55.3%, and 71.73% were female in Japan, South Korea, and Taiwan, respectively. All the three countries sought to tackle these demographic changes to secure workforces through interventions in marriage and family structures, but were faced with challenges. This was mainly due to the significant increase in the tuition fees with the marketization of education and the lack of welfare benefits to support care for children and the elderly population, which have brought substantial financial burdens on families, and hence have thwarted the expectations for a better quality of life through having a family.

All three countries eventually turned to recruiting temporary labor from abroad to supplement their labor force since the late 1980s, when they faced serious labor shortages—particularly in the low-paying and low-technology jobs. Japan was the first to adopt such policy measures, the Industrial Training System, in 1990. Taiwan followed in 1992 with its Employment Services Act, and South Korea followed soon after with the Industrial Trainee Program in 1993. The three programs bore similarities; unless they were skilled migrants, most foreigners were admitted as workers only who, upon completion of their employment contracts, were forbidden from remaining and settling in the country and seeking permanent residency or naturalization. These restrictions have much to do with the three countries preserving *jus sanguinis* citizenship, which accords citizenship on the basis of a blood relationship with the dominant ethnic group in each nation-state, conventionally determined by the male line of kinship. Furthermore, the "guest" workers were not allowed to bring close family members (e.g., spouses or children) with them during their period of legal sojourn. Thus, from the start, these countries introduced an explicit system to control the number of temporary migrants within their borders.

Because of historical ties with their expatriate populations, Japan and South Korea gave preference to people with the same "ethnic" root when recruiting migrants—a system we can term "co-ethnic" migration. Thus, Japan turned first to the "Nikkeijin"—its out-migrants resident in Brazil, Peru, and other Central and South American countries, encouraging "return migration" under specific conditions in the 1990s. Differentiating these Nikkei from other migrants, the government issued a special visa that allowed them to stay in Japan for a long term, eventually permanently. South Korea, upon adoption of its Employment Permit System (EPS) in 2003 to replace the much abused and maligned "guest worker" system, began to accept workers from 15 Asian nations to work in small- and medium-scale labor-intensive industries. However, much like Japan, rather than opening the doors to all Asian citizens equally, they adopted rules that were skewed toward their own "co-ethnic" populations from Northeast China (called "Chosôn-jok" in Korean) and from Central Asia (the "Koryô-in"), which gave particular advantages through what they called the "work and visit system." On the other hand, due to political reasons, despite requests from many employers who would prefer to hire migrants from the same linguistic and cultural background, Taiwanese policy has strictly forbidden the entry of Chinese migrants from the People's Republic of China (PRC). PRC workers are permitted to work only as crewmen and not allowed to set "foot" on Taiwan's land (Tseng 2004). Taiwan looked instead to migrants from Southeast Asian countries, including Indonesia, Thailand, the Philippines, and Vietnam, for human resources.

Another important point that the three nations have in common is the feminization of migration. While migrants used to be predominantly male from less developed countries in Asia to supplement the domestic labor force, the most prominent feature of the new age of migration in East Asia is the drastic rise of female migrants from Asian countries for international marriage, working in the caring professions and light industry. The number of Asian female migrants crossing national boundaries to marry, to work as domestic helpers and nurses, and to perform service labor has increased dramatically since the late 1980s (Parreñas 2001; Ehrenreich and Hochschild 2002; Piper and Roces 2003; Hsia 2004; Constable, ed. 2005; Suzuki 2005). Reproductive and caring labor, which used to be confined to the private and domestic sphere, has increasingly become a marketable commodity with concrete exchange value on the trans-Asian market. This is due not only to the widening of the economic gaps within Asia, which has activated intra-Asian migration in parallel to that from Asia to the West, but also to the crisis of social reproduction experienced in these three East Asian countries.

Japan, South Korea, and Taiwan share the welfare state regime—characterized as predominantly *productivist* developmental state under the influence of Confucianism (Holliday 2000). That is, caring for frail family members including young children and elders is considered to be a family responsibility, typically women's, rather than a social issue to be dealt with by the state. While it is becoming increasingly difficult for women in Japan, South Korea, and Taiwan to stay at home to carry out these care duties within the family, as the rate of female employment and the size of the aging population increase, many married women look for substitutes when they are unable or unwilling to perform these duties. The lack of public intervention has thus turned the rising need for care work into a profitable market niche. Migrant women from less developed countries are therefore recruited to provide reproductive labor for the "maintenance" and "renewal" of productive labor (Burawoy 1976) in these countries, including migrant domestic workers and marriage migrants. This reproduction crisis has resulted in "the restructuring of reproduction," in which women from less developed countries migrate to perform reproductive labor for the more developed countries—that is, in the reverse direction to the restructuring of production (Hsia 2015).

It may seem contradictory that, while implementing policies to prevent the permanent settlement of migrants in their countries, a rapid increase in the number of female marriage migrants has been encouraged in Japan, South Korea, and Taiwan. However, one must understand that deep social changes in the gendered division of labor, which drove this phenomenon of gendered labor migration, had already become prominent in the three countries as early as the early 1980s. A classically patriarchal family structure—where men bear the responsibility for being the family breadwinners while women are homemakers/home-managers—worked to support rapid economic development when jobs were plentiful. However, the position of the male breadwinner became more tenuous as more women began to receive higher levels of education and entered the labor market. The number of lower class men who were no longer able to share in the economic growth and became increasingly disadvantaged in the marriage market rose in both urban and rural areas, while the number of women who could reject marriage as the "natural" life choice grew. Recent studies emphasize this growing devaluation of low-class men on the marriage market from the 1990s onwards, particularly those from rural farming-fishing villages (Lee 2010, 2013; Yen-Fen Tsen 2010).

In Japan, the men who take over farmland from their aged parents have primarily become the domestic partners of international marriages. Of all marriages, 0.4% were international in 1965, 0.93% by 1980, which had jumped to 5.77% by 2005 (Liaw et al. 2010: 53). The rate of international marriages peaked in 2006 at 6.11% of all marriages (40,000 couples) and seems to have stabilized at about 20,000 couples per year. The number of international marriages in 2014 represented 3.3% of the total of all marriages in Japan;[6] 1 in 30 marriages is between a Japanese national and a foreigner. In Japan's case, the difficult work, the maintenance of tradition, and the rural-to-urban migration of young women all contributed to the severity of the problem of unmarried men in the farming villages, especially in the north-eastern provinces. In the 1980s, 56% of the non-Japanese wives were of Korean extraction, but since the 1990s this expanded to include Chinese, Filipina, and Thai women. The Japanese national government lacks any central policy, and all of the "multicultural"-related services have been dealt with by local governments, as discussed in Chapter 4.

Of the three Asian countries, Taiwan has been experiencing the most rapid increase in international marriages, with typically the farmers and men in unskilled manufacturing partnering foreign brides. Beginning in the mid-1980s, and growing rapidly in the 1990s, by 2002, one in every four new marriages in Taiwan was between a domestic citizen and a foreigner, although the percentage decreased after 2003 and has hovered between 15% and 20% of all marriages registered annually. In 2014, 12.3% of all newly wed couples were Taiwanese nationals and foreign spouses, among whom 77.5% were female foreign spouses. The vast majority of foreign spouses are women from Mainland China and Southeast Asian countries, including Vietnam, Indonesia, the Philippines, Thailand, and Cambodia. As of 2015, over 510,000 women had moved to Taiwan through marriage migration.

Following these two countries, South Korea also began to actively recruit foreign brides for farmers and urban working-class men who occupied disadvantaged positions in the domestic marriage market. The term "multicultural family" sprang up in South Korea to describe such cross-border marriages in a context where such foreign women were seen as participants in a national project to sustain the reproduction of Korean families as building blocks of the nation and to compensate for the country's declining population (Kim 2011). As of the end of the year 2013, 73.9% of international brides came from just three countries: China (33.1%), Vietnam (31.5%), and the Philippines (9.2%). Of the 235,942 female marriage migrants, 86,178 (about 30%) have been granted Korean citizenship (Korea Bureau of Statistics 2014).

In Japan, South Korea, and Taiwan, with a strong sense of "ethnic homogeneity," the mounting birth rate of children of mixed heritage as well as the increase of migrants has begun to cause some concern, as it not only seriously challenges the traditional view of "ethnic homogeneity" but also of ethnicity-based citizenship. The next section will discuss this key issue shared among the three countries in detail to provide a renewed perspective to the discussion of multiculturalism.

BEYOND A MONO-ETHNIC NOTION OF CITIZENSHIP

The notion of multiculturalism carries with it a specific historical context. With heightened globalization, the traditional notion that associates citizenship with a single nation-state—a space imagined to be culturally and morally homogenous—has increasingly come under attack. Several scholars claim that national citizenship has lost its importance in the present era of globalization because the exclusionary practices of citizenship are ill-equipped to deal with an age of large-scale, heterogeneous migratory movements. The concept of post-national citizenship has thus been proposed in the hopes that international human rights law would "provide a tool for sculpting a more inclusionary model of citizenship" (Lister 1997: 60).

However, since this proposal is primarily based on the studies of guest workers in Europe, critics have argued that the European experience cannot be easily generalized into a widespread shift toward post-national citizenship (e.g., Joppke 1998; Parreñas 2001; Piper and Roces 2003). It has been pointed out that despite the proliferation of international conventions and human rights instruments, national citizenship, to a large extent, still determines the rights that different categories of migrants are able to exercise (Kofman et al. 2000; Castles and Davidson 2000; Ghai 1999). Moreover, while many guest workers may increasingly enjoy social and civic rights, they often do not possess political rights. Without formal rights to vote or stand for office, immigrants can take little part in the formulation and implementation of policies that may impact, positively or negatively, on their social entitlements and civil liberties.

Multicultural citizenship is an alternative proposed by scholars who recognize both the importance and limits of political citizenship, and is based on the idea that the nation-state incorporates a degree of plurality that allows migrants to retain their cultural identities, provided they conform to political norms. This pluralism does not negate the existence of a dominant culture but recognizes the coexistence of multiple cultures. Kymlicka (1995: 5, 2001) advances a theory of minority rights in the political context of multiculturalism: "A comprehensive theory of justice in a multicultural state will include both universal rights, assigned to individuals regardless of their group membership, and certain group-differentiated rights or 'special status' for minority cultures," because all countries have a "societal culture" that places minority groups in a position of cultural inequality vis-à-vis the majority. This argument assumes the existence of clearly bounded ethnic groups and does not give much consideration to the dynamic processes of dialogic interaction and ethno-cultural commingling. Nevertheless, it may have some relevance to societies like Japan, South Korea, and Taiwan, where the cultural rights of ethnic minorities have not been sufficiently recognized and secured, though how the notion of multicultural citizenship is to be defined and adapted in East Asian contexts remains a challenging question.

In East Asia, citizenship itself continues to be identified with the ethnicized concept of the "nation," and thus, the existence of migrants, returnees, or children of mixed heritage deserves critical attention. It is relevant to larger general issues surrounding the legal rights of citizens and the conditions of belonging as well as the conditions of citizenship in these countries. With the rise in the number of migrants in Japan, South Korea, and Taiwan, more attention has been paid to multicultural policies and discourses. Although the Japanese government has not addressed multicultural policy at a national level, services based upon the notion of "multicultural co-living" (*tabunka-kyōsei*) have been initiated in local communities in Japan since the early 1990s and the government furthered this localized dealing with "foreign residents" in 2006. In the same year, the South Korean government abruptly announced that the nation was in a state of "transition to a multicultural, multi-ethnic society." Translating words into deeds, the government funded and implemented a variety of programs to help migrant women settle in South Korea and established over 200 support centers across the country for these so-called "multicultural families." In the case of Taiwan, in part to distinguish itself from the PRC, in 1997, the constitutional amendment declared that the state recognizes Taiwan being a nation of multi-cultures and should protect cultures of the indigenous peoples. In 2003, the Taiwanese government implemented a multicultural policy to integrate the rapidly growing number of international marriage migrants (Hsia 2013). At the same time, this emergence of a "multiculturalism" discourse in these three countries has prompted new forms of governance to manage the "differences" of ethnic minorities, migrants, and people of mixed ethnic backgrounds. South Korea and Taiwan's policy programs of multicultural accommodation were implemented in a state-led, top-down fashion and without much consultation with the persons directly affected, while there has not been any substantial policy initiative taken by the Japanese government. In such a situation, migrants and people of mixed heritage continue to need to struggle for the procedural rights to acquire citizenship in a full sense. This demonstrates that, while the concept of multicultural citizenship has been and can be co-opted for ethicised governance of multicultural situations, it remains part of the political field in which the discourses of governing and empowering immigrants are constantly contested. In this sense, multicultural citizenship still offers a possibility to be empowering and liberating in East Asian countries, where the concept of citizenship has been equalized with nationality based on blood ties to the dominant ethnic groups.

The ethnic "others" and supporting NGOs/NPOs and citizens' groups have been playing a significant role in advancing multicultural citizenship by contesting discriminatory actions and in campaigning for civil rights in all three countries. In Japan, until the 1980s, the resident "non-citizens" were largely made up of Koreans and Chinese whose families had been brought there, many forcibly, during Japan's colonial expansion prior to 1945. These "foreigners" were subject to strict exclusion, discrimination, and control. Beginning in the 1970s, the "Zainichi" (as the Korean residents in Japan are called) began a number of civil rights actions against the oppression that they were faced with. They protested hiring barriers on the basis of their ethnicity and campaigned against the discriminatory fingerprinting they were forced to undergo. In the 1980s, they campaigned against the lack of suffrage at the national and local levels of government. These civil rights actions paved the way for the arrival of the "co-ethnic" Nikkeijin workers from South America in the 1980s. By the time migrants from Southeast Asia began to arrive in Japan in the 2000s, rights to work, education, and welfare had largely been settled to the benefit of the newcomers.

The labor and cultural rights of migrants to South Korea were also gained through the efforts made by the first groups that arrived. From 2003 to 2004, migrant workers went on strike for 380 days in Myeongdong Cathedral, the main cathedral in Seoul that held a prominent place for South Korean's own struggle for democracy. The strike had two objectives: first, to bring to the attention of ordinary Korean citizens the often violent government policies of immigration crackdowns and deportations, and second, to raise opposition to the newly announced EPS. South Korean media activists also joined the strike, along with members of labor unions and unions in support of migrants. In December 2004, Migrant Worker TV (MWTV) was established. Unlike the cases of many other TV programs featuring the lives of migrants, the migrant workers at MWTV actively participated in the gathering, production, and dissemination of migrant-related news along with supporting a network of activists.

Similarly, in Taiwan, activism and social movements have played a crucial role in the making of multicultural citizenship. The state recognition of the existence of multi-cultures in the 1997 amendment of the Constitution is the result of the continuous campaigns for the rights of the indigenous peoples. Since marriage migrants have become increasingly visible in Taiwan, they have also turned into important actors in the construction of a multicultural Taiwan, through their involvement in several protests organized against unfair treatment by various central governmental agencies. On September 9, 2007, hundreds of immigrant women from Southeast Asia and Mainland China joined in a rally protesting against the financial requirements for applying for citizenship. This rally drew much media attention because it was the first time in Taiwan's history that hundreds of marriage migrants from all over Taiwan came together to hold a street demonstration. Several immigration policies have been changed, thanks to the continuous campaigns led by marriage migrants.

As Hsia (this volume) suggests, the notion of "multicultural citizenship" is useful and significant as an effective framing strategy to make the historically constituted exclusionary model of citizenship more inclusive in East Asian contexts. The idea of multicultural citizenship—though not necessarily pronounced as a goal—can be understood in the contexts of Japan, South Korea, and Taiwan as the collective actions and collaboration taken by migrants, ethnically marginalized people, and people who support them, to advance campaigns for the reform of policies and laws regarding immigration and cultural rights. However, while acknowledging its significance in facilitating such grassroots collective aspiration and practices beyond the idea of mono-ethnic citizenship in these three countries, we also need to attend to the limitations that the notion of multicultural citizenship has in advancing the fundamental transformations in society for better recognizing and dealing with multicultural realities. Particularly challenging but imperative is the advancement of national policies and society-wide learning processes that aim to caringly accept growing cultural diversity and to positively foster the idea and practice of living together in diversity. In addition to recognizing the significant achievement of grassroots practices in engaging the growing multicultural situations in East Asia, we need to consider the uneven but dynamic interactions between policy responses to administer people's inflows and accompanying cultural diversity, the extent to which grassroots collective actions succeed in challenging the exclusive notions of the nation and citizenship, and the ways in which self-empowering practices by diverse subjects in society foster cultural diversity.

STRUCTURE OF SECTIONS AND CHAPTERS

The chapters in this volume will examine these issues of multiculturalism in East Asia based on four key themes: (1) policy responses and their challenges or limitations when faced with multicultural issues; (2) the renewed generation of racialized discourses; (3) multicultural subject-makings; and finally, (4) implications for the social recognition and the empowerment of long-standing ethnic minorities.

The first section focuses on the policy responses to the growing multicultural milieu in Japan, South Korea, and Taiwan and its problems. Due to the increase in labor and marriage migration since the late 1980s, the governments of Japan, South Korea, and Taiwan began developing multicultural laws and policies. Examined together, the cases show both similarities and differences, posing the intriguing question of how to best engage with multiculturalism in those societies that have yet to develop comprehensive multicultural policies and related immigration strategies at the national level.

Wang's chapter shows that Taiwan began dealing with cultural diversity as early as the mid-1990s during its democratization phase, in response to campaigns for the cultural rights of the aboriginals and the immigrants from Mainland China several centuries ago, including the Holo- and Hakka-speaking peoples. This culminated in an amendment to the Constitution and the implementation of related policies. Taiwan was later further challenged by the rapid influx of marriage migrants from both Mainland China and the countries of Southeast Asia.

While Taiwan's response to multiculturalism was marked by gradualism and continuous policy revisions to respond to the changing demographic climate, the response from the South Korean government was more rapid and sudden. Under the Noh government, as Ahn's chapter illustrates, the multicultural law was implemented in 2006 with the abrupt announcement that South Korea was henceforth a "multicultural society." Japan has been the slowest and most reluctant to deal with its multicultural population: Iwabuchi suggests that national policy is yet to be implemented, and instead, multicultural co-living policy initiatives have been taken to support local actors in dealing with multicultural situations without allowing them to rise to the level of a national concern.

These three chapters also show varying ways in which NGOs/NPOs and citizen groups have been intervening in policy decision-making and have been incorporated within the dominant political structures. Taiwan's successful implementation of multicultural policies is, to some extent, an achievement that should be credited to NGOs' and citizen groups' activism, but these policies remain subject to co-optation by governmental agencies when multicultural situations arise (see also Hsia 2013). In South Korea, the government's rapid administrative actions appear to be progressive, but they eventually served to short-circuit and marginalize more progressive activities and views for tackling multicultural issues advanced by local NGOs and citizen groups. In Japan, NGOs/NPOs and the local government remain key players due to the absence of a cohesive national policy, but their activities are low-key and confined to particular local settings.

There are also commonalities to be noted, one of which is the above-mentioned feminized marriage migrant trend. Taiwanese and South Korea multicultural policies tend to focus on the treatment of female migrants in a patriarchal fashion, which excludes male labor and marriage migrants, while the absence of national policy in Japan has not exhibited the same tendencies at the level of policy. Another point that they share is their inability to overcome the traditional ways in which the nation-state is imagined and represented. Assurance of cultural rights, including the right to express one's ethnic solidarity without challenging the legitimacy of the nation-state, to be listened to, and to be recognized on an equal basis with the dominant ethnic groups, has always been the most difficult challenge for multicultural policy. This is because it requires a fundamental change in the way the nation's identity is conceived and communicated through such essential and taken-for-granted processes as education, media representations, and everyday practices. The cases of these three countries reveal the challenges involved in contesting the long-held ethno-racially exclusive construction of the nation and the extent to which these conceptions are embedded in administrative practice and social discourse. In addition to the need for further development of policies promoting multiculturalism, a deeper challenge is with failing to deal "head on" with the multicultural question itself (Hall 2001), which concerns the fostering of egalitarian respect for diversity as a constitutive part of national citizenship. All three countries are faced with the challenges of redefining social membership at the national level in a more open and equal manner.

In relation to this point, the second section endeavors how the rise of multicultural policies and discourses has been generated and developed hand in hand with the notions of "race." Interestingly, the rise of social discourse and related policy in response to growing multicultural situations has been observed in East Asia when the "death" of multiculturalism has been discussed in the West over the past decade. With the rise of right-wing parties in Europe, particularly since 2008 with the global recession, many nation-states around the world began to tighten their immigration policies. This shift in immigration policies was largely unsuccessful and instead only stirred up anti-immigration sentiments among the countries' long-term residents (Castles et al. 2014: 3). A similar trend of racialization of migrants has been detected in East Asia; the chapters by Kawai, Jung, and Liao consider how these processes are closely related to historically constructed narratives of the nation as well as recent attempts to reclaim national identity in an exclusivist, purist fashion against the background of growing antagonism against "foreigners" and "migrants." These chapters share a common line of critically addressing the intersections of nationalism and racism as well as the social constructions of national identity in respective historical contexts. Kawai critically examines whether and how the socially constructed image of the "Other" is reflected on Japanese students' perceptions, whereas Jung focuses on "otherness" in media representations in South Korea, and Liao critically traces othering in Taiwanese migration policies. With strong nationalistic aspirations and discourses of ethnic superiority, the emergence and presence of the "ethnic other" poses a challenging dilemma to many people in redefining their identities. A person's identity can be defined only in reference to, or as different from, various others such as migrants, foreigners, and people of mixed descents. The dichotomy of Japanese and non-Japanese, Korean and member of multicultural family, and Taiwanese and Aborigines, or migrants, are mutually defined. This dichotomized way of understanding "us" and "them" is realizable when the difference is translated into a binary between "superiority" and "inferiority" in terms of blood, descent, gender, race, class, and ethnicity. The emergence of racism is an ongoing process and also the outcome of distorted assertions of their own primordial (based on blood and ethnicity) but contemporary global identities based on the economic success of these nations on a global scale. The authors in this section endeavor to interpret how Asian nationalism (within each of the three countries) and racism are interlocking, drawing their attention to ways in which nation-building and assertion of their global ascendance and economic prosperity or downfall have been uniquely intertwined, or to ways in which "other" Asian people (as the colonized, the migrants, or the laborers) have been constantly positioned/repositioned in the framework and notions of "proper" Japanese/Korean/Taiwanese citizens.

The third section investigates the construction of multicultural subjectivity. Compared to other groups in the foreign population, marriage migrants pose the greatest challenges to the traditionally exclusionary models of citizenship, since transnational marriages involving citizens from different nation-states and their children represent living challenges to the boundaries of nation-states. As Japan, South Korea, and Taiwan have received a significant number of marriage migrants with their children growing up and becoming increasingly visible in society, those who signal "multiculturalism" in a given locale are receiving more attention. While this process of recognizing the multicultural "fact" sometimes results in tokenism and stereotyping, it also encourages the multicultural subjects themselves to feel the desire to actively express their own right to individuality and difference as citizens of the nation-state. The three chapters in this section analyze the ambivalent negotiations of the discourses of the dominant ethnic group when faced with the multicultural transformations of the nation-state, the NGOs' support of the recognition of multicultural possibilities within a given society, and the self-empowering practices of people of mixed heritage.

Kim as well as Horiguchi and Imoto examine how people of mixed race have been constructed as "problems" in society. Kim focuses upon the changing status of the children of marriage migrants in the South Korean military, an exclusively male social institution founded on the principle of Korean ethnic purity, and illustrates how these children labeled "multicultural soldiers" were banned from conscription for doubts about their combat capabilities, allegiance, and loyalty. The military was pushed to amend its policy, and the "multicultural soldiers" began to serve in 2011, and yet, the children of marriage migrants remain under special screening because they are seen as potentially dangerous citizens who cannot acquire full membership in Korean society.

Similarly, Horiguchi and Imoto's chapter shows how racial mixing has historically been a site of stigmatization in modern Japan. In particular, the boundaries of the Japanese race were heavily debated as Japan's colonies expanded in the war period. Proponents of mixed-race marriages argued that the colonized groups would be eradicated through promoting mixed marriages, while opponents feared that the purity of "superior" Japanese "blood" would be degraded through mixing with the "inferior" groups.

In recent years, the images of mixed race have become more "positive," partly because people of mixed race have been constructed as "useful" in the increasingly globalized world. "Multicultural soldiers" have been dispatched overseas to demonstrate Korea's "multicultural capacity" and seen as contributors of Korean military's transnational efforts. The Japanese popular culture industry has valued mixed-race *hafu* celebrities with images of good looks, exoticism, and cosmopolitanism. While these seemingly positive images of mixed race have developed, thanks to their "contribution" to the state and the market, rather than their full membership in society, activist movements of the marriage migrants, youth of mixed heritage and NGO supporters have also significantly helped transform and transgress their symbolic images. Horiguchi and Imoto illustrate how the parents of mixed-race children and the youth of mixed heritage themselves have actively challenged the popularized images of mixed race and become claims-makers of their own subjectivity, for example, by the parents advocating the use of new terms, such as *kokusai-ji* (literally "international children") and *daburu* ("double"), bringing together shared but rarely spoken conflicts of identities.

Social movements, particularly from the grassroots level, have been crucial to the making of the migrants' multicultural subjectivity. Hsia's chapter focuses on analyzing how marriage migrants in Taiwan actively involved in the movement for acquiring the rights and welfare of immigrants and migrants have gradually developed their identities as multiculturalistic subjects, who endeavor to put the ideal of multiculturalism into praxis by being reflexive of their own attendes and behaviors towards other nationalities and ethnicities. Many debates have emerged around the issue of how the host society should deal with the influx of im/migrants of diverse cultural backgrounds. Hsia argues that a problematic implication of such debates is that only the citizens of the host country have to learn to be multiculturalistic, whereas the im/migrants automatically embrace multiculturalism. Hsia's chapter reveals that marriage migrants also have prejudices against other ethnicities and nationalities, and illustrates that it is in the process of their involvement in the social movements that their identities have broadened to become multiculturalistic subjects.

The emergent discussions on multicultural policy to deal with cultural diversity tend to focus on recent migrants and often disregard the existence of other long-standing ethnic minorities in the nation-state. However, the rise of multiculturalism policy has been significantly impacted by the past events concerning historically significant minorities in terms of social (non)recognition, renewed marginalization, and self-empowering strategies. The last section considers these long-standing ethnic minorities by examining the cases of the indigenous Taiwanese in Taiwan, the Chinese-Korean (*Hwagyo*) community that predates any recent migrations, and the Korean residents in Japan (*Zainichi*), whose presence can be traced back to the pre-1945 colonial period.

First of all, the very existence of the long-standing ethnic minorities debunks the myth that these three countries were mono-ethnic and have only recently become multicultural because of the influx of (new) migrants. Secondly, the activism of these long-standing ethnic minorities has significantly contributed to the current discourse of multiculturalism in these countries. Kuan's chapter illustrates how the social movement for indigenous peoples starting in the 1980s has propelled the Taiwan government to institutionalize multicultural policies, and Kawabata argues that the discourse and practice of *tabunka kyōsei* (multicultural co-living) has been embraced through grassroots activities by *Zainichi* Koreans since the 1970s.

Thirdly, by examining the conditions of the long-standing ethnic minorities, the three chapters demonstrate the "cosmetic" nature of current official multicultural policies; the policies legitimate the political regimes and adjust to globalization, and whether they reflect a genuine intention to respect and appreciate differences may be contested. For example, Kuan shows how the multiculturalistic discourse in Taiwan oversimplified indigenous cultures as static in status and overlooked the historical injustice against them, notably the case of land grabbing. Without facing the injustice in the past, the current multicultural discourse that may seem popular on surface may ironically generate backlash against the ethnic minorities. In the Korean case, Shin illustrates how in the past the *Hwagyo* was perceived as the sole "non-Korean" group in the name of nationalism, which led to hardships due to many regulations on property and business as well as displacement in the name of inner-city redevelopment. Korean society remained silent when the *Hwagyo* faced these hardships, but they have started speaking out loudly about *Hwagyo* owning real estate in the face of the rising power of China, leading to aggression on *Hwagyo*. As Kawabata suggests, the neo-nationalists will continue to attack the ethnic minority via discourse of "youth frustration," if the economic depression persists for an extended period.

Lastly, all three chapters in the last section demonstrate that ethnic cultures and identities are not fixed but fluctuate over time because of the changing local, national, regional, and international social-economic and political contexts. As Shin argues, multicultural polices need to overcome the essentialist notion of ethno-national cultures. Moreover, notwithstanding their limitations, it is not productive to oversimplify multicultural policies as mere tokenism.

Kuan shows how the institutionalization of multiculturalism has led to redistribution of governmental resources, which underpins the de-stigmatization and revitalization of indigenous cultures in many aspects. To reimagine what is "multicultural" in a substantial sense, as Kawabata and Kuan suggest, civil groups, particularly the ethnic minorities themselves, need to actively participate in the discourse of multiculturalism, by constantly challenging and altering official multicultural policies as well as problematizing rigidly demarcated "ethnic" boundaries, especially those between "newcomers" and "old-comers."

Joined together, all chapters in this volume elucidate the commonalities and differences regarding some of the key issues around growing multicultural situations and ethnic diversity in Japan, South Korea, and Taiwan. The issues in a trans-East-Asian scope beyond a nation-centric view refresh and deepen our understanding of cultural politics of inclusion and exclusion as well as the possibilities and difficulties to transform the societies by fostering the praxis of living together in diversity. We hope that the fruits of this transnational collaboration demonstrated in this book prompt social scientists and policy makers to recognize the necessity to develop cross-border collaborations to tackle the transnationally shared issues that were previously contained within national borders.

NOTES

1. http://esa.un.org/unmigration/documents/WallChart2013.pdf
2. http://www.moj.go.jp/nyuukokukanri/kouhou/nyuukokukanri04_00057.html
3. http://www.index.go.kr
4. http://sowf.moi.gov.tw/stat/month/m6-05.xls
5. https://www.immigration.gov.tw/public/Attachment/632811431580.xlsx
6. http://www.e-stat.go.jp/SG1/estat/List.do?lid=000001137969

REFERENCES

Burawoy, Michael. 1976. "The Function of Reproduction of Migrant Labor: Comparative Material from Southern Africa and the United States." *American Journal of Sociology*, 81(5): 1050–87.
Castles, Stephen and Alastair Davison. 2000. *Citizenship and Migration: Globalization and the Politics of Belonging*. New York: Routledge.
Constable, Nicole, (ed.). 2005. *Cross-Border Marriages: Gender and Mobility in Transnational Asia*. Philadelphia: University of Pennsylvania Press.
Ehrenreich, Barbara and Arlie Russell Hochschild. 2002. *Global Woman: Nannies, Maids, and Sex Workers in the New Economy*. New York: A Metropolitan/Owl Book.

Eng, Lai Ah., Francis Leo Collins, and Brenda S. A. Yeoh. 2013. *Migration and Diversity in Asian Contexts*. Singapore: ISEAS Publishing.

Holliday, Ian. 2000. "Productivist Welfare Capitalism: Social Policy in East Asia." *Political Studies*, 48(4): 706.

Hsia, Hsiao-Chuan. 2013. "The Tug of War Over Multiculturalism: Contestation between Governing and Empowering Immigrants in Taiwan," in *Migration and Diversity in Asian Contexts*, edited by Lai Ah Eng, Francis Leo Collins and Brenda Yeoh, 130–49. Institute of Southeast Asian Studies Publishing, Singapore.

Hsia, Hsiao-Chuan. 2015. "Reproduction Crisis, Illegality, and Migrant Women under Capitalist Globalization: The Case of Taiwan," in *Migrant Encounters: Intimate Labor, the State and Mobility Across Asia*, edited by Sara Friedman and Pardis Mahdavi, 160–83. University of Pennsylvania Press.

Kim, Hyun Mee. 2011. "The Emergence of the 'Multicultural Family' and the Genderized Citizenship in South Korea," in *Contested Citizenship in East Asia: Developmental Politics, National Unity, and Globalization*, edited by K. S. Chang and B. S. Turner, 203–17. New York: Routledge.

Kim, Nam-Kook, (ed.). 2014. *Multicultural Challenges and Redefining Identity in East Asia*. Surrey, Ashgate Publishing.

Kymlicka, Will and Baogang He, (eds.). 2005. *Multiculturalism in Asia*. New York: Oxford University Press.

Nagy, Stephen Robert. 2014. "Politics of Multiculturalism in East Asia: Reinterpreting Multiculturalism." *Ethnicities*, 14(1): 160–76.

Parreñas, Rhacel Salazar and Joon K. Kim. 2011. "Special Issue: Multicultural East Asia." *Journal of Ethnic and Migration Studies*, 37(10): 1555–693.

Tseng, Yen-Fen. 2004. "Politics of Importing Foreigners: Taiwan's Foreign Labor Policy," in *Migration Between States and Markets*, edited by Han Entzinger, Marco Martiniello, and Catherine Wihtol de Wenden, chapter 7, 101–20. Ashgate Publishers.

Wang, Hong-zen and Shu-ming Chang. 2002. "The Commodification of International Marriages: Cross-border Marriage Business in Taiwan and Vietnam." *International Migration*, 40(6): 93–116.

MULTICULTURALISM POLICY DISCOURSE: CRITICAL INTERROGATION

Chapter 2

Korean Multiculturalism and Its Discontents

Ji-Hyun Ahn

On July 22, 2011, a Norwegian right-wing fundamentalist Anders Behring Breivik committed a horrific act of terrorism, using bombs and guns to attack the governing Labor Party's annual youth camp on Utoya Island in Oslo, Norway, killing more than 70 civilians. The massacre shocked the world. Yet, Breivik pleaded not guilty to criminal charges because he believed that his victims' embrace of immigration was a betrayal to Norway (2012). Breivik believed that the increasing number of immigrants in Norway, especially those who were Muslim, was a major threat to national unity.[1]

In his terrorist manifesto, Breivik mentioned Japan, Taiwan, and South Korea (hereafter, Korea) as "model countries" that had maintained their strong national identity by rejecting multiculturalism. According to a newspaper article from the *Telegraph*,

> In his Q&A section of his manifesto, Breivik answers as to which "current national political system" he admires the most. He writes:
> *I especially admire the Japanese, South Korean and Taiwanese system.* These three countries *reject multiculturalism* outright and have instead focused on maintaining and protecting their monoculture (2011; emphasis added).

Breivik was a mentally ill and violent person whose perception of Japan, Korea, and Taiwan was distorted; nevertheless, his perception that those three countries are racially homogenous was not simply the illogical assumption. Perhaps, this perception *is* the hegemonic national image circulated and shared by many people at the global level. In the case of Korea, for instance, the long-standing myth of "ethnic homogeneity" or "single ethnic nation" has been a primary principle for constructing a unified national identity, excluding various types of racial/ethnic minorities from national imagery.

Unlike Breivik's belief, however, those three countries' ethnoscapes have changed dramatically due to large-scale inter-Asian migration, which challenges the notion of ethnic homogeneity (Kymlicka and He 2005, Chua 1998, Lim 2009). As contributors to this book contend, those three countries have to come to terms with these social changes and rethink a previously hegemonic national identity of racial/ethnic homogeneity. In this process, the idea of multiculturalism, although the term is not always adopted in East Asia as Iwabuchi notes in this volume, has been mobilized by different actors in different contexts to envision a new national identity by accommodating to growing ethnic diversity. For example, in Korea after the government coined the term "multicultural society" in 2006, terms such as "multicultural family," "multicultural education," and "multicultural policy" are now used on a daily basis.

While the Korean government and media have been celebrating the new multicultural face of the nation for the past decade, the rise of anti-multiculturalism as well as hate speech toward racial others both online and offline reminds us that the struggle for a multicultural society creates social conflicts and backlash. This leads to questions like: What does this ardent acceptance of multiculturalism *really* mean to the general public? How does the rise of multiculturalism discourse, which has developed in tandem with policy discussions and implementation, challenge or reinforce the hegemonic understanding of Korea as racially homogenous? How should we envision Korea as a multicultural society?

To consider these questions, Shohat and Stam's (2003) distinction between "multicultural fact" and "multicultural project" is useful. They argue that the multicultural phenomenon as a social fact and multiculturalism as a form of ideology should be distinguished, although they are not entirely separable. Simply put, the multicultural fact or multicultural phenomenon describes a status that diverse cultures coexist, whereas multiculturalism as a project is a political and behavioral norm to be pursued through changes of political system and law (Shohat and Stam 2003). This differentiation also resonates with Hall's distinction between "multicultural question" and "multicultural-ism" (Hall 2000, 2001). Hall writes, "Whereas multiculturalism is addressed principally at ethnic and racial minority people and communities, the multi-cultural question concerns the nature of society as a whole, and thus addresses the changed conditions of everyone" (Hall 2001: 5). In other words, the multicultural question is a matter of how to envisage the future of equality with difference, which requires the whole society to consider and answer collectively. It is obvious that the current situations in Korea, Japan, and Taiwan require us to think hard about multicultural questions that we now face. While multiculturalism has been adopted by the state and a few multicultural policies were legislated within a short period of time to solve social issues related to intensifying ethnic diversity, it seems that the multicultural question of how to nurture equality with difference has barely been discussed in Korea.

This chapter maps out the status of multiculturalism in Korea and considers its problematics to continue our discussion of how to nurture a multicultural environment in Korea. This chapter consists of four sections. First, I present the current racial reconfiguration in relation to the historical context of the long-standing myth of ethnic homogeneity. Second, I discuss how the rise of multiculturalism discourse in relation to the development of multicultural policy has created a national discursive space for conceiving a multicultural society in a highly assimilative way by marginalizing progressive practices and visions that have been developed by NGOs and citizen's groups. Third, I evaluate governmental policy on multiculturalism by focusing on the legislative acts such as the Act on the Treatment of Foreigners in Korea (*jaehan oegugin cheou gibonbeob*) (2007) and the Multicultural Family Support Act (*damunhwa gajeong jiwonbeob*) (2008). I demonstrate how these multicultural policies produce gendered and racialized discrimination and marginalization against certain groups of people. Finally, I conclude the chapter by claiming that we need to (re)appropriate the multiculturalism discourse as a political site where the fight for equality and social justice takes place.

NEW ETHNOSCAPE IN CONTEMPORARY KOREA

Despite the belief that Korea is racially homogeneous, there have been several racial and ethnic groups. There are six categories of racial/ethnic others in Korea (Paik 2011, Park 2011, Eom 2011): ethnic-Chinese (*hwagyo*), Korean-Chinese (*joseonjok*), mixed-race/blood people (*honhyeol*), migrant workers (*ijunodongja*), female marriage migrants (*yeoseong-gyeolhon-iminja*), and North Korean migrants (*bukhan-italjumin*). Although their presence in Korean society has a long history, they have been invisible in public discussion and policy documents because of their otherness.

As one of the oldest ethnic minorities in Korea, the ethnic-Chinese demonstrate the course of strong ethnic nationalism in modern Korea. Some ethnic-Chinese migrated to Korea around the 1880s, but Korea is the only country in which ethnic-Chinese were not able to build and continue their diasporic communities due to Korea's strong ethnocentrism (Eom 2011). One way to block their migration to Korea was to restrict their economic activities. The Korean government placed many restrictions and penalties on the flow of ethnic-Chinese capital into Korea, fearing that the Chinese would make the country ethnically "impure" (see Eom 2011: 140). In light of these restrictions, the ethnic-Chinese found life in Korea onerous and the number of ethnic-Chinese communities gradually diminished after 1972. Another major ethnic minority group is "Amerasians," mixed-race people born to an American GI and a Korean mother after the Korean War. While the ethnic-Chinese were excluded because of their non-Korean nationality, mixed-race/blood Koreans have been discriminated against "full-blood" Koreans due to their marker of otherness inscribed to different skin color. Since there was no government support or policy on Amerasians in postwar Korea, they experienced severe discrimination and destitution; they were marginalized and underrepresented in Korean society for decades (Lee 2008b).

Given that racial/ethnic minorities have long existed in Korea, the notion of "monoracial Korea" does not necessarily refer to a social fact, but implies a hegemonic understanding of Korea as a modern nation-state. That being said, these racial/ethnic minorities experienced severe discrimination for they were not considered to be "full-blood" Koreans under the strong monoracial ideology. Yet this hegemonic understanding of Korea as racially homogenous is not as powerful as it was in the past because of Korea's social transformation since the late 1980s. By then, Korea—which used to be a labor-sending country—turned into a labor-receiving country as a result of economic growth and modernization (Dewind et al. 2012). It was under Kim Young Sam's government (1993–1998) that globalization (*segyehwa*) was introduced. Korea's globalization, like the modernization project in the 1970s and 1980s, was initiated by the state (Kim 2000, Shin 2006). The rhetoric of globalization served to create a national image of a "New Korea," and this led to globalization in many areas such as economy, culture, and politics. Ironically, in the midst of globalization, Korea was struck by the economic crisis of 1997 and had to be temporarily placed under the control of the International Monetary Fund. This economic crisis, which many Asian countries such as Thailand, Indonesia, Hong Kong, and Malaysia also experienced in 1997, led to a more flexible economic and labor system and accelerated the influx of foreign migrant labor into Korea (Moon 2000). Because of the 1997 economic crisis, neoliberal capitalism and transnational movements are restructuring economic and labor relations in Korea (Song 2011).

It is in this context that the rise of multiculturalism in Korea should be understood. Through undergoing the "neoliberal turn" after the economic crisis, global migration has accelerated as Korea seeks a new, cheap labor source from nearby Asian countries. Not only in Korea but also in other developed societies in Asia such as Japan, Singapore, and Hong Kong, the aging population and labor shortages in 3D (difficult, dangerous, and dirty) industries have expedited inter-Asian migration (Kim 2009, Lee 2011). The inter-Asian migration is particularly prevalent not only because of the short geographical distance among the countries but also because of "racial proximity" perceived as such. For this reason, Korean-Chinese were preferred as imported labor in the early stages of immigration because of their similarities with Koreans, such as appearance and language (Park 2011, Freeman 2005).

Since the late 1990s, however, there has been a huge influx of migrant workers especially from nearby Southeast Asian countries (Kim 2009, Shin 2009). This increase of migrant workers was followed by the wave of female marriage migrants, as is the case with Taiwan and Japan to different degrees. International marriage between Koreans and Asians—mostly between Korean men and non-Korean Asian women—has drastically increased since the early twenty-first century as global migration proceeds.

According to the most recent statistics, the total number of (legal) foreign residents in Korea in 2014 was 1,569,470, or 3.1% of the population. Among them, migrant workers (528,587; 34.3%) and marriage migrants (149,764; 9.5%) were two of the largest groups of foreign residents. This rapid increase in migrant workers and international marriages, initiated by the neoliberal restructuring process in the late 1990s, has become an important subject in terms of racial issues and promoted the discursive explosion of multicultural-ism in Korea since 2005 (Han 2007, Kim 2009, Kim 2007, Ahn 2012).

KOREAN MULTICULTURALISM: CIVIC MOVEMENTS AND THE DOMINANT DISCOURSE

To critically reevaluate Korean multiculturalism, we need to understand the rise of the dominant form of multiculturalism discourse in Korea that has been largely shaped and propelled by governmental policies and popular media. While the dominant discourse of multiculturalism promotes cultural diversity in an assimilative manner, adopting a seemingly positive celebratory rhetoric, there have been pushbacks against it as well. Hence, it is important to examine the broader social context in which the term "multiculturalism" acquired its currency as the new face of multicultural Korea and how progres-sive actions and views of civic organizations have been marginalized by the dominant discourse that has been developed by the government and mass media.

Scholars have discussed whether or not Korean multiculturalism is state led. While Oh and others (2007a) define Korean multiculturalism as a state-led policy and criticized its politics, others have insisted that referring to Korean multiculturalism as a state-led policy is not entirely accurate since civic organizations have been deeply engaged with multicultural issues to varying degrees even before the boom of multiculturalism (Yoon 2008, Lee 2007). While a multiculturalism policy was introduced only in 2006—much like Japan but unlike Taiwan, which introduced it in the 1990s in regard to the inclusion of Hakkas and Aborigines—the effort to build a sustainable environment for increasing numbers of immigrants has been practiced by religious organizations and NGOs/NPOs since the late 1980s. Because there was no governmental policy on importing labor until the mid-1990s, religious organizations and human rights NGOs initiated grassroots networks and actions to help migrant workers' social integration from a humanitarian perspective. In the process of building grassroots networks and communities for migrant workers, civic organizations first introduced the term "multiculturalism" in the late 1990s to reflect their needs and called for governmental support (Lee 2007, Oh 2007b). It is also worthwhile to note that in the same year, 2006, when the Korean government first coined the term "multiculturalism" as a policy term, community activists and NGOs initiated one of the first community-based, multicultural experiments, entitled "The Borderless Village" (*gukgyeong eomneun maeul*), which was established in the city of *Ansan*, one of the large cities near Seoul, where migrant workers largely settled. This organization has become a hub for an alternative form of multicultural movement that takes a critical stance toward state-led multicultural policies. Thus, multiculturalism introduced and mobilized by grassroots activists and civic organizations aimed to create social awareness about the human rights of migrant workers who were being mistreated in the workplace and to reconsider Korea's long-standing racism based on ideas of racial purity (Kim 2014: 9).

It was in 1994 that the Korean government implemented the first foreign labor policy, the Industrial Training System (ITS), to tackle the increasing number of undocumented migrant workers. However, because migrant workers were considered students, not workers under the ITS program, it ironically produced more undocumented migrant workers, creating social issues such as low wages, industrial accidents, and labor abuses (Seol 2000). Many NGOs/NPOs criticized the governmental policy regarding migrant workers for not protecting their human and labor rights. This fight for recognition and labor rights resulted in the Employment Permit System (EPS) in 2004 and the abolition of ITS in 2007. Although the Korean government proposed policies regulating incoming labor such as ITS and EPS, these policies were not then exercised under the umbrella of multiculturalism policy. As seen in the case of migrant workers, the Korean government was passive in dealing with the growing foreign population until the mid-2000s, when the increasing numbers of (undocumented) migrant workers became a visible "social problem." Dramatic change came in 2006. In the annual inaugural announcement, President Roh Moo-hyun (2003–2008) announced that "Korea is transforming into a multiethnic society, and the government plans to implement social infrastructure and policies accordingly." This claim was propelled by the urgent need to deal with national issues such as labor shortages in the industrial sector and a low birth rate. To solve these problems, the Korean government formed a committee to establish a basic plan for a multicultural society, recruiting some of its members from civic organizations, and adopted multiculturalism as a policy term. While civic groups and organizations first proposed multiculturalism to nurture a multicultural environment from below, the Korean government seized the moment of transition to a multicultural society for the purpose of accepting more labor forces from other Asian countries and integrating an increasing population of migrants, mixed-race/blood children, and multicultural families in the Korean society (Han 2012: 128).

However, the governmental agenda on multicultural society and multicultural policy diverged from the previous engagement of civic organizations with multicultural situations as its focus shifted from migrant workers (e.g., a fight for labor rights) to multicultural families (e.g., establishing welfare programs). The government's legislation on multiculturalism since 2006 primarily targeted female marriage migrants and multicultural families and their successful assimilation into Korean society, disregarding migrant workers who had immigrated earlier than marriage migrants (Ahn 2013). Migrant workers were perceived as "outside labor" who drain the national income by sending their salary back to their homeland. In contrast, female marriage migrants and multicultural families are considered "useful inside labor" who will eventually be a national asset by replenishing the Korean population (and its labor force). In this shift from labor to the multicultural family, many NGOs/NPOs had to either change their program from migrant workers to female marriage migrants or offer a new project on multicultural families to obtain governmental funding (Yoon 2008). As I will elaborate on shortly, scholars and NGOs have criticized the governmental vision of multiculturalism for its highly gendered practices and because of the coercive nature of its assimilation policy. They argued that without a deeper philosophical foundation about inclusive multiculturalism, governmental multiculturalism policy has been reduced (only) to female marriage migrants and multicultural families, limiting the aim and scope of multiculturalism policy to racialized and gendered assimilation of migrants and their children into Korean society (Kim 2014, Kim 2008, Han 2012).

Together with the multicultural policy discussion, it is important to note that the discursive explosion of multicultural society has been fueled by the media. The Korean press played a key role in constructing the multicultural reality (see Ahn 2012). The Korean press's discursive formation of "Korea as a multicultural society" has functioned as an epistemological endorsement for multiculturalism as a state policy and as a normative practice. In particular, the Korean press has utilized a variety of strategies to construct Korea as a multicultural and global society in line with the government's policy, for instance, by citing statistical data that shows a drastic increase in the foreign population, interviewing multicultural subjects as a way to document multicultural reality, offering a year-long series on multicultural society, and publishing editorials that call for transforming Korea to a multicultural society. Popular media such as TV shows and films have produced content offering (cultural) resources for Koreans to recognize multicultural issues, but they also indicated how the governmental model of multiculturalism has been co-opted by the mainstream media. As Jung discusses in this volume, television programs that focus on the daily lives of female marriage migrants and their multicultural families, such as *Love in Asia* (KBS1 2005–2015), framed them as racialized and feminized subjects who need special care and support to assimilate into Korean society. In addition, the on-screen criminalization of (male) migrant workers and/or illegal migrants is another axis of how migrants are racialized in contemporary Korean mainstream media.

In contrast to mainstream media's stereotyping of racial minorities, alternative media outlets such as radio and Internet have provided a media space for immigrants to voice their own opinions and concerns. The establishment of a few migrants' broadcasting networks—for example, Migrants' Network TV (MNTV) and Migrant Workers Television (MWTV), both established in 2005—demonstrates that while mainstream media continues to stereotype racial others, thereby reinforcing the racial hierarchy, (alternative) media has made it possible for marginalized voices to be heard (Kim 2006). Yet, because this alternative media movement (and others organized by NGOs and progressive activists) does not so much coincide with the government's assimilative view reflected in a multicultural policy, their voices have been marginalized, if not silenced, due to lack of financial support and general publics' indifference to such voices.

Multiculturalism discourse and engagement is never monolithic in Korea. There have been progressive views and actions of multiculturalism to promote human rights of migrants and ethnic minorities, which have been developed by civilian organizations and alternative media. However, a gendered and racialized discourse to manage growing cultural diversity in society has been prevailing since the mid-2000s, when the government launched a series of multiculturalism policies. The next section will discuss the problems of these policies in more detail.

DEVELOPMENT OF MULTICULTURAL POLICY AND ITS PROBLEMATICS

After the first basic plan for a multicultural society and social integration was introduced in 2006, the Korean government quickly enacted two bills that became the core of governmental multicultural policy. In 2007, as foreign residents became more diverse, the government enacted the Act on the

Treatment of Foreigners in Korea, followed by The 1st Basic Plan for Immigration Policy (2008–2012). While previous policies on immigration were framed under the labor policy before 2006, treating migrant workers only from the perspective of economic gain and interests, this act moved beyond labor policy to social integration of foreign residents, broadening its scope to sociocultural integration (Lee 2008a: 117–18). Furthermore, the Multicultural Family Support Act (2008) was passed to support social integration of multicultural families, and The 1st Basic Plan for Multicultural Family Policy (2010–2012) followed.[2] As a continuation of the Plan for Promoting the Social Integration of Female Marriage Migrants" proposed in 2006, one of the core policy actions of the Multicultural Family Support Act was to establish Multicultural Family Support Centers (formerly Female Marriage Migrant Support Centers) at multiple sites from rural to urban including cities and provinces, to build a nationwide support system.[3]

Those two acts make three important points about multicultural policy in Korea. First, Korean multiculturalism has a strong inclination toward assimilation rather than acknowledging cultural differences as constitutive of the nation. Put differently, its main purpose is not to construct a multiethnic state where racial/ethnic diversity and difference are valued on equal basis as the core of national identity. Instead, it is intended to assimilate racial/ethnic minorities for the sake of maintaining hitherto dominant "Koreanness," and the boundary-making process of who needs to be assimilated shapes Korean multiculturalism today. Through this demarcation process, the above two acts/policies constitute a dual system, interrelatedly defining who the "foreigners" and "Koreans" are. As with Japan's "multicultural co-living," both policies rely on an us-and-them or a Korean-and-foreigner dichotomy, simultaneously including and excluding particular types of foreigners as well as Koreans for the sake of building a "new Korea."

According to the Act on the Treatment of Foreigners in Korea, foreigners in Korea are defined as "people who have not obtained Korean citizenship and *legally* stay in Korea for the *purpose of residence* in Korea" (emphasis mine). Undocumented migrant workers as well as documented migrant workers whose status is lawful but who do not stay in Korea for the purpose of residence are excluded. At the same time, any foreign residents who work or live in Korea but are not bound by familial affiliation are also expected to return to their home country and are therefore excluded from the lawful category of "foreigners in Korea." This exclusion reflects a gendered bias of the idea of multicultural family as the act relegates marriage migrants to a separate article as if they require special attention or treatment.

This is closely related to the second point that the multicultural family is at the center of Korean multicultural policy. Whereas the Act on the Treatment of Foreigners in Korea (re)defines lawful boundaries about who "acceptable" foreigners (e.g., high-profile professionals) are by prohibiting the settlement of low-skilled migrant workers, the Multicultural Family Support Act intentionally targets female marriage migrants as subjects of assimilation. Yet, not all types of (international) marriage are acceptable either. According to the Multicultural Family Support Act, a multicultural family is either a family comprised of a married immigrant and a Korean national or a family comprised of a person who obtained permission for naturalization and a Korean national. In either case, the multicultural familial union must contain one Korean national. The marriage between migrant workers or study-abroad students, for instance, is not considered a multicultural family; therefore, their children, even if born in Korea, are not granted Korean citizenship. This clearly shows that Korean citizenship is based on *jus sanguinis*, reinforcing blood lineage to determine Korean citizenship.

The fact that the multicultural family and female marriage migrants have been placed at the center of Korean multiculturalism policy is crucial for understanding Korea's racial reconfiguration because it signifies that female marriage migrants and their mixed-race/blood children (of Asian descent in particular) are the main subjects of Korea's multicultural future. This reflects an international trend that, from the perspective of international division of labor, female workers from developing countries are much mobilized to meet the need for sexual/care labor in developed countries through contract marriages, mail-order brides, and sex workers (see Constable 2005, Ehrenreich and Hochschild 2003). More importantly, female marriage migrants have become the primary subject of Korean multiculturalism policy as they are perceived to be less threatening to the Korean patriarchal system. Korean nationality had long been transmitted patrilineally until the government amended the Nationality Act in 1997.[4] While Korean nationality became both patrilineal and matrilineal since 1997 and the Multicultural Family Support Act is based on this gender equality, the patriarchal practice of nation-building process remains salient. In a patriarchal society like Korea, the current form of international marriage between a Korean male and a non-Korean female is largely acceptable because females and children are usually perceived to be more easily assimilated.

For this reason, scholars and NGOs of female marriage migrants have criticized governmental policy on the multicultural family. They argue that the multicultural policy perpetuates the patriarchal social order by supporting the assimilation of female marriage migrants and their children (Kim 2008, Ahn 2013). Female marriage migrants are required to adopt Korean values, culture, and traditions in order to prove that they are indeed "good Korean citizens." For instance, female marriage migrants are expected to learn how to speak Korean properly, practice traditional courtesy, make *kimchi*, and prepare food for the ancestral rites table through programs offered by the Multicultural

Family Support Center. Moreover, since the Multicultural Family Support Act targets female marriage migrants, another type of multicultural family—a union between a Korean female and a male from a developing country (or male migrant worker)—is underrepresented. Whereas marriage between a Korean female and a White male from the West is considered much more desirable (they are not even called a "multicultural family" but a "global family"), females who married migrant workers particularly from Southeast Asia are stigmatized for legitimating the settlement of migrant workers'—whose residence is restricted—in Korea. Reflecting this widely held bias, policies pertaining to the multicultural family rarely include support or programs for male migrant workers who marry Korean women.

Last but not least, the current multicultural policy has racializing power in tandem with its highly gendered way of assimilation, drawing a new racial line between the multicultural family and Koreans (read: full-blood Koreans). Despite its initial intention, the term "multicultural" has become a stigma for multicultural families and their children. One newspaper reports that in elementary school, the children of multicultural family who have visible difference by appearance were called out by their friends as "Hey, you, *damunhwa* (multiculture)" instead of their name, distinguishing them from rest of the classmates (Yoo and Lee 2013). Since the term *damunhwa* is used in governmental policy on multiculturalism and targets multicultural families, the term has assumed the power of differentiation in terms of bodily difference of children, reproducing racial line between full-blood Koreans and mixed-race/blood Koreans.

This everyday use of *damunhwa* and its racializing power toward children of multicultural family is generated by the fact that multicultural policies frame and treat multicultural families and their children as *beneficiaries* of benevolent social welfare, which makes them into second-class citizens who require special care. In other words, by framing them as beneficiaries of governmental policy, a misleading perception is created that multicultural families eat up the government's budget and pit groups of other beneficiaries (e.g., single-parent families) against each other (Jung 2014, Kim 2011). According to the report (Jung 2014), the government's budget allocated for multicultural family has quadrupled from 31.7 billion to 123.2 billion won since 2008, the year that the Multicultural Family Support Act was introduced. Due to the increased budget, many programs and services have been introduced to foster multicultural family care and childcare. This substantial increase in the budget has been received with hostility from people who are facing job insecurity and hardship (Han 2012). Furthermore, without a sufficient discussion on how to use the resources, this sudden increase in programs created redundancy and wasted resources among ministries (Kim 2011: 235). The government's inability to well manage the budget intensified public antipathy toward migrants and their families as it generated a perception that the government wastes "our" taxes for supporting (im)migrants.

As Wendy Brown (2008) has claimed in the context of the United States, multiculturalism that is based on tolerance easily turns (cultural) differences into a source of hatred because tolerance is a virtue that the haves can extend to the have-nots. This is especially the case when tolerance is related to material support. The policy that treats the multicultural family as a major beneficiary under the framework of the welfare program amplifies social antagonism toward multicultural subjects. It reinforces the general perception that the multicultural policy benefits *only* those who have a different ethnic background and that the multicultural issues concern only "them," not us (Hage 1998), whereby multiculturalism policy works to the detriment of the aim and scope of the multicultural question of how to carve out a communal space for difference in unity.

RECLAIMING MULTICULTURALISM

I have shown that the multiculturalism policy and discourse in Korea was generated as a (new) nation-building project to accommodate intensifying cross-border mobility and accompanied cultural diversity. While more progressive movements from below have predated the rise of multiculturalism in the mid-2000s, they tend to be overpowered by mainstream policy and discourse's strong assimilationist impulse. Indeed, many pro-immigrant NGOs have disappeared due to lack of (governmental) support (Yoon 2008). Or, many NGOs and local governments shifted their agenda to those government-recognized subjects, marginalizing other movements that support migrant workers, since the Korean government appropriated multiculturalism as a state policy and focused on the social integration of female marriage migrants and multicultural families. In a nutshell, a highly racialized and gendered practice of governmental multicultural policies has disregarded the voices from the margins, and it does not tackle the questions of how people of diverse backgrounds can live together as equal members of society. What is more, in a situation where terrorism based on religious and ethnic fundamentalism is on the rise globally and anti-multiculturalism sentiment is becoming more intense domestically, it seems even harder to envision how we can effectively deal with multicultural questions.

Despite or precisely because of this not-so-optimistic situation that we are now in, I argue that it is all the more important to reclaim multiculturalism as a progressive political site of engagement and practice where the fight for social justice—for labor rights and human rights—takes place, challenging and reshaping hitherto dominant vision of multicultural society. Perhaps multiculturalism in Korea signifies the promotion of exclusionary politics in the sense that it only aims to produce a docile gendered and racialized second-class citizen who is mobilized to uphold the norms of the dominant society—to female marriage migrants and their multicultural families. What is needed is not a "pseud-tolerant welfare system" that fallaciously treats them as a major beneficiary of governmental funding, but a full citizenship that constitutes them as equal members of society (Kim 2011). Given that the multicultural question requires a collaborative imagination on how to live together in this increasingly intermingled and hybrid world, it is important to let the populace learn why and how multiculturalism matters as it is not just a social welfare program for a particular ethnic group but a political program for every citizen to make Korea a more democratic and inclusive society. A promising engagement with the multicultural question would advance when we think of multiculturalism not as "their" issue but as "our" issue—when we develop and share a vision of inclusive society, which is lacking in the current multiculturalism policy in Korea.

NOTES

1. See Žižek (2012) for a more detailed analysis of Breivik and the crisis of European identity.

2. The policymaking process was not isolated to civil society or government; it was propelled and supported by academia. Scholars from disciplines such as sociology, education, and politics have participated in committees on multicultural law and policy. In particular, scholars in family sociology, global migration, multicultural education, and social work conducted research on topics around multicultural family and multicultural children allied with the nationwide installation of a Multicultural Family Support Center based on the Multicultural Family Support Act.

3. The center covers diverse services and programs to better help multicultural families and their children such as paperwork for visas and citizenship applications, bilingual education, translation services for female marriage migrants, and cultural festivals.

4. After the amendment of the Nationality Act in 1997, Korean nationality was granted to both patriarchal and matriarchal lineage. Another important amendment of the Nationality Act came in 2010. Dual citizenship is now allowed.

REFERENCES

2011. "Norway Killer Anders Behring Breivik's Cultural References." *The Telegraph*, July 25.

2012. "Anders Breivik Studied Terror Strategies on Internet, Court Hears." *The Independent*, April 20.

Ahn, Ji-Hyun. 2012. "Transforming Korea into Multicultural Society: Reception of Multiculturalism Discourse and its Discursive Disposition in Korea." *Asian Ethnicity*, 13(1): 95–107.

Ahn, Ji-Hyun. 2013. "Global Migration and the Racial Project in Transition: Institutionalizing Racial Difference through Multiculturalism Discourse in South Korea." *Journal of Multicultural Discourses*, 8(1): 29–47.

Brown, Wendy. 2008. *Regulating Aversion: Tolerance in the Age of Identity and Empire*. Princeton: Princeton University Press.

Chua, Beng-Huat. 1998. "Culture, Multiculturalism, and National Identity in Singapore," in *Trajectories: Inter-Asia Cultural Studies*, edited by Kuan-Hsing Chen, 186–205. London; New York: Routledge.

Constable, Nicole, (ed.). 2005. *Cross-Border Marriages: Gender and Mobility in Transnational Asia*. Philadelphia: University of Pennsylvania Press.

Dewind, Josh, Eun Mee Kim, Ronald Skeldon, and In-Jin Yoon. 2012. "Korean Development and Migration." *Journal of Ethnic and Migration Studies*, 38(3): 371–88.

Ehrenreich, Barbara and Arlie Hochschild, (eds.). 2003. *Global Woman: Nannies, Maids, and Sex Workers in the New Economy*. New York: Metropolitan Books.

Eom, Han-Jin. 2011. *Damunhwa Sahoelon [Multicultural Society Theory]*. Seoul: Sowha. (in Korean).

Freeman, Caren. 2005. "Marrying Up and Marrying Down: The Paradoxes of Marital Mobility for Chosonjok Brides in South Korea," in *Cross-Border Marriages: Gender and Mobility in Transnational Asia*, edited by Nicole Constable, 80–100. Philadelphia: University of Pennsylvania Press.

Hage, Ghassan. 1998. *White Nation: Fantasies of White Supremacy in a Multicultural Society*. Annandale: Pluto Press.

Hall, Stuart. 2000. "Conclusion: The Multi-cultural Question," in *Un/Settled Multiculturalisms: Diasporas, Entanglements, Transruptions*, edited by Barnor Hesse, 209–41. London: Zed Books.

Hall, Stuart. 2001. *The Multicultural Question*. Available from http://www.open.ac.uk/socialsciences/pavis/papers.php.

Han, Geon-Soo. 2007. "Multicultural Korea: Celebration or Challenge of Multiethnic Shift in Contemporary Korea?" *Korea Journal*, 47(4): 32–63.

Han, Geon-Soo. 2012. "Hangugsahoeui damunhwajuui hyeomojeunggwa silpaelon [Multiculturephobia and the Discourse of Failure of Multiculturalism in Korea]." *Multiculture and Human*, 1(1): 113–43. (in Korean).

Jung, Hyo Sik. 2014. "Haemada ttwineun damunhwa yesan . . . Hanbumogajeong yeogchabyeol nollan [Budget for multiculturalism leaps annually . . . A Controversy on reverse-discrimination over a single-parent family]." *JoongAng Ilbo*, Febuary 10, 16. (in Korean).

Kim, Andrew Eungi. 2009. "Global Migration and South Korea: Foreign Workers, Foreign Brides and the Making of a Multicultural Society." *Ethnic and Racial Studies*, 32(1): 70–92.

Kim, Hye-Soon. 2008. "Gyeolhonijuyeoseonggwa hangugui damunhwasahoe silheom [Migrant Brides and Making of a Multicultural Society]." *Korean Sociology*, 42(2): 36–71. (in Korean).

Kim, Hyun Mee. 2007. "The State and Migrant Women: Diverging Hopes in the Making of 'Multicultural Families' in Contemporary Korea." *Korea Journal*, 47(4): 100–22.

Kim, Hyun Mee. 2014. Injongjuui hwagsangwa guggaeobseum [Spread of Racism and the Stateless]. Alternative *Report of NGO on Racism in South Korea*, 6–9. (in Korean).

Kim, Jung Sun. 2011. "Simingwon eobsneun bogjijeongchaegeuloseo 'hangugsig' damunhwajuuie daehan bipanjeog gochal [The Critical Study of 'Korean style' Multiculturalism as Welfare Policy Excluding Citizenship]." *Economy and Society*, 92(12): 205–46. (in Korean).

Kim, Samuel. 2000. "Korea and Globalization (*Segyehwa*): A Framework for Analysis," in *Korea's Globalization*, edited by Samuel Kim, 1–28. Oxford: Cambridge University Press.

Kim, Young-Chan. 2006. "Ijunodongja midieoui munhwajeongchijeog hamui [Mapping the Cultural Politics of the Migrant Workers' Media]." *Studies of Broadcasting Culture* 18(1): 37–59. (in Korean).

Kymlicka, Will and Baogang He. 2005. *Multiculturalism in Asia*. Oxford: Oxford University Press.

Lee, Hey-Kyung. 2008a. "International Marriage and the State in South Korea: Focusing on Governmental Policy." *Citizenship Studies*, 12(1): 107–23.

Lee, Mary. 2008b. "Mixed Race Peoples in the Korean National Imaginary and Family." *Korean Studies*, 32: 56–85.

Lee, Seon Ok. 2007. "Hangugeseoui ijunodongundonggwa damunhwajuui [Migrant Workers' Movement and Multiculturalism in Korea]," in *Multiculturalism in South Korea: A Critical Review*, edited by Kyung Seok Oh, 81–107. Kyŏnggi-do P'aju-si: Hanul. (in Korean).

Lee, Yean-Ju. 2011. "Overview of Trends and Policies on International Migration to East Asia: Comparing Japan, Taiwan and South Korea." *Asian and Pacific Migration Journal*, 20(2): 117–31.

Lim, Timothy. 2009. "Who is Korean? Migration, Immigration, and the Challenge of Multiculturalism in Homogeneous Societies." *Asia-Pacific Journal*, 30(1): July 27.

Moon, Katharine. 2000. "Strangers in the Midst of Globalization," in *Korea's Globalization*, edited by Samuel Kim, 147–69. Oxford: Cambridge University Press.

Oh, Kyung Seok, (ed.). 2007a. *Hangugeseoui damunhwajuui: Hyeonsilgwa jaengjeom [Multiculturalism in South Korea: A Critical Review]*. Kyŏnggi-do P'aju-si: Hanul. (in Korean).

Oh, Kyung Seok. 2007b. "Eotteon damunhwajuuiinga?: Damunhwasahoe nonuie gwanhan bipanjeog jomang [What Kind of Multiculturalism is it?: A Critical Perspective on Multicultural Society]," in *Multiculturalism in South Korea: A Critical Review*, edited by Kyung Seok Oh, 21–56. Kyŏnggi-do P'aju-si: Hanul. (in Korean).

Paik, Young-Gyung. 2011. "'Not-Quite Korean' Children in 'Almost Korean' Families: The Fear of Decreasing Population and State Multiculturalism in South

Korea," in *New Millennium South Korea: Neoliberal Capitalism and Transnational Movements*, edited by Jesook Song, 130–41. New York: Routledge.

Park, Hyun Ok. 2011. "For the Rights of 'Colonial Returnees': Korean Chinese, Decolonization, and Neoliberal Democracy in South Korea," in *New Millennium South Korea: Neoliberal Capitalism and Transnational Movements*, edited by Jesook Song, 115–29. New York: Routledge.

Seol, Dong-Hoon. 2000. "Past and Present of Foreign Workers in Korea 1987–2000." *Asia Solidarity Quarterly*, 2: 6–31.

Shin, Gi-Wook. 2006. *Ethnic Nationalism in Korea*. Stanford, California: Stanford University Press.

Shin, Jiwon. 2009. "The Gendered and Racialized Division in the Korean Labour Market: The Case of Migrant Workers in the Catering Sector." *East Asia*, 26: 93–111.

Shohat, Ella and Robert Stam, (eds.). 2003. *Multiculturalism, Postcoloniality, and Transnational Media*. New Brunswick, NJ: Rutgers University Press.

Song, Jesook, (ed.). 2011. *New Millennium South Korea: Neoliberal Capitalism and Transnational Movements*. New York: Routledge.

Yoo, Keun-Hyoung and Saem-Mul Lee. 2013. "Yeojeonhi seoleoun damunhwa janyeodeul - Jiwojiji anhneun juhonggeulssi [The children of multicultural family still feel sorrowful (Part 1): The indelible scarlet letter]." *DongA Ilbo*, May 6. (in Korean).

Yoon, In-Jin. 2008. "Hangugjeog damunhwajuuiui jeongaewa teugseong [The Development and Characteristics of Multiculturalism in South Korea: With a Focus on the Relationship of the State and Civil Society]." *Korean Sociology*, 42(2): 72–103. (in Korean).

Žižek, Slavoj. 2012. *The Year of Dreaming Dangerously*. London; New York: Verso.

Chapter 3

Multicultural Taiwan

Policy Developments and Challenges

Li-Jung Wang

INTRODUCTION

Since the 1990s, multiculturalism has been regarded as the new administrative method to resolve the long-standing cultural conflicts by embracing multiple cultural differences in Taiwan under an all-encompassing idea of "multicultural Taiwan." Initially, the key intent of multicultural Taiwan in the 1990s was to achieve social integration and ensure the living equality of the "Four Great Ethnic Groups": the indigenous Taiwanese, the Hakkas, the Mainlanders, and the Hokkeins.[1] The idea eventually influenced some important cultural policies in Taiwan. In 1996, the Council of Indigenous People (CIP) was established to protect the rights of the indigenous people. The establishment of the Hakka Affair Council (HAC) in 2001 represented the second step in the development of multicultural Taiwan.

However, multicultural Taiwan has faced new challenges from the increased number of migrant workers and foreign brides since the late 1990s, who mostly came from China and Southeast Asian countries. As of June 2015, roughly 500,000 migrant workers (out of a total population of approximately 23 million in Taiwan) and 50,325 foreign spouses from China, Indonesia, Thailand, Vietnam, and the Philippines have attracted significant attention (National Immigrant Agency, 2015).[2] To deal with this new phase of multicultural Taiwan, the National Immigration Agency (NIA) was established in 2007 to improve the counseling assistance provided to the immigrants.

In this study, we explored the multicultural policy developments and changes in Taiwan and focused on the new challenges faced by the migrant workers and foreign brides. The series of multicultural institutionalization policies in Taiwan showcased the vigorous multiculturalism developments made possible by the successful efforts of nongovernmental organizations

(NGOs) and citizen's groups to secure cultural rights. Yet, it remains a question whether multicultural policies can effectively tackle the marginalization and cultural difference issues, and reconstruct Taiwan's national identity to one that is inclusive of multiple cultures. Similar to cases in South Korea and Japan discussed in this section, this chapter will argue that Taiwan's situation also shows a significant gap between the actual multicultural policies and the intensified multicultural-related problems in reality, albeit in a specific intricate manner. This chapter is divided into three parts. The first part provides the historical background of the multicultural Taiwan concept and the relevant policy developments. The second part further describes the multicultural policies and citizenship legislation developments in order to meet the growing cultural diversities due to the increased numbers of migrants in Taiwan from China and Southeast Asian countries. The third part discusses the new challenges faced by multicultural Taiwan in terms of transnationalism, hybrid cultures, and multiple identities that the immigrant groups, migrant workers, foreign brides, and their children have embraced beyond the national boundaries.

HISTORICAL BACKGROUND OF MULTICULTURAL TAIWAN

Multiculturalism has been regarded as a significant issue for an inclusive national membership and citizenship as well as the practical policies needed to administer cultural diversity in the contemporary society. In terms of practical policies, Canada and Australia have started to pursue active multicultural policies since the 1970s. Subsequently, other Western countries have also begun to consider the ethno-racial diversity of long-standing minority groups and immigrants as well as gender and sexual differences in formulating their cultural policies. Complementary to actual policy implementation, the "politics of differences" provides the theoretical consideration on how the notion of multiculturalism challenges some traditional views of "universal citizenship" and "liberal equality" (Young 1990). Parekh (1998) defined "multicultural society" with five normative measures. First, such a society should not subject its cultural communities to any intended or unintended discriminations, and should provide equal respect and opportunities for minorities to flourish. Second, a multicultural society should ensure social justice and equal access to political power for its minority communities and encourage interethnic and interreligious cooperation in all walks of life, especially in politics. Third, the institutions of the state, especially the civil services, the army, the police, and the judiciary, should be completely impartial and insulated from ethnic and religious pressure. While these three measures are primarily concerned with equality and social integration, the other two measures are more concerned about respecting the differences and "multicultural issues" (Hall 2001). A multicultural society should encourage its citizens to take an open-minded and extensive view of their cultural identity so that the citizens of diverse ethnic and cultural backgrounds would cease to feel threatened by the cultural differences and embrace it instead. Finally, national identity should evolve in an open and inclusive manner without excluding or delegitimizing any ethnic communities. National symbols, rituals, and events should reflect the cultural diversity of the society wherever possible.[3]

In the context of Taiwan, multiculturalism policies have been developed relatively earlier compared to those of South Korea and Japan. In 1997, the Taiwanese government declared Taiwan as a multicultural country in its Constitution with two key objectives. The first objective was an attempt to create a new national identity to resolve the conflicts between the Mainland Chinese nationalism[4] and the Taiwanese consciousness,[5] which has developed since the establishment of the Kuomintang (KMT) government during the postwar era. The conflicts and confusions surrounding the national identity were clearly highlighted by the political debates over unification with or independence from China, and such debates have seriously divided the populace of Taiwan. The second objective was to use multiculturalism to create new political legitimacy and social justice based on ethnic equality during democratization movements since the 1980s. Inequality among the various ethnic groups, especially for the aborigines and Hakkas in Taiwan with subservient positions, was regarded as a major issue to be resolved toward the development of democratization in Taiwan. Multiculturalism was thus perceived as a good method to protect the rights of the various ethnic minorities and ease tensions between social integration and ethnic separation.

The Democratic Progressive Party (DPP), which returned to power in 2016, is the main opposition party to the KMT (the ruling party in Taiwan from 1949 to 2000 and from 2008 to 2016). The Ethnicity and Cultural Policy proposed by the DPP in 1992 issued a challenge to the Chinese nationalism expounded by the KMT and eventually made some impacts during the 1997 Constitution reform in two key points.[6] First, the proposal stated that the government should encourage the development of a multicultural society so that no single ethnic group is permitted to dominate or degrade the cultural values of the other ethnic groups for the purpose of maintaining its own hegemonic status. Second, the cohabitation of diverse ethnic groups in a nation-state should constitute the core of modern citizenship, and the national identity should not be constructed based on a singular notion of national culture or the blood kinship of a dominant ethnic group (DPP 1992: 77–9). This proposal provided more space and freedom for the "Four Great Ethnic Groups" and became the critical foundation of multiculturalism development in Taiwan. The cultural rights issues have become increasingly more important in the concept of citizenship. Numerous new laws and policies[7] were promulgated in order to improve the cultural rights of the minority groups. The Council of Cultural Affairs (or the Ministry of Culture) is the primary cultural policy maker in Taiwan, but the Hakka Affairs Council (HAC), the Council of Indigenous Peoples (CIP), and the Council of Labor Affairs (CLA) have all played some important roles in terms of influencing the national identity–related cultural policies.

Under the rubric of multicultural Taiwan, the government presently provides significant support to the Hakkas in order to win their votes during elections. Since 2001, the HAC has established a number of policies to improve cultural participation.[8] In 2010, the HAC instituted important laws for the Hakka people under the Hakka Fundamental Act to improve their cultural rights in terms of Hakka history reevaluation; the promotion of Hakka cultural heritage, language, and media communication; and the Hakka's representation in the national administrative system. The development of the Hakka-related multicultural policies encouraged the Hakka people to break away from the traditional stigmas and cultivate their own cultural identity. In particular, the HAC has constructed numerous cultural events and media programs that later became critical channels for the people to access and participate in the Hakka cultural life and reconstruct the Hakka identity (Wang 2007).

Since the mid-1980s, the Taiwanese indigenous social movement had struggled for 10 years in demanding social rights, land rights, language rights, identity rights, and so on. With the decline of the KMT-driven Chinese nationalism, the social recognition of the aboriginal people in Taiwan further gave rise to policies that promote aboriginal culture. In 1992, the CCA held the first "Artistic Season for the Mountainous Peoples" event. Between 1990 and 1992, the aboriginal music and dance performance called "Series for the Dance and Music of the Taiwanese Aborigines" was included in the National Theatre programs. Furthermore, through Constitution revisions, numerous new indigenous rights became protected under new laws and regulations such as the Act of Indigenous Education, the Act of Indigenous Development, and the Fundamental Act of Indigenous Peoples. The CIP was established in 1996 as the central authority for promulgating indigenous people–related policies, protecting the rights of the indigenous peoples, and providing a whole picture of the indigenous cultural development needs.[9] Aboriginal cultures that had been viewed as tribal customs have thus became officially recognized in Taiwan.

While the constitutional revisions and the development of the related multicultural policies were significant landmarks toward the construction of multicultural Taiwan, some problem still remain in reality, especially in terms of respect for the cultural difference of the aborigines in Taiwan. In 1994, former president Deng-Hui Lee made a speech during the first aboriginal cultural meeting of the CCA:

The Taiwanese aborigines cannot exist apart from the Taiwanese society. . . . However, they have to "melt" into the Taiwanese society. The problems of any ethnic group are the problems of the whole Taiwanese society; thus no one can remain uninvolved. Additionally, the aborigines are a part of "our" society. Therefore, I hope that everyone (the aborigines) can contribute to "our" country and work for the construction of a new "Community of Destiny." (Lee, Deng-Hui 1994)

This statement illustrated how the aboriginal culture was used as a symbol of the new highly assimilative national identity in Taiwan, as connoted by the word "melt." Multicultural policies in Taiwan encourage the minorities to express their culture to the public. Such policies have achieved the promotion of group-differentiated rights to some extent, especially in terms of recognizing poly-ethnic cultural rights and identities (see Kymlicka 1995).[10] Yet the current multicultural policies only facilitate the organization of events that showcase cultural diversity,[11] and steep funds are allocated for these events without seriously promoting the public's recognition of the Taiwanese aborigines on equal terms. The aborigines are invariably invited to perform or celebrate alongside other ethnic groups on national holidays or ceremonies to show that the new Taiwan has indeed become a multicultural country. As Hage (1996) argued in the Australian context, it is a cosmo-multiculturalism in which "ethnic" culture is put onto display to be consumed and approved of by the majority group. Multicultural Taiwan policy implementation has eventually blurred the line between protecting aboriginal culture and dominating cultural development by the government. The Taiwanese government has enacted laws to encourage and support the indigenous peoples to maintain and develop their culture, but such laws tended to result in the government exerting greater power and control over the indigenous population that it was trying to "help" in terms of "ethnic culture" development (Chen, Shun-Ling 2002: 194). Multicultural policies in Taiwan eventually required the indigenous people to select certain traditions and cultures and modify them in order to cater to the administrative rules and official tests because these people need the support and funding from the government. Taiwan's indigenous peoples thus face a dilemma. On the one hand, the resources and assistance of the government assist them in practicing cultural rights; on the other hand, their cultural autonomy and circumstances in which it can be exerted remain under government control (Wang 2014).

Not only the indigenous peoples face challenges in "the politics of recognition," but they also have to deal with "the politics of redistribution" (Zhang, Pei-Lun 2007). Most of the indigenous people struggle with financial problems, so they are very concerned about economic development and social welfare as well as cultural issues.[12] According to a research conducted in 2010, the average income for the citizens of Taiwan is approximately three times higher than that of the indigenous peoples (CIP 2010).[13] Multicultural Policy in Taiwan only focuses on the maintenance and development of "ethnic cultures" that actually function as a tool to conceal economic inequality (Chao Kang 2006). It is important to consider redistribution and cultural recognition simultaneously, and the demands of social justice should be based on equal social and cultural participations (Fraser 2005: 73).

NEW CULTURAL DIVERSITY AND POLICY CHALLENGES

Multicultural Taiwan was initially based on the "Four Great Ethnic Groups," but it faces some challenges from the new immigrant groups. From the mid-1990s, migrant workers and marriage migrants from South East Asian countries such as the Philippines, Thailand, Indonesia, Vietnam, and Malaysia have introduced new cultures into Taiwan. As of 2015, about 500,000 migrant workers live in Taiwan, which consist more than 2% of the total population of Taiwan. This is nearly on a similar footing with Taiwan's indigenous peoples in terms of their numbers. In 1994, the Taiwanese government eliminated the restrictions on "foreign brides" entering into Taiwan from Indonesia, Thailand, Vietnam, and the Philippines; this new group, comprising mostly Taiwanese husbands and Southeast Asian wives (50,325 in 2015), has also attracted significant attention. According to statistics from the Ministries of the Interior, new birth ratio from foreign brides accounted for 13.8% in 2004, children from foreign brides accounted for 11% in 2007, and new birth ratio from foreign brides accounted for 6.5% in 2014. Over the decade, the new birth ratio from foreign brides in Taiwan has decreased by 7.3% (Statistical Office of the Ministries of the Interior, 2012).[14] According to the National Institute on Aging, over 13% of the new generation around 25 years of age will come from migrant families by 2030.[15] The ethnic composition of Taiwan no longer fits into the "Four Great Ethnic Groups" touted by the government policies, and it now includes the substantial number of those who have Southeast Asian backgrounds. In terms of the reconception of national identity in Taiwan, how the government treats these migrants and integrates them into the society can be viewed as a renewed litmus test for the construction of multicultural Taiwan. Foreign brides and their children have significantly posed challenges to the hitherto definition of being "Taiwanese."

New immigrant groups have posed further challenges to the concept of the "Taiwanese citizenship" based on the notion of a homogeneously bounded nation. The growing human mobility and the associated transnational connections maintained by many people have also posed profound challenges to the classical model of national citizenship in terms of both legal rights and cultural identity politics (Joppke 1998: 23–24). Taiwan's government has just begun to protect and improve the basic human rights for immigrant groups. In 1999, the formulation of the Immigration Act and the revision of the Nationality Act finally established the basic laws and administrative system needed to protect the rights of migrant brides. In 2003, the Ministry of the Interior promulgated the guidance measures for brides from foreign countries and Mainland China, which became the main reference for the immigrant marriages and the family-related services provided by the government. In 2004, the Foreign Brides Assistance Fund was established to provide foreign bride families with 3 billion NT dollars per year for 10 years (Pan, Shu-man 2013). In 2007, the NIA was established to supervise migrant affairs. However, many studies have illustrated the drawbacks of these migrant-related laws and regulations, and showed that the migrant communities in Taiwan are still struggling for social welfare, political participation, and cultural rights (Wan-Ying, Yang and Ya-Wen, Chang 2014: 52). In this situation, the NGOs specializing in human rights and labor movements have been working hard to protect the rights of foreign brides and migrant workers. For example, in 2003, numerous NGOs successfully pushed the government to revise the parts of the Immigration Act that contained discriminatory and anti-immigrant provisions (Hsia 2009).

Moreover, many studies indicated that such policies tended to treat migrant families as "social problems" or "inferior citizens" in Taiwan (e.g., Wan-Ying, Yang and Ya-Wen, Chang 2014: 52). The Ministry of the Interior proposed the foreign spouse counseling measure on September 10, 2004. The eight key orientations of the measure include: Life Adaptation Counseling, Eugenics and Medical Care, Employment Rights Protection, Education and Culture Upgrade, Parenting Assistance, Personal Safety Protection, Sound Legal System, and Concept Advocacy Implementation. The implications behind the policy were that foreign spouses must clarify the suspicion of "fake" marriage, overcome physiological problems, and upgrade their parenting capacities to meet a superior Taiwanese standard. For example, Medical Care instructs foreign spouses how to take care of physical and mental health, and to have their children take a medical check of developmental disorder. Parenting assistance, which aims to assist them to improve children's intellectual capabilities through after-school tutoring, also assumes them to be inferior and works to put an "underdog" stigma on them.

This biased assumption reflects on widely held negative stereotypes of migrants associated with "social problems" or "inferior citizens" in Taiwan. Taiwan's mainstream media tended to represent such images for the migrants and associate them with social problems such as crime rate increases, abuse of welfare system, and degradation of the educational level in Taiwan (Zhang, 2014: 8; Hsia 2000). For example, a major local daily represents migrants as follows:

The fact that an increasing number of Taiwanese men go to Southeast Asia to marry women who are poorly educated, insipid, and lacking in beauty reflects upon the many problems inherent in the social structure, the marriage system, and the relationships between men and women in Taiwan (China Times, 21/11/1995).

With the growing number of children of foreign spouses, many primary schools face new challenges. This new category of students face difficulties in learning language (their mothers are not able to teach them Mandarin), which increases the burden for teachers. . . . Concerns regarding how primary schools can overcome this new problem with the limited available resources are worrying many teachers and principals. (China Times 22/12/2003)

Foreign spouses have also been portrayed and advertised as "sexual commodities" for Taiwanese men by agencies that arranges overseas marriages. Some agencies even offered polygamy services and refunds for unsatisfactory matches. Furthermore, foreign spouses are viewed as causing a challenge to the traditional family values (Xue, and Lin 2003). Yang and Chang (2014) point out that many people believe that the advent of the foreign bride option has led many people in Taiwan to change their attitudes about marriage by encouraging men to evaluate prospective spouses (from Southeast Asia and Mainland China) for functional considerations, such as "easy to control," "industriousness," and "trouble saving" (i.e., some men feel that they should get married without the trouble of romance). And foreign spouses are thought to be responsible for destroying traditional relationships between men and women. Given that marriages involving foreign spouses have been statistically shown to have a higher risk of divorce, conservative scholars also worry that a continued trend to accept more foreign spouses will reduce the overall quality of marriages in Taiwan (Xue and Lin 2003). In any case, it is foreign spouses that are to be blamed for causing the deterioration of "our" society.

Under the strong pressures from the NGOs that support migrant families, the Taiwanese government has recently started to tackle social prejudices against migrants by paying more attention to issues such as respecting and recognizing the cultural differences of the foreign spouses on equal terms and encouraging the mainstream society to respect and understand their multicultural backgrounds. New immigrants have officially been recognized as the "fifth biggest group" and a part of the multicultural Taiwan, as stated by Mr. Hong-Yuan Lee (minister of the interior from 2012 to 2014):

International marriages have become popular in Taiwan in recent years under the globalization trend and have influenced Taiwan's social demographics. New Immigrants are now the fifth largest community in Taiwan and have become an emerging power in the society. Since 2010, our government has provided more assistance and aids to our migrant friends in hopes that the children of the new generation can gain identity, recognition, and attentions from our society. . . . We hope to create a friendlier society and attract more migrant friends to Taiwan. (2013)

Thus in 2011, the NIA established The Life Adaption Assistance Plan for Foreign Spouses to facilitate the multicultural society, promote respect for migrant cultures, protect the migrants' human rights, and help the migrants to adapt to life in Taiwan. In 2013, the NIA established the "Torch Program" to offer comprehensive supports to new immigrants such as fund assistance for foreign spouses; settlement services for foreign or Chinese spouses upon their first arrival to Taiwan and 10 categories of information that includes social welfare, healthcare, medical care, group consultation, and learning programs; and assistance for the new immigrants to find jobs and secure their employment. The program also provides policies that promote the diverse cultures from the immigrant's home countries. The local governments start to support cultural festivals for immigrant groups such as the "Southeast Asia Cultural Carnival" performed at Taoyuan City in 2014 that combined several Thai, Vietnam, and Indonesian traditional ceremonies, which was attended by over 89,000 migrant workers. Public TV (funded by government) on channel 13 also produces some programs that introduce and promote a deeper understanding of foreign cultures. Furthermore, the Ministry of Culture held professional training courses to advocate the equality of cultural rights in local cultural centers in 2013 to promote cultural understanding for new migrants from Southeast Asia in the local community.

Throughout the process, the difficulty of understanding the cultural complexity of migrants from Southeast Asia became apparent (Zhang 2014: 117). Taiwan's Southeast Asian immigrants primarily migrated from Thailand, Vietnam, Indonesia, the Philippines, Cambodia, and so on. The cultures and religions from these countries are very different from those in Taiwan, especially for Muslims from Indonesia. The Taiwanese people understand very little about the Islamic culture, which caused employers to force Indonesian migrants to eat pork and many residents in Taipei to complain about the foreign workers gathering at the Taipei Railway Station for Ramadan celebration[16] (Zhang 2014: 90–95). Therefore, many NGOs have been organizing events to improve the understanding and promote respect toward the Southeast Asia societies and cultures in Taiwan and further facilitate exchanges between Southeast Asian immigrants and the people of Taiwan. For example, the *Four Way Voices Newspaper* (in Vietnamese, Thai, Tagalog, Cambodian, and Burmese languages) provides a good channel for immigrants to express their feelings and experiences in Taiwan, and more Taiwanese people pay attention to them. The newspaper was originally published by *Taiwan Lihpao Daily* (a newspaper established by a university). Subsequently, the leading members started to participate in the cultural promotions of new immigrant groups, such as literature, music, and dances, and the activities had been gradually developing into the establishment of NGO, *Four Way Voices Culture and Creativity*. At present, the primary members operate the "Brilliant Time" bookstore, whose objective is to serve as a new immigrant cultural exchange platform as well as promote the relevant policies and new immigrant cultures. The *Four Way Voices Newspaper* also organizes "the Back to Grandmother's Home plan" to encourage second-generation immigrants with Southeast Asian backgrounds to visit their homelands in order to strengthen their links with the relatives and cultures in their homelands, and this plan is supported by the governmental funding. These developments have showcased the contributions made by the NGOs to the promotion of cultural rights and recognition of new migrants in Taiwan society and progress of the relevant policies by the government.

MULTIPLE IDENTITIES AND CULTURAL HYBRIDITY UNDER MULTICULTURAL TAIWAN

The multiple identities and cultural hybridity of migrants from Southeast Asia pose even more difficult challenges to multicultural Taiwan. This is suggestive of a widely observed trend-signal to problematize the conventional national identity conceived based on territories. As Steven Vertovec (2001: 573) indicated, with the ease of cross-border mobility, transnational connections fostered by migrants have significant impacts "on the construction, negotiation, and reproduction of individual and group identities." Indeed, migrants are reconstructing their national and cultural identities by negotiating their transnational connection with "home" and their mundane experiences in Taiwan. As Chiu (2003) observed, while the foreign spouses in Taiwan are separated from their "home" society, they are unable to completely assimilate into the Taiwanese society and must continue to construct their identities intricately by synthesizing the cultures of and their experiences in both their homeland and in Taiwan. Furthermore, the key sources of the foreign spouses' cultural identities cover more than just their nationality and ethnicity. They also include gender, class, family relations, work environment, and the social network throughout their everyday experiences in Taiwan as well as their transnational connections with "home" (Chiu 2003: 287–88).

These new Taiwanese citizens have built a sense of multiple belongings and embodied cultural hybridization and bilingualism, all of which have challenged the definition of being "Taiwanese" and the "Taiwanese culture." Specifically, the cultural hybridity and the multiple identities of the second generation are critical issues in Taiwan today. As the new second generations reached adulthood (after reaching adult age from the 1990s until now), they have begun to express their own hybrid identities through literature, arts, films, and popular music.[17] The second-generation migrants no longer remain as "problems" of the Taiwanese society or as the "others" portrayed by the media. They are rethinking about their parents' migration processes and their impacts on themselves, and reimagining Taiwan through their own stories.

Yu-Chin Chen, a writer with a Chinese father and an Indonesian mother who is active in the literature field, expressed her experiences and identities as a child of a "migrant marriage" as follows:

> My concept of Southeast Asian transnational marriages when I was little was exactly as what were written (in Chinese) on the cement walls outside of the houses: Foreign spouses \ guarantee virgin \ no added price \ NT$180 thousand total \ if one flees, marry another one. Under these circumstances, it was extremely difficult to say anything to my friends at school. At the time, no one made fun of me for having a foreign bride as a mother. They mostly ask suspiciously, "Is your mom Taiwanese?" I always smiled and answered, "What do you think?"[18]

As a second-generation migrant, Yu-Chin Chen has actively and publicly rejected the stereotypes of migrants portrayed by the mainstream media. She believes in the power of words and hopes to find the new second generations hidden among the sea of people in order to start the "New Second Generation Book Writing for the New Second Generation" event. Chen's greeting remark on Facebook shows her hope to find those who share similar backgrounds with her and are willing to write new second-generation migrant-related stories. "Regardless if you came from Southeast Asia, from South to North, from Taiwan to China, or from East to West; there may be some similarities or ignorance about our parents. Everyone is welcome to comment!"[19] Many of the second-generation migrants also hope to have the opportunities to express their voices through the mainstream media. Some new TV and radio programs have started to broadcast various stories of the second-generation migrants and enable them to discuss their hybrid cultures and multiple identities from their life experiences. For example, an online program supported by the local government of Taipei called the "Small Media Solider" has invited second-generation migrants to share their life experiences, cultures, and arts in Southeastern Asian languages. The program also teaches them how to use media to tell their stories. Through these opportunities, the new second generation strive to remove the stigmas in Taiwan society and firmly establish their own subjectivity while starting to develop a new sense of belonging to society and formulate a new form of cultural identity in Taiwan.

The newly developed hybrid cultures across the national boundaries have posed serious challenges to a homogenous or unified notion of the Taiwanese national identity and the definition of "Taiwanese culture." For example, the literatures based on the experiences of immigrant groups in Taiwan are starting to become recognized as an essential part of the "Taiwanese literature."

As Zhang indicated, "The Taiwanese literature has been influenced by new trends that comprised different languages and historical memories from the new immigrant groups in recent years. Meanwhile, the second-generation migrants are changing the literature of Taiwan through expression of new cultural identities and experiences based on their Southeastern Asian backgrounds" (2013).[20] The first Taiwan Literature Award for Migrants was held in the National Museum of Taiwan Literature in 2014. In a speech made in an official capacity, Mr. Zhi-Cong Weng (the curator of the National Museum of Taiwan Literature) indicated that the first Taiwan Literature Award for Migrants illustrated how the government has taken immigrant literature very seriously. Migrant worker literature is not just writing about the author's personal life, but it is also a part of the Taiwanese literature.[21] One of the prominent writers is Yu-Chin Chen. With a Chinese Mainlander father and an Indonesian mother, she has won numerous literary awards in Taiwan since 2014. Her 2015 piece *Taipei People-to-Be* depicts the identity problems and hardship to work in a "foreign land" that her parents faced when they migrated to Taiwan. It humorously describes her parents' everyday lives with identity uncertainties and cultural mixing through the eyes of a girl who is growing up in a multilingual and multicultural environment that comprised the Fuzhou, Indonesian, Hakka, Mandarin, and English languages—her father watches national dramas of Taiwan before going to the night market to sell his hometown flavor Kompyangs (salty cakes) while speaking Hokkein, and her mother from Indonesia goes to the local market to buy groceries without understanding any of the Taiwanese greetings. *Taipei People-to-Be* was later revised into a popular teen comics version. Through such literary pieces like Chen's, the intercultural experiences of people with Southeast Asian backgrounds have gradually become acknowledged as part of cultural diversity enriching Taiwanese society.

While these changes are promising in facilitating the heterogeneous formations of identity and culture in Taiwan, much more should be accomplished. The new immigrant experiences indicated that individual identities would continue to shift with the historical, social, cultural, scenario, and memory choices. The difference in cultural identification between the generations will be even more sharply articulated. In the future, the identification issues of migrants and their children will become even more complicated and continue to blur clearly demarcated ethnic boundaries. Homi Bhabha (1994) used *inter*national culture as a starting point not based on the exoticism, multiculturalism, or diversity of cultures, but according to the inscription and articulation of culture's hybridity. The Taiwanese society or cultural policy should take seriously how to transform the dominant definition of "Taiwanese" in order to better deal with ethnic and cultural heterogeneity of people in Taiwan and to respect individual differences on equal terms.

CONCLUSION

Compared to South Korea and Japan, the Taiwanese government has issued more policies and welfare supports to promote multicultural citizenship since the 1990s. Yet, despite being more active in multicultural policy implementations, similar to South Korea and Japan, Taiwan also faces the key issue of how to tackle the multicultural question. The presence of the Taiwanese aborigines, the Hakkas, and the immigrant groups in Taiwan requires the national identity of Taiwan to reconsider and fairly reflect the heterogeneity of the members of the society. However, there are policy limitations in dealing with the people living together despite their differences. In reality, Taiwan is still facing challenges in tackling the gaps between multiculturalism and the multicultural questions. The indigenous peoples in Taiwan face a dilemma that the government's support to maintain and develop indigenous cultures tended to create an "ethnic culture" that is more easily acceptable by the public. Increasing number of immigrant groups with Southeast Asian backgrounds present further challenges to addressing questions such as, what is the Taiwanese identity, what constitutes national culture, and how can Taiwan accommodate itself to welcome the cohabitation of people with diverse sociocultural backgrounds while recognizing the transnationalism and cultural hybridity that the first- and second-generation migrants from Southeast Asian countries have come to embrace as a part of the society. The multicultural policy of Taiwan has been facing new multicultural questions. The multicultural policy must constantly be readjusted and revised to deal with residual and emerging challenges to go beyond an exclusive and singular notion of "Taiwan" and "Taiwanese."

Multicultural policy development is an intricate matter because cultures are always changing, unstable, and fluid across diffident boundaries. It is my contention that cultural policies need to emphasize on the intersections, intermixing, and crossovers between different cultural perspectives and traditions in order to produce the social dynamics for the form of cultural diversity that is constantly interpenetrating one another with new and unpredictable consequences. In addition, the government of Taiwan should also incorporate the identities and imaginations of the marginal groups and enable them to establish their own positions in Taiwan. It is especially imperative whether and how the migrants' experiences and formation of multiple identities can be conceived as a national issue that all people of Taiwan must take seriously. Two interrelated processes will be needed to promote an inclusive multicultural society in Taiwan. The first process is to attend and listen to the voices and experiences of the indigenous people as well as the new immigrants carefully and allow their cultures, identities, and viewpoints to be included in the narratives and imaginations of the national identity in Taiwan. The second process focuses on how Taiwan can create a national space to pro-vide opportunities for different groups to exchange, dialog, understand, and share their historical memories, social dilemmas, and diverse experiences in terms of being "Taiwanese." Such exchanges and dialogs between all citizens of Taiwan are indispensable for the mainstream society to truly respect the feelings and experiences of the marginal groups and seriously confront the discriminations and prejudices against them.

NOTES

1. "Four Ethnic Groups" refers the four main ethnic groups: Taiwanese aborigines, the Hakka, the Hokkeins, and the Mainlanders. To aid the reader unfamiliar with the situation in Taiwan, I will provide a short history of these four ethnic groups. *Taiwanese aborigines:* Taiwanese aborigines are native to the island of Taiwan. They are Austro-nesian and are of Malayo-Polynesian descent. They share a very close blood relation-ship and appearance with other aboriginal people in Malaysia, the Philippines, and some islands around the Pacific Ocean. Their population accounted for approximately 2% to 3% of the entire population of Taiwan. *The Mainlanders:* The Mainlanders were those people who came to Taiwan with the KMT government around 1945–1949. They included administrators of the KMT party, government members, military men and their families, and people who wanted to run away from war. And their popula-tion is 12% to 15% of the whole population in Taiwan. That is less than the Hokkeins and the Hakka. *The Hakka:* The Hakka is a special ethnic group with a long history in Mainland China. Most people believe the following about the Hakka: They come from the northern part of Mainland China; they moved on more than five occasions on a large scale to the south. The Hakka arrived in Taiwan about 300 years ago, later than the Hokkeins. Their population is 15% to 18% of Taiwan, making it the second largest group. *The Hokkeins:* The Hokkeins are the largest ethnic group in Taiwan at around 65% of the total population. Their ancestors emigrated from the Fu-Jian province in the southeastern part of Mainland China in the seventeenth century (400 years ago).

2. From NIA. website: http://www.ris.gov.tw/346

3. Bhikhu Parekh (1998), "A Commitment to Cultural Pluralism," Speech for UNESCO, Stockholm, Sweden, 30 March–2 April 1998, at website http://www.unesco.sweden.org/conference/Papers/Paper1.htm. I will discuss the Parekh's model in Taiwan's case.

4. From 1949 to the 1970s, the KMT government kept the very strong control to cultural policy directly by the KMT party and administrative institutions, such as cen-sorship of media or publication and the establishment of cultural and arts associations under the control of KMT party. In addition, the president was the main and highest manager of cultural affairs to make and issue cultural policy without any cultural sector in the central government, and cultural policies were explicit and dominated by political consideration, party interests, and Chinese identity. Therefore, the ten-sion between Chinese nationalism and Taiwanese consciousness leads to the conflict between two "ethnic groups": The Ben Sheng (local to Taiwan)/Wai Sheng (external to Taiwan). The Ben Sheng (local to Taiwan)/Wai Sheng (external to Taiwan) divide

has been the basis of difference in Taiwan since 1949. The Ben Sheng people lived in Taiwan before 1949, including most of the Fulo, Hakka, and Aboriginal groups. The Wai Sheng people moved to Taiwan from Mainland China in 1949. Wai Sheng culture came to be viewed as a representative of Chinese culture and the official culture in Taiwan. The dominant policy for the construction of a national culture brought about different results for the Ben Sheng and Wai Sheng people: the Wai Sheng people had only one culture—national culture—but the Ben Sheng people were forced to give up their culture until 1970. The national culture was not their culture, but was a source of oppression for them. Thus, the Wei-Sheng culture became the official or national culture, and its diversity was ignored and limited.

5. From 1970 to 1990, the KMT government faced many challenges from civil society for more freedom and democracy, and they need to use more meticulous and implicit ways to interfere with cultural affairs. The KMT government claimed that the establishment of CCA (Committee of Cultural Affair) and local cultural centers was to provide better and more cultural services and art activities to people, rather than control culture or promote Chinese identity. Faced with the challenge of Taiwanese consciousness, the KMT government improves community consciousness to reduce the conflicts between Chinese identity and Taiwanese identity.

6. The Kuomintang Party (KMT) has already faced numerous challenges while representing China in the 1970s. These challenges include the acceptance of the People's Republic of China as the representative of China in 1971 and the United States severing diplomatic ties with Taiwan to accept China in 1979. The Taiwanese society started to question and challenge KMT's original Chinese Nationalism policies, and forced the KMT to start to respond to the upsurge of Taiwanese consciousness and localization demands. The Democratic Progressive Party (DDP) that represents the local consciousness proposed constitutional suggestions that are more congruous to ethnic equality and supported by the Taiwanese society. The KMT must also adhere to the prevailing social atmosphere and cannot continue to Maintain the Chinese mainlander dominance.

7. Numerous cultural policies are designed to protect the various cultural rights of the indigenous peoples. The government has strived to revive traditional indigenous festivals, maintain indigenous cultural heritage, redefine tribal histories, and support the indigenous population and uphold their rights to cultural participation. The establishment of indigenous TV broadcasts has promoted the right to participate in cultural life, the right to cultural identity, and the right to represent their groups. At the same time, the government has instigated a number of cultural policies aimed at reviving the indigenous languages, such as the bonus points in the educational systems and the language certificate in the employment market to improve the motivation of the younger generations to learn traditional languages (Lee, Tai-Yuan 2003).

8. Measures in the Plan to Promote the Hakka Culture within Six Years (HAC 2002) include: helping to establish Hakka cultural workshops and artists villages, setting up Hakka cultural centers to help local governments and communities promote Hakka culture, and reconstructing Hakka cultural life by improving Hakka cultural activities, recording Hakka cultural life, and creating traditional Hakka culture (HAC 2002: 6–12). Since then, the main cultural policies of the HAC from 2002 to 2010 have included: the improvement of Hakka language education, the development of a Hakka academic community, the improvement of Hakka media (TV and radio), the

development of Hakka industries and economy such as Hakka tourism and Hakka festivals, and the construction of a global Hakka network (HAC 2010). From the HAC website: http://www.hakka.gov.tw/public/Data/032514321871.pdf (in Chinese).

9. The Department of Education and Culture in the CIP has several responsibilities: to consider, work out, and negotiate indigenous education and culture; to research, preserve, and spread the indigenous language; to train and cultivate the skills of the indigenous people; and to improve and support indigenous media, cultural organizations, and activities. The main duties of the CIP are to formulate laws and policies to support the development of indigenous cultures and to sponsor the indigenous cultural and educational groups.

10. For example, some special representation rights are given to the indigenous peoples in Taiwan, such as the exclusive right to hunt in National Parks. The revision of the Act of National Parks on November 29, 2000, removed the limitation on hunting by indigenous peoples. From the website: http://web.pts.org.tw/~abori/archives/001209/index.html (in Chinese). Discussions of self-governance by the indigenous peoples began in 1997 and continue until this day. The Act for Self-government continues to be discussed in the government and parliament. As of September 2010, there was still no clear conclusion and legislation. From the website: http://www.libertytimes.com.tw/2010/new/sep/23/today-p4.htm (in Chinese).

11. In July 1997, the National Assembly amended Paragraph 9, Article 10, of the Constitution to declare the "the nation has affirmed multiculturalism and actively development measures to maintain and develop Aboriginal languages and culture." Based on this legal source, the Council of Indigenous People has continued to develop the Aboriginal Education Act, Aboriginal Development Act, Aboriginal Self-governance Act drafts, and so on, in order to safeguard the interests of the indigenous peoples.

12. For example, numerous indigenous parents believe that it is not necessary to teach their mother tongue to their children. If the parents have money to do so, they tend to send their children to urban areas to learn Mandarin Chinese or English (Huang, Zhi-wei and Xiong, Tong-Xin 2003).

13. From the CIP website: http://www.apc.gov.tw/main/docList/docList.jsp?cateI D=A001114&linkParent=49&linkSelf=339&linkRoot=4 (in Chinese).

14 http://www.moi.gov.tw/stat/

15. http://city.udn.com/55272/5131588#ixzz3KiVxIkU4

16. Thanks to NGO groups' supportive activities, the Taipei Railway Station has been acknowledged as the location for Indonesian Muslims Ramadan celebrations and many Taipei residents also participate in it.

17. For example, Abby Lu, whose mother is Spanish and Filipino mixed and whose father is Chinese and Filipino mixed, formed a band to promote rock & roll in Taiwan, and their music represents a new Taiwanese pop music. The new immigrants' multi-style Taiwanese pop music that uses Western instruments and traditional Filipino instruments interchangeably embraces the Filipino optimistic attitude and the Spanish passion to form an Oriental/Latin musical enchantment with a tint of American jazz and rock flavor.

18. from the website : http://www.storm.mg/lifestyle/60058 (You-Jin Chen special article: "I am a new second generation – Fujian veteran father × Chinese immigrant mother from Indonesia").

19. From the website: http://www.cw.com.tw/article/article.action?id=5069246#st hash.0jp6h8hC.dpuf
20. From the website: http://2014tlam-tw.blogspot.tw/2014/02/o-2012474430-20117201110-20124201220133.html#more
21. From the website: http://www.moc.gov.tw/information_250_14404.html

REFERENCES

Bhabha, Homi K. 1994. *The Location of Culture*. London: Routledge.

Chiou, Shwu-Wen. 1999. "Zai Di Guo Ji Hau' Riben Nong Cun FeilVbin Xin Ning [Local Internationalization: The Philippines Spouses in Japanese Villages]." *Contemporary*, 141(1): 108–17. (in Chinese).

Cheng, Shu-Lin. 2002. *Yuanzhuming Yun Dong Zhong Quan Li Fa Zhi Hua De Kun Ju [The Difficult Position of Law legislation in the Taiwan's Indigenous Movements: And the Discussion of Self-Government of Taiwan's Indigenous Peoples]*. MA Thesis. Graduate School of Law. National Taiwan University.

Fraser, Nancy. 2003. "Social Justice in the Age of Identity Politics," in *Redistribution or Recognition? A Political-Philosophical Exchange*, edited by Nancy Fraser and Axel Honneth. London and New York: Verso.

Fraser, Nancy. 2005. "Reframing Global Justice." *New Left Review*, 36, Nov/Dec.

Democratic Progress Party. 1992. *Multi-Ethnic Relationship and Multi-Cultures—the Ethnic and Cultural Policy of DPP*. Taipei, DPP.

Hsia, Hsiao-Chuan. 2000. "Zi Ben Guo Ji Hua Xia De Guo Ji Hun Yin: Yi Taiwan De Wai Jin Xinning Xian Xiang Wei Li [Transnational Marriage and the Internationalisation of Capital - The Case of the Foreign Bride Phenomenon in Taiwan)." *Taiwan: A Radical Quarterly in Social Studies*, 39: 45–92. (in Chinese).

Hsia, Hsiao-Chuan. 2009. "Foreign Spouses, Multiple Citizenship and the Immigrant Movement in Taiwan." *Asian and Pacific Migration Journal*, 18(1): 17–46.

Hsia, Hsiao-Chuan. 2013. "'Wo Men' Han 'Ta Men' De Jiao Hui [The Meeting of 'We' and 'They']," in *"Li: Wo Men De Mai Mai, Tai Men De Yi Sheng [Separation: Our Business and Their Whole Life]*," edited by Four Way Voices, 6–8. Taipei: Chinese Times Publisher.

Huang, Zhi-Wei and Xiong, Tong-Xin. 2003. "Taiwan Yuanzhumin Jiao Yu De Lun Shu: Duo Yuan Wei Hua Si Chao De Fan Si [Discussion of Indigenous Education: Reflections on Multicultural Thought]." *Indigenous Education Quarterly*, 29: 55–76. (in Chinese).

Joppke, C. 1998. "Immigration Challenges the Nation-State," in *Challenge to the Nation-State: Immigration in Western Europe and the United States*, edited by Christian Joppke, 5–39. Oxford: Oxford University Press.

Kang Chao. 2006. "Duo Yuan Wei Hua De Xiu Ci, Xheng Zhi He Li Lun [Multiculturalism: Rhetoric, Politics and Conceptualization]." *Taiwan: A Radical Quarterly in Social Studies*, 62: 147–89. (in Chinese).

Kymlicka, Will. 1995. *Multicultural Citizenship: A Liberal Theory of Minority Rights*. Oxford: Oxford University Press.

Lee, Dan-Hui. 1994. "Quanguo Yuanzhumin Wei Hua Hui Yi Yan Jiang [The speech at the National Meeting of Aboriginal Culture]." 11, April, Pingtung: the Cultural Park of Aboriginal Peoples. (in Chinese).

Lee, Hong-Yuan. 2013. "Presentation: Building an Immigrant-friendly Environment, Light the Torches for New Immigrants across the Country," in *2013 International Conference on Immigrant Policy and New Immigrants Torch Program Achievement Exhibition*, Date: Tuesday, November 19th, 2013, Venue: GIS National Taiwan University Convention Center.

Lee, Tai-Yen. 2003. *Taiwan Yuanzhumain Yu Yan Neng Li Ren Zheng Zhi Du Zhi Ping Gu [Evaluation to the Accreditation of the Indigenous Languages Proficiency in Taiwan]*. MA Thesis, National Chengchi University. (in Chinese).

Muetzelfeldt, M. and G. Smith. 2002. "Civil Society and Global Governance: The Possibilities for Global Citizenship." *Citizenship Studies*, 6(1): 55–75.

Pan, Shu-man. 2013. "Crossroads of Multicultural Citizenship Practice: Dilemmas and Possibility," in *2013 International Conference on Immigration Policy and New Immigrants Torch Program Achievements Exhibition*, Tuesday, November 19th, 2013, Venue: GIS National Taiwan University Convention Center, Taipei.

Parekh, Bhikhu. 1998. "A Commitment to Cultural Pluralism," Speech for UNESCO, Stockholm, Sweden, 30 March–2 April 1998, at web site http://www.unesco.sweden.org/conference/Papers/Paper1.htm.

Vertovec, S. 1999. "Conceiving and Researching Transnationalism." *Ethnic and Racial Studies*, 22(2): 447–62.

Vertovec, S. 2001. "Transnationlism and Identity." *Journal of Ethnic and Migration Studiesno*, 27(4): 573–82.

Wang, Li-Jung. 2007. "Diaspora, Identity and Cultural Citizenship: The Hakkas in Multicultural Taiwan." *Ethnic and Racial Studies*, 30(5): 875–95.

Wang, Li-Jung. 2014. "Cultural Rights and Citizenship in Cultural Policy: Taiwan and China." *International Journal of Cultural Policy*, 29(1): 21–39.

Wei, Mei-Chuan. 2009. "Duo Yuan Wei Hua Zhu Yi Zai Taiwan Qi Lun Shu Qui Yan, Nei Rong, Yan Bian Yu Dui Taiwan Min Zhu Zheng Zhi De Ying Xinang Zhi Chu Tan [Multiculturalism in Taiwan: A Preliminary Study of Its Origins, Evolution, and Impact on Taiwan's Democratic Politics)." *Taiwan: A Radical Quarterly in Social Studies*, 75: 287–319. (in Chinese).

Xue, C. T. and Lin H. F. 2003. "The Change of Family in Taiwan: Foreign Spouses." *Journal of National Policy*, October, 2003.

Yang, Wan-Ying and Ya-Wen, Chang. 2014. "Wei She Me Fan Dui Yi Gong/ Yi Ming? Li Yi Chong Tu Hao Wen Hua Paichi? [Who oppose Immigration? Interest Conflict and Cultural Exclusion Explanations]." *Taiwanese Journal of Political Sciences*, 60: 43–84. (in Chinese).

Young, Iris Marion. 1990. *Justice and the Politics of Difference*. New Jersey: Princeton University Press.

Zhang, Zheng. 2014. *Wai Po Jia Yung Shi: Tai Wan Re Bi Xiu De Dongnanyan Xue Fen [Something's Up at Grandma's Home: Compulsory Southeastern Credit for The Taiwanese]*. Taipei: Owl Publishing House.

Zhang, Pei-Lun. 2007. "Yuanzhumain Jiao Yu You Hui Dai Yu Tan Tao [The Discussion on the Educational Affirmative Policy of Indigenous Peoples]." *Taiwan Indigenous Studies Review*, 2: 47–64. (in Chinese).

Chapter 4

Multicultural Co-living (*tabunka kyosei*) in Japan

Localized Engagement without Multiculturalism

Koichi Iwabuchi

In many Western countries, multiculturalism as a policy and social aspiration to promote an egalitarian recognition and equal treatment of cultural diversity sharply declined in the first decade of the twenty-first century. The ever-growing mobility of people crossing national borders, on the one hand, makes cultural diversity within national borders more multifaceted and complicated and puts the cogency of the notion of multiculturalism "with its rather static connotation of coexisting but mutually exclusive cultural communities" (Ang 2009: 19) into critical scrutiny.

Multiculturalism has also been under strong attack, especially after September 11, 2001, as it is considered divisive to national unity and harmful to national security, hence the governments reinforcing national border control regimes and stressing national integration. This rhetoric of national crisis sensationally amplifies people's sense of anxiety and longing for a secure and peaceful community to live in; however, this anxiety is not entirely groundless but has been provoked by the escalating speed and scale of socio-economic change and instability under the processes of globalization, which push forward transnational mobility and interconnection of people, capital, ideas, and images.

However, the predicament of multiculturalism does not erase the significance of engaging with multicultural situations, but ever-intensifying cultural diversity even more strongly underlines its imperativeness. This is indicative of Hall's (2000) differentiation of the multicultural question from multiculturalism, which Ahn mentions in Chapter 1. While multiculturalism is "the strategies and policies adopted to govern or manage the problems of diversity and multiplicity" (Hall 2000: 209), an imperative project that each society needs to engage is the multicultural question: a question of "how people from different cultures, different backgrounds, with different languages, different religious beliefs, produced by different and highly uneven histories, live together and attempt to build a common life while retaining something of their 'original identity'" (Hall 2000: 210). Under the current situation in which multiculturalism as a policy declines, it is required to develop a better conceptual tool and associated social praxis to effectively engage the multicultural question toward the creation of a more inclusive public space in which hitherto marginalized voices are justly heard and commonly shared and which promotes the dialogue among diverse citizens. Recent argument of "everyday multiculturalism" is one such attempt. It is an attentive examination of people's mundane practice of living together in difference and negotiating with cultural diversity to understand how the multicultural question is incompletely but actively enacted and worked out in society beyond multiculturalism policy and discourse (e.g., Wise and Velayutham 2009; Harris 2009). The understanding of such mundane practices offers precious insights into further advancement of the multicultural question.

While mostly developed in the Western context, the examination of everyday multiculturalism is also significant in East Asia. Yet, it requires a careful contextualization in terms of the relationship of the (un)development of multiculturalism policy and the nongovernmental local engagement with multicultural situations. Due to increasing visibility of migrants from other parts of Asia, the management of growing multicultural situations has come to be officially discussed in Japan, South Korea, and Taiwan in the new millennium, though the term "multiculturalism" is not always adopted. While this situation appears to be contrastive to that of many Western societies where multiculturalism has come under serious disapproval, it is a belated and unsatisfactory policy response to growing human mobility and accompanied cultural diversity. In Japan, although the postwar governments have been consistently disinclined to adopt an immigration policy, the number of foreign nationals residing in the country has been nearly constantly increasing due to labor migration and international marriage since the late 1980s when the strong Japanese economy attracted many migrants especially from other Asian countries. Accordingly, in addition to long-existing ethnic minorities, the number of foreign-national residents, migrants, and "mixed blood" (*haafu*) younger people (see Iwabuchi 2014) has been noticeably increasing. A sharply declining birth rate and a rapidly aging population have also been generating a push from business sectors to accept more labor and skilled migrants to maintain Japan's economic strength. Thus, immigration and multicultural situations will continue to be a vital policy agenda and social issues in Japan in the years to come, but the current Japanese government still neither officially acknowledges Japan as an immigrant country nor develops a substantial policy to accept migrants and do justice to existing cultural diversity—even less so compared to South Korean and Taiwanese counterparts as discussed in other two chapters of this section. Eventually, the empowering practice to support the lives of migrants and ethnic minorities and enhance the praxis of "living together in difference" has been occurring at the local level. When the Japanese government took the initiative in a policy discussion of "multicultural co-living" (*tabunka kyosei*), it newly endorsed the significance of localities and local players such as local governments, NGOs/NPOs, and citizens' groups to deal with multicultural situations. Yet it eventually shows a lingering posture to refuse to acknowledge the multicultural question as a national matter.

In this situation, the Japanese case poses an intriguing question of whether and how everyday multiculturalism is relevant to the consideration of the engagement with multicultural situations in a society where multiculturalism and related immigration and social integration policy have not been institutionally developed on a national level. This chapter will argue that in the context that the Japanese government refuses to make immigration issues and multiculturalism a national policy agenda, Japan's everyday multiculturalism has been developed in tandem with the absence of multiculturalism policy, and in this sense, everyday multiculturalism is administered as localized engagement by the government's nonengagement. Acknowledging that the grassroots practices are an important feature of Japan's engagement with the multicultural question, I will suggest that they should be advanced in a way to seriously tackle a persisting binary perception of "Japanese" and "foreigners" and put forward a vision of Japan as an inclusive society in which people of diverse ethno-cultural backgrounds live together and participate as constitutive members of the nation.

GOVERNMENT'S UN-ENGAGEMENT WITH MULTICULTURAL REALITY

Although Japan has a strong inclination to officially represent itself as a homogenous nation, it has been a multicultural and multiethnic nation. Japan was a formally self-recognized multiethnic empire before 1945, and no small number of ethnic minorities has long lived in Japan such as resident Koreans and Chinese; Ainu people, who were officially recognized as indigenous people in 2008; as well as the people of marginalized regions like Okinawa. However, after losing its colonies and under the umbrella of the US Cold War policy, Japan reimagined itself as an ethno-racially homogenous nation without seriously facing the aftermath of its colonialism and enthusiastically advanced to achieve economic development (Iwabuchi 1994). In the postwar period, the strict border control over ethno-inflow limited the number of people migrating into Japan and the term *imin*—literally meaning immigration and immigrant—has not been used in official state policy agendas. Whenever it is used, it refers to emigration—those Japanese nationals who leave for other countries, especially those who emigrated to Hawaii, California, and Latin American countries in the prewar era.

Although the postwar setting has constructed a widely held view that Japan is not a country of immigration, the situation changed significantly in the late 1980s. Attracted by the strong Japanese economy and yen, many people from Asia and Latin America (mostly Japanese-Brazilians and Japanese-Peruvians, descendants of those who emigrated in the early twentieth century) as well as other parts of the world entered Japan not just as tourists, expatriates, or students, but also as workers and marriage migrants, in both urban and rural areas, who intended to live in Japan for a long time or permanently. Since then, the number of foreign-national residents has been nearly constantly increasing in Japan, despite the lingering financial and economic crisis since the collapse of the so-called bubble economy after the mid-1990s and the bankruptcy of Lehman Brothers in 2008 that has dampened job opportunities for migrants, and the Great East Japan Earthquake in March 2011 that discouraged some people who would like to migrate. While the number has been slightly decreasing since 2006, international marriage consists of about 3% to 4% of newly married couples each year, and in Tokyo and Aichi the percentage was around 5 in 2013.[1] Currently, according to data from the Ministry of Justice's website, the number of foreign nationals living in Japan was about 2.12 million at the end of 2014, while it was 1.22 million as of 1991.[2] Although the share of foreign-national residents in the total population is not high compared to many Western countries, the size of the ethnic and racialized minority population would be much larger when naturalized immigrants, children whose father and/or mother is originally from foreign countries and ethnic minorities born with Japanese nationality are included.

Furthermore, Japan is currently facing rather a drastic change of social demography due to the sharp decline of the birth rate and consequent aging of the population, change which any modern society has never experienced before. Consequently, there is a growing demand, especially from business sectors, to accept more migrants as labor forces. A 2000 report by the Department of Economic and Social Affairs, United Nations Secretariat, suggested the necessity for Japan to accept about 500,000 migrants every year in the coming 50 years if Japan is to keep its economic activities intact (United Nations 2000). In 2008, some members of the Liberal Democratic Party then in government also proposed a more relaxed migration policy to accept 10 million migrants (about 10% of the population) in the coming 50 years. While this proposal has never been taken seriously by policy makers, there has been a gradual shift in policy to accept more migrant workers, especially skilled migrants. Most recently, the government has decided to accept temporary construction workers for the preparation for Tokyo Olympic 2020, but the demand is no longer limited to the so-called 3k (or 3d) jobs (*kiken, kitanai, kitsui* = dangerous, dirty, difficult). It extends to nurses and caregivers for the elderly as well as other skilled and managerial jobs to maintain Japanese economy and welfare system. Since 2006, the government has entered Economic Partnership Agreements (EPA) with the Philippines, Indonesia, and Vietnam to bring in caregivers and has plans to expand these agreements. In 2014, a new visa was launched to attract more highly skilled foreign workers by allowing them to stay in Japan permanently. As in other Western countries, immigration has eventually become a socially and economically imperative issue in Japan.

MULTICULTURAL CO-LIVING AND THE SIGNIFICANCE OF THE LOCAL

Under the situation that the amplification of multicultural reality in Japan is a long-term trend and escalating cultural diversity has become conspicuous, the Japanese government became belatedly started policy discussion to administer foreign nationals living in Japan. In 2005, the Committee for the Promotion of Multicultural Co-living was established by the Ministry of Internal Affairs and Communications of Japan and in the subsequent year its report "Towards the Local Development of Multicultural Co-living" was submitted to the government. The report states the aim of multicultural co-living (*tabunka kyosei*) as follows: "People of various nationalities and ethnicities live as members of local communities by striving to mutually recognize differences and construct equal relationships." This initiative was positively received as the first step for the government to be involved with the multicultural situation in Japan by encouraging and supporting local governments to offer appropriate services for foreign-national residents such as interpreting, language education, housing, and health care. Particularly considered worthy of note is the first official use of the term *seikatsusha/chiiki jumin* (residents of local communities), replacing the hitherto notion of *gaikokujin* (foreigner), usage of which has an implication that foreigners living in Japan were a social problem.

It should be noted, however, that the government's multicultural co-living initiative does not accompany substantial national policies. Which is to say, unlike Taiwan and South Korea, the Japanese government neither yet officially recognizes Japan as a multicultural society nor intends to develop comprehensive policies to address ongoing inequality and discrimination against them and promote social integration, not to mention multiculturalism policy. The government effortlessly commissions actual support for and handling of foreign nationals living in Japan to local governments and NGOs/NPOs working in the area and recognizes them simply as local residents, not as members of the nation. Multicultural co-living thus lacks the engagement with both multiculturalism and the multicultural question on the national level. At the same time, the policy initiative's underlining on the local as a site of multicultural engagement actually reflects the fact that multicultural issues have been actively dealt with by the local and grassroots actors. While, as I will discuss later, there is obviously the limitation of such local initiative to tackle the multicultural question without national institutional arrangements, the significance of localities as a site in which mundane practices of the multicultural question and everyday multiculturalism are taking place should not be underestimated in the Japanese context.

It needs to be noted that the term *kyosei* ("co-living" or "living together"), which was used for the government's policy initiative, has its origin in activities developed from grassroots. The term *kyosei* was first advocated by various groups and social movements such as feminism, the Ainu people, and *minamata* (mercury poisoning) disease since the 1970s. *Tabunka kyosei* became a practice-driven catchphrase after the Great Hanshin-Awaji Earthquake in 1995 when citizens of diverse descents such as resident Koreans and Vietnamese worked together with Japanese local communities to support the victims and revive the suffering areas. *Tabunka kyosei* was also adopted by local governments in cities such as Kawasaki and Hamamatsu, and NGOs, NPOs, and citizens' groups since the late-1980s to support the lives of migrants, foreign nationals, and ethnic/racial minorities who lack fundamental citizenship rights and access to social and welfare services in the absence of national policy. Paying attention to grassroots supporting activities and movements in the local is thus crucial to understand multicultural engagements in the Japanese context. It also reveals how they have expanded citizenship in the local community for certain ethnic minorities and migrants in the absence of national policy and institution.

Localities are also significant sites for discerning how the negotiation with cultural diversity is practiced through community participation and mundane negotiation over cultural differences. Being in line with the argument of "everyday multiculturalism" though they do not refer to the term, Matsumiya and Yamamoto (2007) stress the necessity to examine actual interactions, which is not necessarily of a harmonious kind, between Japanese and foreign residents in the local communities to well grasp what is actually going on in everyday life. While some Japanese people have negative images of foreign residents and tend to be unwilling to live together with them in the same community, Matsumiya and Yamamoto (2007) argue, Japanese residents' dispositions on the "consciousness level" do not straightforwardly direct their actual practices on the "interpersonal reciprocal level." There is in reality a space in which residents, Japanese or not, meet, converse, and work with each other to handle various issues that they are facing in everyday life.

Matsumiya and Yamamoto's (2007) stress on the local negotiation process is suggestive of the differentiation of urban and national citizenship. Like Robins (2000), Ang distinguishes urban citizenship—"politics of presence" that "centers around the everyday pragmatic and affective dimensions of 'rights to the city'"—from national citizenship—"politics of representation" that is "generally defined in terms of a formal demarcation of national belonging (such as the possession of a passport and the ability to vote)" (2006: 33). Ang thus defines the city "as [a] lived physical and social space" in contrast to the nation as an abstract imagined community:

> While concepts of national citizenship are delimited in absolutist terms of inclusion and exclusion, urban citizenship encompasses the process of living with difference, rather than its negation, handling actual heterogeneity rather than imposing imaginary homogeneity or commonality. (Ang 2006: 39)

Politics of presence highlights how citizenship is actually practiced and negotiated in the urban space, which is not fully contained by the national politics of representation.

Needless to say, we cannot entirely isolate urban or local citizenship from national citizenship. National citizenship still has an unambiguously dominant governing power that has some impacts on the formulation of local/ urban citizenship. However, an investigation of politics of presence propels us to rethink what it means to belong to society and how people learn to negotiate with each other over the issues of living together in differences. As Appiah (2005) argues, it explicates the process of learning cosmopolitanism through mundane actions—cosmopolitanism that is not a detached, elite kind, but rooted in everyday practices and stimulates mutual transformations of the perception of self–other relationships. While actual encounters might be highly conflict-laden, "conversation doesn't have to lead to consensus about anything, especially not values: it's enough that it helps people get used to one another" (Appiah 2010: 85). Indeed, the urban space can be considered "the place where cosmopolitan orientations are most likely to take roots" (Stevenson 2003a: 60) as it is a vibrant site in which people learn from each other how to live together through daily interactions. Likewise, Matsumiya and Yamamoto (2007) contend that a view that puts too much stress on irreducible cultural differences and/or managing cultural diversity disguised as celebration would lose sight of the day-to-day practices of multicultural coliving as it does not well attend to how the "etiquette of co-living" has been mutually learned and formed.

MULTICULTURAL CO-LIVING WITHOUT
MULTICULTURALISM

The grassroots practices of multicultural co-living in the Japanese context appear to be comparable to everyday multiculturalism in the local space. However, there is a crucial difference between them in terms of the development of multiculturalism policy and related discourses and actions. The discussions of everyday multiculturalism, and Hall's multicultural question too, are founded on a tacit assumption that ethnic minorities are granted, if not fully, institutionalized entitlements as citizens or residents of the country under multiculturalism policy and social integration policy on the national level—although the issue of cultural recognition is arguably hardest to achieve by policy and legislation. However, this is not the case with East Asian societies, especially in Japan, as noted above. Let me reiterate that Japan's multicultural co-living policy discussion does not involve any national government's policy engagement while enhancing the relevance of the grassroots activities at the local level in a way to isolate them from the development of multicultural questions as a national matter. How can the notion of everyday multiculturalism be relevant to a society like Japan, which has not developed an immigration policy and has no preexisting institutions that deal with cultural diversity and where citizenship is fundamentally equated with nationality based on *jus sanguinis*?

This is not to deny the significance of the localities as the vital context within which the citizenship of migrants and ethnically marginalized people are expanded and multicultural co-living is actually practiced in the absence of national policies and institutional arrangements. However, the point is that Japan's case urges differentiated considerations of the significance of localities for it is questionable whether grassroots-driven practices and support for multicultural co-living in localities are sufficient to fully engage multicultural situations and the multicultural question. To say nothing of nationality law and immigration policy that secures entitlements of social welfare and health insurance, comprehensive nationwide programs are required to foster and enhance respect for cultural diversity by developing multicultural education curriculums and antiracism (and anti-hate-speech due to the recent rise of hate speech movements in Japan) regulation as well as media services that reflect diverse voices. Since the actual operation of these programs are all tightly controlled by the state, a central question is whether and how the grassroots practices of multicultural co-living in localities could lead to compelling and collaborating with the government to develop such programs and what kind of critique is needed for the actualization of this bottom-up transformation.

The multicultural co-living policy initiative has been widely criticized by Japanese scholars and activists as unsubstantial and cosmetic (see

Morris-Suzuki 2003). It does not bring about any change in the idea of national membership and actually masks deeply structured discrimination and inequality. This point is often associated with the critique of multicultural co-living for being shallowly culture centered by paying much attention to culture and ethnicity, whereby urgent socioeconomic problems such as poverty and unemployment or access to social security and health insurance that migrants face tend to be obscured (Kajita, Tanno, Higuchi 2005). In condemning multicultural co-living policy initiative for failing to give a due attention to actually existing practices at the local level, Matsumiya and Yamamoto (2007) also argue that the central issue to be analyzed is not a cultural one (i.e., ethnicity and difference) as emphasized by the multicultural co-living discourse. Indeed, the government is rightly criticized for its superficially culture-centered vision of multicultural co-living that masks socioeconomic difficulties and inequality and loses sight of mundane interaction and negotiation processes. However, it is somehow misleading to say that multicultural co-living policy puts "culture" in the center stage as some critics seem to assume. Rather, a critique should also be made against the lack of engagement with the multicultural question, which has never been pursued in Japan's multicultural co-living initiative. While the social, economic, and civic aspects of citizenship entitlement and distribution are urgent and fundamental matters, earnestly underlining the cultural aspects in critical engagement with multicultural co-living is, I would argue, also imperative to go beyond the co-option of the localized promotion of multicultural co-living by the state governance that seeks to keep an essentialized notion of the "Japanese" intact.

BEYOND THE TENACIOUS OPPOSITION OF "JAPANESE" AND "FOREIGNERS"

Hatano (2006) criticizes multicultural co-living policy initiative's superficial emphasis on "multiculture" and harmonious co-living among groups of different cultures as it slyly celebrate cultural diversity only for the majority by the majority, which makes no fundamental change in the conception of the nation. This is akin to what Hage (1998) calls "multiculturalism of having," in which the dominant group can claim the power to control, tolerate, and consume cultural diversity in society without fundamentally changing the social structure. It is opposite to "multiculturalism of being" in which everyone fully recognizes cultural diversity as fundamentally constitutive of society and is responsible for self-reflexively changing their own view of self/other relations and transforming society in an inclusive manner. More fundamentally, rejecting to make the multicultural question a national issue, the multicultural co-living initiative shrewdly evades the question of who Japanese citizens are—"proper" members of the nation—whereby the rigid boundary between "Japanese" and "foreigners" is kept intact. Adopting the term "local residents," the government appears willing to assist local actors in creating a better social environment where foreign residents can live smoothly and nonthreateningly, but a new category of local residents neither attests to the inclusion of those with cultural differences as members of the national society nor discards the polarized definition of "Japanese" and "foreigners."

In this regard, it should be noted that there is an obvious continuity between the policy of multicultural co-living and that of "local internationalization" policy in the 1990s. At that time, the national government also pursued a policy to support local governments in accommodating the increasing number of foreigners staying and living in their areas with an aim to advance international cultural exchange within Japan. This bipolarized identification of cultural diversity in terms of Japanese and foreigners goes back even further, to the internationalization discourses of the 1970s and 1980s. The internationalizing aspiration of the government eventually evoked further national feeling and posturing, as it did not question, but rather strengthened the clearly demarcated cultural boundaries between nationals and "foreign others" (Iwabuchi 1994).

Being in line with the long-standing dominant discourse of internationalism, the Japanese government's refusal to make the multicultural question a national matter in the multicultural co-living initiative newly reinforces an institutionalized implicit polarization of "foreigner" and "Japanese," which eventually works as a "prototype" for multicultural co-living policy (Kashiwazaki 2009: 283–85). The policy question of accepting migrants and foreign-national residents tends to be discussed in terms of community planning of letting "foreigners" live and work smoothly in localities rather than accepting them as a member of Japanese society. Seriously challenging such view is also crucial to give a due attention to cultural differences of those who have Japanese nationalities by birth or by naturalization, as multicultural co-living policy and discourse tend to be inattentive to them by putting a focus on recent migrants and ethnic minorities of non-Japanese nationals. Even settled migrants and ethnic minorities with Japanese nationality are still regarded as "foreigners" or named by other categorizations such as *haafu* (mixed race) and *zainichi* (resident Koreans), which do not recognize them as the member of Japanese nation; they are still in but not of Japan.

A clearly demarcated distinction between Japanese and foreign tends to be not seriously interrogated or implicitly shared in some instances by local governments and NGOs/NPOs. As Kashiwazaki (2011: 50–54) notes, in contrast to their achievements in "the dissociation of an array of citizenship rights from the possession of Japanese nationality . . . the[ir] effort to redefine Japanese nationality is relatively weak." While exclusive nationalism, strong forces of assimilation, and the unequivocal association of nationality and citizenship have been much criticized in Japan, the *gaikokujin* (foreigner) category based on the assumption of Japanese as ethnically homogeneous is not much fundamentally questioned. Some NGOs, such as Solidarity Network with Migrants Japan (*Ijuuren*), has become more critical of the categorization of "foreigners" and replaced it with "migrant workers and citizens of foreign nations." Yet a more fundamental interrogation and transformation of the hitherto defined ethno-racial boundaries of who is "Japanese" needs to be made in order to advance the recognition of wide-ranging cultural differences on equal basis beyond a "foreigner" category.

TOWARD COLLECTIVE ENGAGEMENT WITH
THE MULTICULTURAL QUESTION

As Taylor (1992) argues, we need to ensure two interrelated kinds of equality to do justice to multicultural situations: equal dignity, which is related with the universalist entitlement of citizenship and civic rights, and equal respect, which is more concerned with fair recognition of cultural difference and living together in diversity. As the Japanese case of multicultural co-living without multiculturalism shows, the governments' disavowal to make the multicultural question a national matter is the most essential source of impediment to develop both. This is not to underestimate the grassroots endeavor to take care of multicultural situations. In the Japanese context, the turn to local residency is tactically important as well for going beyond the nationality-constricted notion of citizenship, as it is rigidly defined by its essentialized equation with nationality, ethnicity/race, and language. Grassroots activities in localities thus have played a crucial role in the expansion of some citizenship rights for foreign residents by dissociating "an array of citizenship rights from the possession of Japanese nationality" (Kashiwazaki 2011: 50). This commitment is becoming even more significant as further activation of migration and cross-border mobilities, which has been increasing the number of residents with (or without) various kinds of legal status, highlights the renewed necessity to reconsider the exclusive association of citizenship with nationality. Everyday multiculturalism that has been activated by supportive practices of multicultural co-living as well as mundane negotiation over cultural difference in localities would in the long run lead to the heightening of the national consciousness about cultural differences within Japan and the development of immigration policy (Shipper 2008). However, the grassroots practices alone are not sufficient to fully engage with equal recognition of cultural difference and living together in diversity. They need to be further developed into a national aspiration by distinctly promoting a society-wide project over the redefinition of who is a Japanese citizen, what are the multicultural questions that Japanese society needs to tackle, and how to create and share a democratic vision of Japan as a multicultural society in its full spectrum.

Given that no further development of multicultural co-living policy has been made and there is no prospect of this occurring in the near future or at least under the current government, we are required to consider how to substantially reinforce the already existing local practices and Japan's grassroots multicultural co-living in a bottom-up manner. Toward this end, the notion of cultural citizenship as a dialogic learning process gives us some productive suggestion. While the discussion of citizenship has focused on the formal aspects of political, civil, and social rights and the duties of the citizen, cultural citizenship first and foremost aims to seriously tackle an exclusive assumption of the membership of the nation by interrogating "who is silenced, marginalized, stereotyped and rendered invisible" and to "foster dialogue, complexity and communication in place of silence and homogeneity" (Stevenson 2003b: 345). Yet a crucial question of "how" remains, especially as cultural aspects of citizenship are the most difficult to tackle by policy and legislation. Hence, Delanty's (2007) point that cultural citizenship should be conceived as a "learning process" is rather suggestive. It aims to transcend and unlearn officially sanctioned dominant-cultural codes, categories, and values and facilitate people's self-reflexive reformation toward the construction of a more egalitarian and inclusive society: "One of the most important dimensions of citizenship concerns the language, cultural models, narratives, discourses that people use to make sense of their society, interpret their place in it, and construct courses of action" (Delanty 2007: 6). Such a learning process is not just an individual practice but a collective social praxis, for it functions as "a medium of social construction by which individual learning becomes translated and coordinated into collective learning and ultimately becomes realized in social institutions" (Delanty 2002: 66). Such a collective learning process would be imperative to go beyond the multicultural co-living without multiculturalism.

How to develop such a learning process of living together in difference in society still remains an urgent task for everyone concerned. We researchers have to strive for practicing everyday multiculturalism at various levels and sites of society by critically integrating the empirical and the aspirational and by collaborating with various social actors outside of schools and universities, in order to further develop already existing multicultural co-living and collective learning process to make Japan a more inclusive and democratic society. And the examination of the state of everyday multiculturalism or multicultural engagement without adequate multiculturalism policy in Japan, South Korea, and Taiwan in this section is also significant towards the nurturing of the mundane practice of engaging the multicultural question collaboratively and transnationally, which has not been well nurtured within the framework of the nation-state.

NOTES

1. http://www.e-stat.go.jp/SG1/estat/List.do?lid=000001127023
2. http://www.moj.go.jp/nyuukokukanri/kouhou/nyuukokukanri04_00050.html (accessed January 2015).

REFERENCES

Ang, Ien. 2006. "Nation, Migration, and the City: Mediating Urban Citizenship," in *City and Media: Cultural Perspectives on Urban Identities in a Mediatized World*, edited by Electronically Published Proceedings of the ESF-LiU Conference. Vadstena, Sweden, 2006. www.ep.liu.se/ecp/020/ (accessed May 2014).

Ang, Ien. 2009. "Provocation—Beyond Multiculturalism: A Journey to Nowhere?" *Humanities Research*, XV(2): 17–21.

Appiah, Kwame Anthony. 2010. *Cosmopolitanism: Ethics in a World of Strangers*. New York: WW Norton.

Delanty, Gerard. 2002. "Two Conceptions of Cultural Citizenship: A Review of Recent Literature on Culture and Citizenship." *Global Review of Ethnopolitics*, 1: 60–66.

Delanty, Gerard. 2007. "Citizenship as a Learning Process: Disciplinary Citizenship versus Cultural Citizenship." *Eurozine*, http://eurozine.com/pdf/2007-06-30-delanty-en.pdf (accessed April 2014).

Hage, Ghassan. 1998. *White Nation*. Sydney: Pluto Press.

Hall, Stuart. 2000. "Conclusion: The Multi-Cultural Questions," in *Un/Settled Multiculturalisms: Diasporas, Entanglements, Transruptions*. London: Zed Books.

Harris, Anita. 2013. *Young People and Everyday Multiculturalism*. New York: Routlege.

Hatano, Ririan Terumi. 2006. "Zainichi Burajirujin wo torimaku "tabunka kyōsei" no shomondai [Issues of Multicultural Co-living for Japanese Brazilians]," in *Kyōsei no naijitsu: Hihanteki shakaigengogaku kara no Toikake [Debunking "Co-living": Appraisal from a View Point of Critical Social Linguistics]*, edited by K. Ueda and J. Yamashita. Tokyo: Sangensha.

Iwabuchi, K. 1994. "Complicit Exoticism: Japan and its Other." *Continuum: Australian Journal of Media and Popular Culture*, 8(2): 49–82.

Iwabuchi, K., (ed.). 2014. *Hafu towa Dareka: Jinshu Konkō, Media Hyōshō, Kōshōjissen [Who are Hafu?: Mixed Race, Media Representations, Negotiation Practices]*. Tokyo: Seikyusha. (In Japanese).

Kajita, Takamichi, Tanno Kiyoto, Higuchi Naoto. 2005. *Kao no mienai teijūka: Nikkei Burajirujin to kokka/sijou/imin nettowāku [Invisible Settlement: Brazilians and the State/Market/Migrant Networks]*. Nagoya: Nagoya University Press.

Kashiwazaki, Chikako. 2011. "Internationalism and Transnationalism: Responses to Immigration in Japan," in *Migration and Integration: Japan in Comparative Perspective*, edited by G. Vogt and G. Roberts. Tokyo: Deutsches Institut für Japanstudien.

Matsumiya, Ashita and Kaori Yamamoto. 2007. "Chiiki jūmin to shiteno gaikokujin wo megutte [Foreigners as Local Residents]," in *Proceedings of Cultural Typhoon, Nagoya*, Association for Cultural Typhoon, 23–39.

Morris-Suzuki, Tessa. 2003. "Immigration and Citizenship in Contemporary Japan," in *Japan: Change and Continuity*, edited by J. Maswood, J. Graham and H. Miyajima. London: Routledge Curzon.

Robins, Kevin. 2000. "To London: The City Beyond the Nation," in *British Cultural Studies: Geography, Nationality, and Identity*, edited by D. Morley and K. Robins. Oxford: Oxford University Press.

Shipper, Apichai W. 2008. *Fighting for Foreigners: Immigration and Its Impact on Japanese Democracy*. Ithaca, NY: Cornell University Press.

Stevenson, Nick. 2003a. *Cultural Citizenship. Cosmopolitan Questions*. Maidenhead: Open University Press.

Stevenson, Nick. 2003b. "Cultural Citizenship in the 'Cultural' Society: A Cosmopolitan Approach." *Citizenship Studies*, 7(3): 331–48.

Taylor, Charles. 1992. "The Politics of Recognition," in *Multiculturalism: Examining the Politics of Recognition*, edited by A. Gutmann. Princeton, NJ: Princeton University Press.

United Nations. 2000. *Replacement Migration: Is it A Solution to Declining and Ageing Populations?* Department of Economic and Social Affairs, Population Division. http://www.un.org/en/development/desa/population/publications/ageing/replacement-migration.shtml (accessed April 2014).

Wise, Amanda and Selvaraj Velayutham, (eds.). 2009. *Everyday Multiculturalism*. Houndsmills, England: Palgrave Macmillan.

Section 2

RACIALIZATION OF
MULTICULTURAL SITUATIONS

Chapter 5

The Racialization of Multicultural Families by Media in a Multicultural Nation

Hyesil Jung

The Korean government announced that the Korean society is multicultural after Statics Korea reported that the population of foreign residents was over 1 million in 2007.[1] A year later, Korea's parliament enacted a law to support multicultural families, and thus far, the Korean government's policies reflect the agenda to pursue multiculturalism. As a result, mainstreams media has been portrayed that the Korean Society is going to stage of multi-racial and multi-ethnic society. However, Korean society has not yet reached an agreement on what is meant by "multiculturalism" and has not found the way how to coexist Korean and migrants.

Korean society looks over the diversity of migrants, but only focuses on hierarchy of migrant's economic status and nationality. This hierarchy is easily divided between migrants who are laborers or not, Asian or not, and especially marital migrant or not. These divisions affect the Immigration Control Act (ICA) and Visa Entry policy for foreigners. Above all ICA give the priority a marriage migrant who could get a membership of Korean as a family. Therefore, the policy of multiculturalism is not for all diverse migrants from around the world. Instead, it only focuses on marital migrants and their family who is called by legal title of "multicultural family," except for migrant labor and refugees. Alternatively, Korean society has an ambiguous attitude toward multicultural families, which is seen in the methods of both inclusion and exclusion. Such an attitude can also be easily be seen through the media coverage on the topic, which indicates how the Korean society wants to differentiate the multicultural families from Korean families while also expecting their assimilation into the Korean society.

Racism is commonly defined as "the belief that biological differences between races determine an individual's abilities." According to this definition, there are implications that a certain race is superior to others; thus, inequalities between races are thought to be a natural result of hierarchy. However, in order to examine racial discrimination in Korea, it is necessary to take an approach different from that of traditional racism. Whereas the notion of traditional racism is focused on "groups categorized by physical features," racial discrimination in Korea is the discrimination against other racial groups (especially people of African descent), and discrimination within the same racial group occurs at the same time. There is discrimination against Asians, who is meant be the term "Asians." It can be argued that this could be better explained with concepts of discrimination based on nationalism or ethnic discrimination, but it can still be regarded as an aspect of racism as it defines certain people as inferior and discriminates against them.[2] Therefore, racism of Korea is different from traditional racism of Western society. This is because racial discrimination within same race and the appearance is indistinguishable feature. The process of racialization is an ongoing phenomenon, which involves calling attention to values similar to that of racial distinction, and stigmatize minority such as migrants by labeling a race. In this regard, the Korean government's multicultural policies are worth nothing. That is, Korea's multicultural policies involve the active use of racist metaphors that stir up racism.[3]

In particular, multicultural families are categorized as a minority group that are inferior to Korean and Western migrants and their members, who are married migrants and children were born or adopted, are always labeled such as the term "multicultural" so that they could possibly never be identified as a real Korean and their diverse identities are removed.

This chapter explores why the Korean society has an ambivalent attitude towards multicultural families and how they are racialized by mass media. Namely what is the media's mechanism of racializing the multicultural families and how the mass media is produce a certain images of multicultural families in Korean society. This chapter presents a discourse analysis of the results taken from my participation in two different projects monitoring both television and news coverage. The first took place between May and October 2012 for the National Human Rights Commission, and the second in 2014 in preparation for the UN Special Rapporteur's report on contemporary forms of racism. Monitoring takes place and makes sense only in the context of serious social problems such as racism. This not only requires insight into media discourse structures and processing, but especially warrants focus on the social problem itself. Discourse actually affects social belief of a group, including prejudices and racist ideologies.[4]

The aim of this chapter is to find how media categorized and intensifies multicultural families as an other race different from Korean. Therefore, my works focuses on the Korean identity, and demonstrates how an multicultural families are racialized in Korean society and by media.

WHO IS A KOREAN?

Korean society has long held the belief that Korea is a homogeneous society since the Tan-gun era.[5] This belief always is an indulgence for justifying their exclusion to strangers. The myth of pure blood in Korea society removes or canceals various histories that includes: Japanese women marrying Korean men after liberation from Japan's colonial rule, the Chinese referred to as "Hwagyo" have lived in Korea for more than hundred years, Korean women who married U.S. soldiers and their mixed—race children. All of these groups have had the option of leaving or living in Korea, but if they want choose the latter, then they are rendered voiceless, invisibilized, and without rights. They are excluded from military service, are unable to be naturalized as Koreans due to their different ethnic backgrounds, and are deemed "half-blooded" Koreans. They are also isolated from the public school system, as well as from social life. Coexistence necessitates changes in both the immigration system and the nationality law.

It is difficult to accept migrant laborers and marital migrants as members of Korean society despite the needs of industry and marriage market. These immigrants are newcomers from Asia, and some migrants are compatriots of their forefathers who originated from Korea. But the immigration system and the nationality law must be revised legally in order for there to be coexistence with each other. Some migrant laborers are treated as temporary residents who will return to their country after they finish their period of employment so that they aren't able to stay in this land unless they marry a Korean or be an illegal migrant laborer. In contrast with these migrant laborers, compatriots such as Korean-Chinese individuals have a privileged legal advantage to get qualification for work or could be naturalized by recovered Korean national-ity. This legal advantage is given to compatriots on the basis of the law for Overseas.[6] Clearly, this opportunity is a result of ethnocentrism of Korea, which their lineage of family must prove that their identity belongs to Korea's national identity.

But we have to pay attention marred immigrants who are easily access to citizenship of Korea. They are included as Korean family so that supported through legal system and policy for integration of Korean society. The first step in the process of "Be Korean" is learning the Korean language, and the second is learning the Korean culture. This process is used by the Centre for Multicultural Family, which has about 220 centers nationwide supported by the Ministry of Gender Equality and Family on the basis of the law to support multicultural families. This is not optional; therefore, if any married immigrant wants stable stay as a citizen of Korea and wants Korean nationality, it is their duty to pass a rite of passage for social integration. But it is also an opportunity that is given only to married immigrants who are the member of multicultural families.

Mary Douglas (1997) argues that the concept of society is strong image and the society have ability to dominant members and to make act by inner rights. And this image delineates the boundary line between outside, inside, and periphery zone in a society control over the border and people. And also borders are markers of identity of a modern state. This important role of border, in the creation and the maintenance of the nation and state, is one reason why borders have also become a term within narrative discourses of nationalism and identity (Malcolm Anderson 1996, recited from book of borders). Historically, Korean society maintains the inside border so that make stranger as the outsider of inside because of their ethnic identity or hybridism. But the outsider of inside is suddenly identified as multicultural existence as newcomers cross border of outside. These people are rearranged according to their visa status and possibility whether they get nationality or not and their positions are relocated according to their ethnic identity and family lineage. The border of outside and inside is multilayered and complicated no matter whether this border is a fact or a symbol. But what's clear is that all these people are an outsider or a periphery of inside, although some of them have Korean nationality. This is because their royalty is so doubtful and their purposes of stay are only for economic reason. And also their children are not qualified to be true Korean.

The term "multicultural" in the Korean society refers to a specific group of people. The Support for Multicultural Families Act specifically designates families whose members are migrants married to Korean citizens and whose children were born to them or adopted. The use of this term has deviated its purpose, and has become applied narrowly, primarily referring to either married migrant men from Asia (originally migrant workers) and married migrant women (generally marriage through religious groups or marriage broker) and is differentiated from international marriages with Western Europeans. This has been combined with other words to form new terminology such as multicultural family, multicultural neighbor, multicultural children, multicultural youth, multicultural kids, multicultural student, multicultural soldier, multicultural married couple, and so on. It seems as if it is used to categorize racial groups in Korean and multicultural societies similar to how blacks and whites are categorized, which shows, with implications of racial hierarchy, that families with members from Western Europe are considered different from those with only Koreans. In 2012, the Ministry of Strategy and Finance announced that it will establish a new law, which will prohibit discrimination against "multicultural people." This law has been controversial because of the term of "multicultural people (Damunhwain)." Many activists who work for migrants have insisted the necessity for the law of antiracism, but the government has proposed another law in spite of similar content that prohibits the discrimination against migrants. This terminology is so discriminative that it makes all migrant collectively identify differently with Koreans and puts them into a certain image despite their diversity. As a result of this distinction between "multicultural people (Damunhwain)" and Korean, this law makes people divide "we" and "others" so that this division is also racism against migrants. Then the law itself involves contradictive contents; therefore, naming migrants as group is also drawing a line of demarcation as symbol border and boundary and showing that who are Korean or not.

RACIALIZING THE PROCESS OF MASS MEDIA AGAINST MULTICULTURAL FAMILIES

Mass media offers easy access to information in everyday life, and its impact is having an effect on the awareness and value judgment of Koreans. In addition, Internet penetration and usage is high in the Korean society, and media such as press reports, television, and film are easily accessible through smart-phones. Therefore, these kinds of accessibility lead to the formation of discourse in SNS and impact through rapid reproduction. For this reason, issues covered in the media are sometimes distributed without verification of authenticity, and in most cases the damage has already been done even when corrections are made afterward. Mass media circulation and sharing among the ingroup of ethnic prejudices and ideologies with the ingroup presuppose mass communication, or, expression or (re-)production via the mass media.[7] Therefore, it is important to consider how media covers the multicultural families and makes them distinct from Koreans through the stereotype, prejudice, image distortion, stigmatization, scapegoating, and cultural belittlement.

As argued previously, the term "multicultural" has become a word that refers to a specific group of people. They are members of multicultural families. The term "multicultural" has been combined with other words to form new terminology such as multicultural neighbor, multicultural children, multicultural youth, multicultural kids, multicultural students, multicultural soldier, and so on. It seems as if it is used to categorize racial groups into Koreans, multicultural families in the same way as black and white, which shows, with implications of racial hierarchy, that members of families from Western Europe are considered different from those with only Koreans. Mass media is used to assign collective identity of "multicultural families" and represent a certain image about them. The role of this media is connected with racism against multicultural families. Racism as an ideological formation should be endlessly materialized into concrete discourses and representation, and mass media are essential tools in this process.[8] Multicultural families are identified without racial division by media. It has been considered that the members of multicultural families are Asian even though they are diverse married migrants from any country including Western Europe legally. Why people regard the multicultural families as Asian? In this context, Asian is not regional in meaning, but it is symbolic, which means a poor, a nonelite, a beneficiary of state welfare program, a lower class, and so on.

The mass media intensifies the categorization of multicultural families by objecting them in a way that multicultural families are regarded as another race, different from Koreans or other migrants. Media holds significant influence in our daily lives, and it infiltrates our perceptions and understanding with continuous messages that impact our belief and value systems. It becomes important to look at whether or not media also impacts race and racism in our society.[9] Therefore, the National Human Rights Commission demanded the evaluation of these programs in order for these programs to pursue multicultural understanding and schematize the image of multicultural family. From May to October in 2012 and 2013, the National Human Rights Commission monitored these kinds of television programs. According to this result of monitoring, the National Human Rights Commission recommended that major media organization such as KBS, MBC, and SBS as well as other general broadcast and channels pay special attention to the use of the negative identity and should not show discriminative expression about immigrant and foreigners. In particular, the "multiculture (*damunwha*)" is an incorrect term to use without social agreement between each other in Korean society as a discriminative term to refer the adults and children who are the member of international marriage families.[10]

There are three major media such as KBS, MBC, and the educational channel EBS, which have some kinds of programs about multicultural families. The title of the programs are "Love in Asia (Reobeuin Asia)"[11] (KBS1), "A project of hope for multi-culture (Damunhwa Himang Peurojekteu)" (MBC), and "Multi-cultural hot battle between mother-in-law with daughter-in-law 다문화고부열전>" (EBS). Many married migrants appeared in these television programs, but performers are married migrant women for the most part. This program draws a sketch of their life as a uniform image of a wife who comes from the poorest region and a husband who helps the wife's family, and they have a piteous story. These performers who are migrant women must show how much they have assimilated the Korean culture so that they cook Korean food such as kimchi and doenjang chigae as well as doing well for their parents-in-law. And other programs for children such as "TV Kindergarten

TV (Yuch'iwŏn)" (KBS2) cast the children of multicultural family to teach Korean alphabets and sentence (Han'gŭl). Their parents are from China, Vietnam, Philippine, Pakistan, Uzbekistan, and so on, so that they are supposed to not speak the Korean language well. This arose simply from their tag that the children of multicultural families have poor school performance because of their insufficient ability to speak and write Korean language.

Therefore, the more these programs are aired on television, the more the multicultural family is divided from Korean. In this way, media identifies the multicultural families and gives the message that they must be assimilated into Korean society.

Turner argues that multiculturalists may claim to stand for a liberating recognition of the de facto heterogeneity of the cultural and ethnic makeup of contemporary metropolitan societies, and to call for a critical retheorizing of the relation of culture and political society that accommodate, rather than ignore or repress, the multiplicity of identities and social groups comprised by such society. Multiculturalism, in this form, becomes a vantage point for unique critical insights into the nature of contemporary national cultures, as well as current developments and transformations of culture associated with transnational developments in media technology, commodity consumption, and other political and economic changes. Because culture has come to serve as the basis of both imagined communities and individual identities deemed to be "authentic" in contrast to repressive, aliens, or otherwise "inauthentic" normative codes, social institutions, and political structures.[12] But it is not important in Korean society whether multiculturalists are right, because they don't sufficiently consider how the culture is related to racism and also have insufficient sensitivity of racism. Furthermore, the media sometimes overlook a fact that Korean and multicultural families are contemporary and stuff a culture of native places of migrants.

Multiculturalism is the concept, which means coexistence between the identities of majority with minority. It is needed to argue how cultural diversity and specialty can coexist in a nation and a society. The goal of this concept is to reach an acknowledgment of minorities in the culture, through forming a system, a policy, a law, and so on, so that it can achieve social integration. This means that multiculturalism is the concept of admitting the rights of minority in the majority and accepting exception of them as a Right.[13] As seen from the examples above, however, the term "multicultural" doesn't include cultural diversity of minorities. It is just used to refer to and describe collective identity about members of multicultural families. In this situation, the term "multicultural" does not describe the cultural diversity and also the individual characters of married immigrants and their children. This term means that they are from an Asian country and come for marriage but can never be fully Korean.

There were two television program: one is "Love in Asia (Reobeuin Asia)" and another is "Talk with Beauties (Minyeodeurui Suda)." The former program casts a married migrant woman who is a member of a multicultural family from Asia, and the latter program cast an elite migrant woman such as a foreign student, diplomat, professor, employee of foreign invested company, and so on from Western Europe and Asia. One program shows the married migrant women of members of multicultural families are objects of assimilation to be integrated socially, but the other program shows elite migrant women are subjects of evaluation to assess the Korean culture. Both of them have performers from Asia; however, there is no way the viewers accept differently the image between married migrant women with elite migrant women because of their position showed by media. It is important whether these Asian women belong to members of multicultural families or not in the context of media's direction. Therefore, the multicultural families are segregated from Asian, other migrant, and Korean families because of their gender, class, and social position. Despite some of them come from China, Japan, Vietnam, Philippines, Mongolia, Cambodia, Nepal, etc and their cultures are so diverse that they need to also understand each other, they are still categorized as one group as multicultural families have a certain image framed by stigmatization.

This image is intensified by news reports that reproduce social discourses narrativizing multicultural families is minority, weak, victims, isolated, sacrificed, and so on. Collins says that the media is key in perpetuating controlling images that enable the domination of minority groups. The use of controlling images is important to understanding racism in the news media, as it is a tool that has been historically used by those seeking to preserve that racial status quo persists in contemporary media practices.[14] Even though some of the multicultural families succeed in their workplace, school, the fields of sports, and arts, they become an issue because they are members of multicultural families. Then they are called multicultural students, multicultural artists, multicultural athletes, multicultural entertainers, and so on. So the idea of "multicultural" becomes a stigma and a symbol of social standing to them as well as racial division too difficult to overcome. From July 1, 2012, to July 31, 2014, the articles of national and local daily newspapers, daily economic newspapers, Internet newspapers, and three main broadcasting companies were analyzed for the Conference about Racism of Korea in 2014. In the article search result, there were 30,656 articles in the past two years that could be found by using "multicultural families" as a keyword. Also multicultural families have been used as a related search keyword to target support (6,963 articles) and disadvantaged (3,573 articles) groups, which leads to concerns that the image of poverty may be reinforced, and this shows clear aspect of hierarchical racism. This type of media coverage reinforces narrow, negative views that multicultural families are eating away tax money or that they are targets of welfare.[15] In this process, their diverse ethnic, educational, and cultural backgrounds are largely ignored. They are treated collectively as the interracially married women and men to Koreans regardless of where they are from. The way media represent these multicultural families well demonstrated how the media construct the meaning of the other. Always, their meaning is shaped from the standpoint of dominant group, the members of the mainstream society.[16]

WHY MULTICULTURAL FAMILIES ARE RACIALIZED ?

Some schools of thought regards racism as discrimination against people of color, based on white superiority. Korean society also has forms of racism, but many experts explain that this racism is based on the belief that Korea is a homogeneous nation rather than concepts of white supremacy. As a result, Korean people sometimes discriminate against foreigners as well as multicultural families, not only because of their skin color but also because of their "exotic" appearance. Therefore, appearance is often referred to in case of bullying at school of children from multicultural families. However, this cannot be deemed as a sufficient explanation since the majority of marriage migrants are Asian from China, Japan, and Mogolia and are not easily distinguished from other Koreans.

In particular, accounts of racism in Korean is often differentiated by accounts of Korea's relationship with Western power and the sense of defeat brought about by Japanese imperialism. The "yellow superiority" felt by Koreans over other races is the result of an inferiority complex about white and Japanese people. In other words, the racism of Koreans is historically internalized Western racism and exclusive nationalism.[17] First, the exclusive nationalism was that which spread during the independence movement. In order to shore up public support, independence movement needed the myth of the homogeneous Korean society and a hierarchical nationhood of Koreans.[18] These historical experiences affect both the consciousness and the unconsciousness of Koreans, which explains the characteristics of racism in Korea and why the Korean society segregates multicultural families from Korean families. Consequently, multicultural families are categorized by discriminative policies and the biased collective media image of Korea as a multicultural nation.

According to Etien Balibar, the organization of racists denies that their name is racist and instead insists that they are nationalist. The power initiative nationalism starts from inner-directed intolerance. Nationalism as a dominant discourse is controlled fundamentally by elite. This is an ideology that it represents for the benefit of a few privileged and elite groups. And nationalism is a mechanism that it makes people agree and subordinate to the dominant group's hegemony spontaneously. This mechanism is connected with forming an exclusive consciousness such as nationalistic sentiment to maintain a cultural purity and established tradition, racism, or xenophobia.[19] So it is no surprise that the anti-multicultural policy group called themselves nationalist as patriotic citizens and justified their xenophobic attitudes. They exaggerated the rate of migrant crime, opposed multicultural policy, and raised concerns that children of multicultural families will later grow up to become rebels, criminals, or social outcasts. They also insisted that multicultural policies are forms of reverse discrimination against Koreans.

Surprisingly, in Korean some scholars who write high school textbooks students insist that "open nationalism" can coexist with multiculturalism.[20] They try to argue that nationalism does not have to be abandoned, and Korea's ethnic identity can be maintained together with a diversity of migrant ethnic identities. Their position is impossible from outset given that one of the main reasons for the exclustions of migrants is based on the belief that Koreans are ethnically homogeneous. So that open nationalism is just another path into ethnocentrism, which implies that those who share ethnicity and bloodline may embrace other people's generous attitudes. Members of society who have identified with others sharing ethnic identities will come to feel a sense of repulsion toward those who are different, and violence could be used against noncitizen the moment bounds of consideration and tolerance are broken. This is clearly racial discrimination, and it must be concerned that this is articulated as a as part of ethnic identity.[21]

Many Koreans possess both a sense of fear and superiority against multicultural families because they are not pure, "real" Koreans. Multicultural families are also classified them as one large group separate from Korean families, even though the race, ethnicity, or nationality of multicultural families in Korea is diverse. Multicultural families are not accepted as real Koreans even if they have Korean citizenship or they were born in Korea and even if their appearance is indistinguishable from that of Koreans. Multicultural families are racialized in Korea and exposed the racism of Korea, concealed beneath the consciousness of political leaders and the public.

Earlier in this chapter, I demonstrated why and how media racializeds multicultural families in South Korea, in the decade following its pronouncement to be a multicultural society. That said, racialization does not only come from the media as judgments against multicultural families also stem from nationalism, and the myth of Tan-gun, the belief that Korean ethnic identity is extended via a pure-blood lineage. As a result, Koreans possess both a sense of fear and superiority against multicultural families because they are not pure, "real" Korean. This nationalism affects the consciousness of Koreans and is intensified by the machinations of mass media. Multicultural families are classified as one large group separate from Korean families, even though race, ethnicity or nationality of multicultural families in Korea is diverse. Multicultural families are not accepted real Koreans even if they have Korean citizenship, they were born in Korea, or even if their appearance is indistinguishable from that of Koreans. Multicultural families are racialized in Korea, and exposed to the racism of Korea concealed beneath the consciousness of political leaders and the public.

Therefore, members of multicultural families are categorized into a group different from Koreans, as well as other foreigners, and have placed them in an ambivalent stance in social status.

Despite the fact that some members of this multicultural nation have been naturalized or were born on this land, the background of one their parents may be Korean, the term "multicultural" is combined with other words to concentrate on members of multicultural families. Instead of emphasizing diversity, multicultural denotes a disadvantaged difference, racialized boundaries and stigmatization, and a social problem that requires assimilation into Korean society for social integration. Mass media further cleaves multicultural families from Koreans and deals with them differently from other foreigners, and casting them as special perfomars on television programs and or source of a news issue in what is clearly a process of ongoing racialization instead of focusing on an equitable distribution of political and legal rights. I urge us to consider that the project of multiculturalism that Korea needs to take on is not one about assimilating families that are deemed multicultural, but rather articulating Korea as a multicultural nation that requires the cultivation of coexistence and cultural diversity.

NOTES

1. http://www.moj.go.kr/HP/COM/bbs_03/ListShowData.do?strNbodCd=noti0005&strWrtNo=1276&strAnsNo=A&strNbodCd=noti0005&strFilePath=moj/&strRtnURL=MOJ_30200000&strOrgGbnCd=100000&strThisPage=10&strNbodCdGbn=24.Aug.2007, news release by Ministry of Justice.

2. Park, Kyungtae, "Racism and racial discrimination in the Republic of Korea," *Alternative Report: NGO Alternative Report on Racism in Korea*, 2014, 4–5.

3. Kim, Hyunmee, "The Spread Racism and 'No Country,'" *Alternative Report: NGO Alternative Report on Racism in Korea*, 2014, 6–9.

4. Van Dijk, Teun A, "Media, Racism and Monitoring," in *International Media Monitoring*, edited by Kaarle Nodenstreng and Michael Griffin. (Creskill, NJ: Hampton Press, 1999).

5. This is legend about Dangun's founding Dangun Joseon, the first country in Korea history. For a long time Korean learned that we are homogeneous people from this Dangun.

6. This law is enacted in 1999 and revised 2008 and 2014.

7. Van Dijk, Teun A, "Mediating racism: The role of the media in the reproduction of racism," Short version In R. Wodak (ed.), *Language, Power and Ideolosy* (1989), 199–226.

8. Joen, Gyu Chan, "A study on the formation of universal ideology of racism and media," *Media and Society*, Summer 9 volume 3 number, 2007: 73–105.

9. Kulaszewicz, Kassia E., "Racism and the Media: A Textual Analysis," Master of Social Work Clinical Research Papers, School of Social Work (2015).

10. http://www.humanrights.go.kr/04_sub/body02.jsp/ 11. December. 2013, news release by the National Commission Human Rights.

11. This program was ended on 22, Feb, 2015. This program showed for 10 years from 2005 to 2015.

12. Turner, Terence, "Anthropology and Multiculturalism: What is Anthropology That Multiculturalists Should Be Mindful of It?" *Cultural Anthropology*, vol. 8, no 4. 411–29, 1993.

13. Lee Kwangsuk, *Multicultural Administration Theory*, Seoul: Jomyung Munwhasa, 2014.

14. Rose, Joshep P., "The New Racism in the Media: a Discourse Analysis of Newspaper Commentary on Race, Presidential Politics, and Welfare Reform" Thesis, GEORGIA State University (2014) recited from Collins, Patricia Hill (1991, 2005): 8–9.

15. Jung, Hyesil, "Racism in the Media" *Alternative Report: NGO Alternative Report on Racism in Korea* (2014): 10–22.

16. Yang, Jung Hye, "Representation of Migrating Women: News Depiction of Inter racially Married Asian Women to Korean," Media, Gender & Culture, Korea Women Communication Society No. 7, 2007: 47–77.

17. Ha, Sang-bok, "Yellow Skin, White Personae: Historical Reflexivity and Muliticulturalism of Indicated Racism of Korea," *Humane Studies*, no. 33, 2012.

18. Seol, Dong-hun, "Sociology of the 'Mixed-Blood': Hierarchical Nationhood of the Koreans," *Humanity Studies*, vol. 52, Young Nam University, 2007.

19. Lee, Jimyeong, *Who is singing the Nationalism?* 2004: 43.

20. "Open nationalism can be explained through 'diversity' and 'independence.' First, 'open' means an open attitude toward those both inside and outside of ethnic group, and this signifies the acceptance of diversity. 'Nationalism' implies that the independence of one's ethnic group is maintained. Open nationalism refers to engaging in exchange and cooperation with diverse ethnic groups and countries, while maintaining ethnic identity. While open nationalism focuses on ethnicity, its purpose is not only to bring prosperity to the ethnic group through the rules of nationalism, but to achieve justice as a form of 'introspective nationalism.' Nationalism, along with understanding of other cultures, can coexist with multiculturalism." (High School Life and Ethics, Kyohak Publishing, 279, p. 2014) recited from Lee, Myorang, "Racism and racial discrimination in the school curriculum" *Alternative Report: NGO Alternative Report on Racism in Korea*, Multicultural Administration 2014, p. 23–34.

21. Above book.

REFERENCES

Ha, Sang-bok. 2012. "Hwangsaek Pibu, Baeksaek Ga-myeon: Hangugui Naemyeonhwadoen Injongjuuiui Yeoksajeok Gochalgwa Damunhwajuui [Yellow Skin, White Masks: A Historical Consideration of Internalized Racism and Multiculturalism in South Korea]." *Studies in Humanities*, 33: 525–56.

Joen, Gye Chan. 2001. "Injongjuuiui Jeonjigujeok Hyeongseonggwa Midieo Yeongwanseonge Gwanhan Yeon-gu [A study on the formation of universal ideology of racism and media]." *Media and Society*, 9(3): 73–105.

Judith, Buttler and Gayatri, Spivak. 2008. *Nu-ga Minjokgukgareul Noraehaneun-ga? [Who sings the Nation-state?]*. Seoul: Sanchaekja, translated by Hae Yeon Choo.

Jung, Hyesil. 2014. "Midieo Sogui Injongjuui [Racism in the Media]." *Alternative NGO Report on Racism in South Korea*, 10–22.

Kim, Hyun Mee. 2014. "Injongjuui Hwaksangwa Gukgaeopseum [Spread of Racism and the Statelessness]." *Alternative NGO Report on Racism in South Korea*, 6–9.

Kulazewicz, Kassia E. 2015. "Racism and the Media: A Textual Analysis," Master thesis of Social Work Clinical Research Papers, *School of Social Work*, St. Catherine University.

Lee, Kwangsuk. 2014. *Damunhwa Haengjeongnon [Multicultural Administration Theory]*, Seoul: Jomyung Munwhasa.

Lee, Jimyeong. 2004. *Neomchyeonaneun Minjok Sarajineun Juche [Overflow Nationalism and Disappearing Subjectivity]*. Seoul: Chacksesang.

Lee, Myorang. 2014. "Gyogwaseo Sogui Injongjuuiwa Injongchabyeol [Racism and racial discrimination in the school curriculum]." *Alternative NGO Report on Racism in South Korea*, 11–18.

Park, Kyungtae. 2014. "Hangugui Injongjuuiwa Injongchabyeol [Racism and racial discrimination in the Republic of Korea]." *Alternative NGO Report on Racism in South Korea*, 4–5.

Rose, Joshep P. 2014. *The New Racism in the Media: A Discourse Analysis of Newspaper Commentary on Race*. Master thesis of Sociology, Georgia State University.

Seol, Dong-hun. 2007. "Honjong Hogeun Honhyeore Daehan Inmunhakjeok Seongchal; Honhyeorinui Sahoehak: Hanguginui Wigyejeok Minjokseong [Sociology of the 'Mixed – Blood': Hierarchical Nationhood of the Koreans]." *Humanity Studies*, 52: 125–60.

Turner, Terence. 1993. "Anthropology and Multiculturalism: What is Anthropology That Multiculturalists Should Be Mindful of It?," *Cultural Anthropology*, 8: 411–29.

Van Dijk, Teun A. 1989. "Mediating Racism: The Role of the Media in the Reproduction of Racism," in *Language, Power and Ideology*, edited by R. Wodak, 199–226. Amsterdam: John Benjamins Publishing Company.

Van Dijk, Teun A. 1999. "Media, Racism and Monitoring," in *International Media Monitoring*, edited by Kaale Nodenstreng and Michael Griffin, 307–14. Creskill, NJ: Hampton Press.

Chapter 6

Enacting Race and the Nation in Taiwan

How Immigration Laws Embody the Dark Side of the Nation-building Process in Taiwan

Bruce Yuan-Hao Liao

Building a Taiwan-based nationalism appeared to be a significant political ideology since 1990s. Taiwan[1] nationalists not only intended to prove that Taiwan is politically independent from China, but also wanted to announce Taiwan's unique identity. Nevertheless, due to the international and domestic constraint of realpolitik, any attempt to establish formal Taiwan nation was impossible to succeed. Therefore, nationalists turned out adopting a subtler and more notorious approach in realizing their dream—enacting an immigration legal scheme that is exclusionary, nativist, xenophobic, and classism based.

This chapter introduces the various statutes and court rulings regarding immigration and nationality, and tries to reveal how they manifest the deeply rooted nativism and racism in the policy makers' minds. Many Taiwanese considered that the great amount of marital immigrants, who came primarily from Southeast Asia and Mainland China, are inferior people. They treated migrant workers in a similar way.[2] As a result, those laws made during 1990s and 2008 largely have the following features: (1) presuming marital immigrants and migrant workers are inferior so that "screening mechanism" is needed to guarantee Taiwanese identity and security; (2) treating immigrants as "exceptions" to Rule of Law—normal legal protections, such as due process, equal protection, and judicial review, would be inapplicable to those inferior people; (3) reluctance to allow them to get the formal status of "Taiwanese," that is, the citizenship of the Republic of China, or the permanent resident status; therefore, Taiwan's pure identity and quality can be maintained; (4) blatant regional and class discrimination, without regard to the equality commitment in the Constitution and international law.

Nationalism, racism, ethnic-national identity, and law are highly inter-woven in Taiwan. Most Taiwanese don't even notice that they've treated migrants as other (inferior) "races." They always regard marital immigrants as essential distinct groups from "Taiwanese," notwithstanding many of those immigrants have the same ancestry with "We Taiwanese." Worse, even after the marital immigrants legally acquired the Taiwanese citizenship via naturalization, they are largely deemed "foreign spouses" forever. That is, they are treated as a category, or race, which is permanent non-Taiwanese. Since Taiwan is a "democracy," the government must adopt the electorates' desire into law. Thus, the immigration law of Taiwan enacted this kind of national-ethnic-racism.

After introducing the legal scheme and the discriminatory nature thereof, the author analyzes how the laws and the Taiwan society mutually reinforced the racism, nativism, and classism prevailing in Taiwan at that time. The chapter also shows the efforts made by these immigrants and migrant work-ers to challenge Taiwan people's prejudice. These "new residents" not only changed certain immigration laws, but even transformed certain notorious mindset hidden in the Taiwan nationalism. Thanks to "their" effort, Taiwan has been gradually inclusive and diverse.

I. BACKGROUND—TAIWAN NATIONALISM, RACISM, AND IMMIGRATION POLICY

Taiwan lifted the martial law in 1987. Since then, the KMT[3] authoritarian regime formally turned into a democracy in which various political parties and ideologies could lawfully compete with each other. Pursuing the "Taiwan subjectivity" virtually became the Zeitgeist then. Though Taiwanese had dif-ferent opinions over whether Taiwan should declare de jure independence (from China), it's fair to say that most Taiwanese support certain kind of national identity of Taiwan. That is, Taiwan was experiencing a nation-build-ing process despite the absence of creating a new country formally.

Any country that seeks raising the nationalist awareness would emphasize the uniqueness of its culture and the political autonomy. Taiwanese were desperately looking for the definition of "Taiwanese." "Who is Taiwanese" or "Who loves Taiwan" thus became the Taiwanese's primary anxieties. For a nation like Taiwan, to find the "Otherness" or even an "Enemy" for the sake of establishment of its national identity is not surprising.

At the same time, more and more marital immigrants came to Taiwan. Most of them were from Mainland China and the Southeast Asia.[4] It gave rise to the nationalist anxiety of Taiwan: not only these immigrants were not the typical Taiwanese (as the Han-Chinese or the Holo People), but also their children will become the new ethnic group (Hsia and Huang 2010). The hostile relationship between Taiwan and Mainland China amplified the anxiety, especially for the attitude toward "mainland spouses."

Law, as a system of social expression, oftentimes manifests the desire and thought of the time (Karst 1993). Also, immigration policy generally reveals how "we the people" define ourselves (Hing 2004). Therefore, when Taiwan people wanted to confirm their unique identity, immigration laws became a critical site. It must be noted that the concept of "Taiwan People" is itself a multiethnic and fluid one, and Taiwan has been ruled by Holland, the Imperial China, the Empire of Japan, and the ROC government. Thus, it is hard to distinguish Taiwan people from outsiders by blood, skin color, or ancestry; only legal fiat can arbitrarily but legitimately define the newcomers as outsiders so as to make the old residents superior. The immigration legal system can simply single out noncitizens to essentialize their otherness and inferiority. Immigrants' otherness was therefore legally constructed, and this is a kind of socially constructed racism. That is why immigration law, border control, and racial discrimination have been interwoven in history (Chavez 2013; Johnson 2004).

Taiwan's legislature passed or amended various laws then; all of them treated the marital immigrants as different (inferior) race-ethnic groups, though most marital immigrants from Mainland China were, like most native-born Taiwanese, the Han People. In this regard, nationalism and racism are interwoven, because the notion of "race" was not based upon biological differences but social perception. As long as Taiwanese see marital migrants as "different" from Taiwanese, that is definitely about race and ethnicity.

Ironically enough, another feature that made Taiwanese proud was its "democratization." Universal suffrage, rule of law, constitutional review, freedom of speech, and equal protection of laws have been integrated into Taiwan's political system in the 1990s. Nevertheless, how could a democracy believing in equality treat thousands of residents so disadvantageously? To accommodate the essential conflict, Taiwan policy makers and the general citizens employ nationalism to justify such discrimination: we treat them differently due to national sovereignty; our democracy is applicable to "us," not "them." In other words, boundary-defining takes precedence over universal value; therefore, it's normal to discriminate against "other kind of people" without repugnance to equality and liberty.

Against this background, the government adopted a hostile attitude toward marital immigrants since 1990s. The former president Teng-hui Lee put much emphasis on "localization" and "Taiwan identity." The following Chen administration, led by the pro-independence Democratic Progressive Party, held an even tougher stance toward immigrants, especially those who came from Mainland China. Until the KMT President Ma Ying-jeou was elected in 2008, the Taiwan government's hostile stance just changed a little bit. This history indicated the relationship between "nationalism" and "nativist-exclusionary racism." Taiwan nationalism, combined with such racism, gave rise to the discriminatory immigration laws in 1990s.

The most significant legislations passed in this era include: Act Governing Relations between the People of the Taiwan Area and the Mainland Area of 1992 (hereinafter Cross-Strait Relations Act), the Immigration Act of 1999, and the Nationality Act Amendments of 2000. The main driving forces of passing those laws are: mass infusion of migrants, democratization, and the transformation of Taiwan-China relationships. Because Taiwan had been an authoritarian regime before 1990, the government was able to control the national border without complicated statutes. Ever since the government lifted the martial law, the legislature just passed a very rough "National Security Act" to control the border. However, the policy makers soon discovered that the National Security Act was too simple to deal with the multifaceted immigration problem; therefore, to make a more comprehensive legal regime was inevitable. In this vein, the aforementioned statutes were passed in governing immigrants from different regions—the Cross-Strait Relations Act dealt with Mainland Chinese; the other statutes aimed at foreigners and stateless persons. They regulated the whole process of immigration, including entry, residence, citizenship and naturalization, and removal matters.

This chapter will then introduce how they (and other laws) embodied Taiwan's nativist-exclusionary racism. Some of them were revised and turned into more reasonable measures after 2008, due to the changing social perception toward marital immigrants.

II. LAWS DISCRIMINATING AGAINST IMMIGRANTS

A. The Arbitrary Interviewing System

Like most nation-states, Taiwan government filters immigrants via the so-called "interview" mechanism. The consulates located in respectful foreign countries were in charge of interviewing foreigners applying for immigration visas; the National Immigration Agency (NIA) is responsible for interviewing every Mainland Chinese entering Taiwan territory. The former processes were implemented abroad and the latter at the airport and NIA locations.

The interviewing officials' legal jurisdiction is to determine whether the marriage is a sham one. However, they virtually enjoy unconstrained discretion in making "pass" or "fail" decisions. There's no precise legal standards defining or discerning "sham marriage"; their decisions to fail the applicants generally don't consider precise reasons and records of findings;

the interviewing proceedings are secret and confidential so as to avoid any meaningful public scrutiny. Worse, due to the aforementioned conditions, plus the imminent enforced removal or exclusion, the post hoc administrative and judicial reviews appear meaningless.

In addition, the basic mindset of those interviewing officials seemed antagonistic toward immigrant applicants from Southeast Asia and Mainland China. The applicants have not been regarded as our sisters or potential equal members; rather, they were largely presumed law-breakers, criminals, or resource-predators. That's why the officials were tempted to show hostility or even humiliating attitude in interviewing the applicants, notwithstanding the fact that those women are Taiwanese' "another half." When journalists or social activists inquired government officials' attitude and arbitrariness, they oftentimes responded with a very arrogant stance: We are defending the scarce resource and the quality of population of Taiwan!

Ironically, even the NIA or consulate officials could not guarantee the effectiveness of the interview mechanism. How can the officials distinguish real marriages from sham marriages in a short period and in light of few dialogs? Since it's a standardless decision-making, who can evaluate whether the excluded one is indeed the traffickers' accomplice rather than a primitive, shy, and stammered woman?

In addition, because of the U.S. Department of State's annually released "Trafficking in Person Report," the government increasingly put emphasis on the dubious interview mechanism, especially when the government is impotent to eliminate the international trafficking syndicates and reluctant to provide more humanitarian protection to the victims of trafficking. Alleging that we filtered out more "illegal immigrants" therefore became the cheap strategy to answer the American Boss' inquiry. Nevertheless, they did these things at the expense of family unification rights of immigrant sisters and their Taiwanese husbands.

B. Deportation and Detention without Due Process

In modern democracies, one of the most critical features to distinguish citizens from aliens is that the latter is subject to deportation. As long as the punishment of "banishment" or "exile" has faded away, only foreigners could be expelled from the national territory.

For one thing, deportation is no doubt the nation-states' prerogative against the nonmembers; for another, deportation could make devastating effect on resident aliens. Especially immigrants have largely rooted in the host country for a very long time, to deport them is tantamount to destroying their (and their family members') life. Furthermore, since other innocent residents, citizens or noncitizens, have already established interwoven relationships with those potential deportees, the deportation decision will likely hurt innocent ones simultaneously. In sum, unlike excluding someone's entry in the first place, deporting a resident alien is worth more human rights concerns.

Under Taiwan's immigration laws, marriage immigrants are subject to deportation to the same extent with other aliens. The law does not make any differentiation among various categories of foreigners, and there appears no difference in practice either. Immigrants, especially marital immigrants, and their special needs and situations had been rarely, if ever, taken into account in making and enforcing deportation orders.

1. Unfair Grounds for Deportation

I would like to introduce some of the harshest and most unfair provisions regarding deportable grounds here.

First, to get a contagious disease such as AIDS, SARS, or even syphilis could be the reason to be removed, without regard to how the resident aliens have been infected. An Act even provided that any HIV-positive alien "shall" be deported (in comparison with the Immigration Act's "may" provision).

Certain foreign spouses were expelled due to the infection of HIV, even though they were infected by their Taiwanese husbands. Later, the legislature amended the law to exempt the foreign spouses from the mandatory deportation order so long as she is able to prove that it's her husband who infected her. But they are still subject to the Immigration Act's "discretionary" deportation. Since foreign spouses had no right to get infectious disease such as AIDS, they tended to conceal their infection.

Second, the catchall provisions—forbidding foreigners engaging in any activities inconsistent with the specific admission purpose—in immigration laws have been erroneously interpreted to restrict any foreigners' freedom of expression. Those officials absurdly alleged that foreigners are inherently prohibited to conduct any political activities in host countries, so that they are not allowed to attend any political expressive action. Practically, the immigration authority has expelled or threatened to expel some foreigners taking part in social or political protest. Though only few aliens have been deported simply because of getting involved in parades or demonstrations since the martial law has been lifted, the occasional and selective use of this weapon does have its chilling effect. In many occasions where immigrants went to the street to protest the relevant policies, foreign spouses, the true stakeholders, were reluctant or hesitant to speak in front of the masses simply because they don't have the Card.

The immigration authority frequently misused this sort of "inconsistency" provision. Mainland Chinese spouses would be removed if they work somewhere without authorization. However, there's no statutory language explicitly providing "unauthorized work" to be the deportable ground. The immigration authorities always charged them as "engaging in activities inconsistent with the admission purpose" and accordingly sent them back to Mainland China. The more ridiculous case is that several mainland spouses were deported because of group gambling; a misdemeanor could be fined up to NTD 9,000 at most. The ground to deport them was also the "inconsistency" provision!

In any event, deporting marriage immigrants in terms of "inconsistency" provision is in essence mumbo jumbo! Marriage immigrants came here to be permanent residents! They were meant to stay here in doing everything like citizens. Since their purpose must be general, how could the government say that they can just do certain "specific purpose"? Or, does it imply that the immigration authorities consider marriage immigrants as reproduction instrument only so that they cannot do anything other than taking care of her family directly?

The third problem is that divorce or the death of their Taiwanese spouses (mostly the husbands) could automatically lead to the expiration of the visa and the right of stay. Since few (if any) immigrants have obtained the permanent resident status, they must renew the resident certification annually or two years apart. Once the marriage relationship terminated, the immigration authorities in general would not renew the certificate regardless of the reason why the marriage ends. Even if the immigrant sisters were a battered woman, and domestic violence was the cause of divorce, she must go back to her homeland. Likewise, in case that her husband passed away, she can't reside in this island any longer, notwithstanding the fact she's lived here for more than 10 years! It appears that the law barely tolerates immigrants' existence solely because of the wedlock, or more precisely, because she belongs to a Taiwanese man?

This legal practice is not only unfair to those divorcees and widows; it also creates the incentive for foreign spouses to tolerate domestic violence and other abusive actions. Squarely because her fate—whether they can keep residing in this place—totally depends on the state of matrimony, the husband therefore gets a critical leverage to control and even abuse her. She can't afford to "vote by foot"—just leave the wedlock—unless she is courageous to pay the huge price of leaving this country.

2. Absence of Due Process

Since deportation decision influences immigrants' liberty and life so much, it is natural to design some procedures in ensuring the impartiality and accuracy of the decision. As for the transient detention measure, it is more needed to have due process guarantee in that detention restricts people's personal freedom.

In light of Taiwan's Constitution, the government cannot constitutionally restrict people's personal freedom or bodily integrity without the court's order in the first instance. No matter in criminal detention or in civil custody, a court's prior involvement is mandatory except when there's a very emergent situation. A couple of administrative detention measures—including prosecutors' authority to detain the suspect—have been struck down by the constitutional court. Moreover, Article 8 of the ROC Constitution, which guarantees personal freedom, does not limit to protect citizens. It is agreed that personal freedom is a universal human rights; the constitutional guarantees, therefore, must be applied to the noncitizens as well.

In addition to restriction of personal freedom, the constitutional court also required all administrative decisions infringing the rights or liberties of people must satisfy the minimal due process requirement. Especially "the right to be heard" and "the right to judicial review" are the most paramount mechanisms among others. Though the Administrative Procedure Act exempts the "foreigners' entry and leave" from the procedural requirements of the Act, the relevant measures still have to comply with the constitutional standard of minimum standard.

Sadly, if we evaluate Taiwan's immigration laws and practices in terms of the aforesaid constitutional requirements developed by the constitutional court, it appears that the immigration laws and practices are in another planet! They are almost totally repugnant to every constitutional principle regarding due process!

In making and enforcing deportation decisions, immigration authorities did not need to hold any hearing; neither do they have to make specific record of fact-finding. The more notorious thing is that the post hoc judicial review is virtually useless because deportation decisions are usually enforced very soon, even to foreign spouses. The total time for going through all administrative and judicial remedies could be more than 2 years; no deportee can afford such a lengthy process. It is fair to say that Taiwan's immigration authorities have unilateral, virtually absolute power to remove whoever they want to expel. I have studied a number of deportation cases and wondered if they can pass the judicial muster, but the reality is that no judge has the chance to review them.

Detention must be another tragedy. The governing statutes authorize the NIA officials to detain aliens before enforcing the deportation orders. No court order was necessary in detaining any aliens. The detainee even had no right to habeas review. Worse, the immigration authorities can indefinitely detain the aliens without sending them back to the country of origin. Oftentimes, one of the absurd reasons of detention was simply that the detainee can't afford (or is unwilling) to pay the airfare.

C. Denial of Social Rights

In practice, the government denied to give foreigners many government/ social benefits, especially the social welfare benefits. They are eligible for the National Health Care Insurance, but they can't apply for social assistance program benefits designed to help the poor, the disabled, and the abused people. However, the relevant statues do not exclude aliens explicitly. The government officials take for granted that social welfare benefits are for citizens only; even this assumption is without any statutory ground!

In terms of policy analysis, it still makes no sense to deny territorially present aliens in applying for social welfare, because most of these benefits are need based and have nothing to do with citizenship/alienage.

Ironically enough, the government refused to give immigrant sisters the right to social benefits; it nevertheless created a special fund called "Fund to Take Care of Foreign Spouses" (hereafter the Fund) as the funding source of marriage immigrants' social benefits. Due to the Fund, many local governments which had refused to give foreign spouses any statutory benefits in the first place began to provide such benefits since then. In terms of legal logic, if the foreigners are ineligible for those benefits by law, how could they become eligible for the same benefits simply because there is more money? The reasonable inference is that legality doesn't matter as it appeared; "resources allocation" and "foreignness" are the core, real concerns.

It is worth mentioning that the Fund was not created by any statute but only an administrative measure. Therefore, the government can withdraw it anytime and determine its allocation at will. It's not the immigrant sisters' "entitlement" but simply the "mercy" from the benevolent (so to speak) government. The fact that policy makers are willing to create an ad hoc Fund but reluctant to include immigrant sisters into the official, formal social benefit system also embodies their mindset and background assumption: immigrants could be the "subjects" to be taken care of; they can't be the equal, dignified "person" or "right-holder." The former may passively receive benevolent almsgiving; the latter will actively claim rights!

Before 2009, marital immigrants from Mainland China faced the other significant obstacle—highly limited right to work. Generally, these Mainland Chinese immigrants were not allowed to work in the "union stage" (usually the first two years) at all; after the "union stage," they are in the "residence stage" (at least 4 years in length) in which they can work under very limited situations, such as the family income is under the poverty line. They must get the full-fledged right to work until they go into the "Lengthy Residence Stage" (after another 2 years in length). In case that the Taiwanese husband is a low-income person, the immigrant wife would be under pressure to work and earn money. However, as long as the law categorically prohibited the right to work in the union stage, Mainland Chinese spouses got to take the risk of being deported in order to support the family (or/and her original family in Mainland China).

In comparison with marriage immigrants coming from the rest of the globe—in which they may work without limitation—the policy treated Mainland Chinese immigrants as second-class aliens. Many of them would be far more vulnerable in terms of economic condition, if they really obey the law. Unauthorized working was the primary reasons for the immigration authorities to deport Mainland Chinese spouses before 2008.

Such a restriction is unnecessary and illegitimate. Right to work not only adds the income of immigrants but also indicates the human dignity in a capitalist society like Taiwan. Deprivation of such right is equal to denying their right to pursue happiness. Furthermore, Mainland Chinese spouses' works, like other foreign spouses, could fill the rent of Taiwan's social security net and therefore increase the overall productivity. In fact, no empirical studies thus far could determine whether and to what extent Mainland Chinese spouses would reduce the native-born Taiwanese's working opportunities. The policy was made not upon economics or sociology, but on political hostility toward Mainland China.

D. Obstacles to Naturalization

Taiwan's immigration laws (including the statutes themselves plus the affiliated regulations) impose several requirements of naturalization. In addition to the period of continued residency (3 years in length), coming of age, and the good moral behavior requirements, there are two substantial obstacles worth mentioning here.

One is the "test" requirement for foreign spouses (not including Mainland Chinese spouses). The Nationality Act provides that an immigrant sister must pass the test of (1) basic language skill and (2) basic knowledge regarding citizens' rights and obligations.

Immigrants' rights advocates strongly protested this requirement when the legislature just passed it to be an additional, new condition of naturalization. The test requirement presumed the inferiority of immigrant sisters and the superiority of "us"—we can examine "your" quality. It implicitly suggests foreign spouses' unwillingness or incapability to learn Chinese; it also implies that they need to be educated to be members of our political community.

These assumptions are contradictory to the truth. The reality is that virtually every immigrant sister is anxious to speak, apprehend, read, and write Chinese (including Mandarin or other primary languages fashionable in Taiwan) fluently. After all, there's no "Vietnam Town," "Thailand Street," or other kinds of enclaves for immigrants to live by their mother tongue in

Taiwan. The reason why some sisters still can't speak Chinese well is not their laziness or refusal of integration, but the lack of necessary resource and support to learn a language. Working-class or farmer families are earning livelihood desperately all the time. To attend "language class" is more than a luxury to them. How can the government (and part of the general public) condemn their poor Chinese before it creates a friendly, accessible learning environment?

Moreover, as for "basic knowledge regarding citizens' rights and obligations," how to determine the content of the test? How to design and implement a test appropriate for measuring the "basic knowledge"? As long as Taiwan's political and legal status is always unclear and ambiguous, our government structure is chaotic, plus the weird performance that many politicians slander the Constitution for their political capitals, how could the law ask the immigrants to have such knowledge about "citizens' rights and obligations"? As a faculty member teaching constitutional law in law schools for a couple of years, I myself sometimes can't be sure what our "rights and obligations" are.

As a result, absurd enough, the test contains lots of questions totally irrelevant with the notion of "citizenship." It included fiddle-faddle questions such as the speed limit in free way, the legal condition to feed pets, and so on and so forth. I, among other native-born Taiwanese, would not pass the test without reading designated materials in advance. Does it mean that we are unqualified to be a Taiwanese? Why doesn't the government just enact a new law requiring all citizens, native-born or immigrant, to take a citizenship renewal test annually to ensure the quality of national population?

Also, in accordance with the Nationality Act and its then-subsidiary regulations, a foreign marital immigrant was not allowed to get ROC (Taiwan) citizenship without providing the certificate proving that her family has either (1) NTD 410,000 deposit or (2) monthly income more than NTD 34,000. Immigrants and the relevant NGOs have opposed the "financial certification" requirement for a long time. The requirement constituted one of the primary obstacles for the immigrant sisters to get the National ID Card (hereafter the Card), which is Taiwan citizens' exclusive prerogative.

The "financial certificate" requirement shared the same evilness as the aforementioned test. In facing immigrant sisters and other social activist groups' charge, the government's official response—it's so benevolent enough, in policy makers' eyes—usually consists of:

a. The requirement is nominal, simply the basic living standard in Taiwan. Immigrants without such minimal financial support could not live well.
b. Some officials implied (or even expressed) that the foreign spouse or her husband can borrow money to get bank saving certificate.

The reality is that this class discriminatory provision made many immigrant families unlikely to get the Card in the foreseeable future. It sent a very clear and demeaning message to them that you (the foreign spouses and their Taiwanese husband) are too poor to be a Taiwanese. At the same time, if you were a native-born Taiwanese (rather than an immigrant), you would not need a test or the financial certificate to justify your citizenship. Native-born Taiwanese would never be asked to renew their citizenship, nor do they need to prove their "quality" in any sense. The superiority of Taiwanese was thus established via the test and financial requirements. Taiwanese, as a kind of human race, became a precious asset through legal construction!

E. Second-Class Citizenship—Discrimination after Naturalization

Getting the Card doesn't guarantee the wonderful land. Except social discrimination and obstacles, the law even discriminates against the naturalized citizens in certain regards.

The most remarkable is that an ex–Mainland Chinese spouse is still ineligible to be *any* public officials for 10 years since she/he got citizenship. The law not only excludes those ex–Mainland Chinese to be high-ranking or politically charged officials, but also denies their eligibility to be inferior civil service employees. Moreover, in terms of the personnel authorities' interpretive rulings, they even cannot be the contract-based temporaries! An ex–Mainland Chinese woman Ms Hsieh, who has got the citizenship and the Card, wanted to work for the government. She amazingly passed the very-hard-to-pass civil service examination and was assigned to be a primary personnel official in a public elementary school. However, the government turned out discharging her for she was from Mainland China and her ROC citizenship was not old enough.

This is squarely a discrimination based upon national origin. For one thing, the naturalized citizens from other "nations" would not be subject to such rigorous restraints—any foreigner, as long as he/she got the ROC citizenship via naturalization, is eligible to all inferior and middle-level civil service positions. By contrast, the law totally bans the Mainland Chinese immigrants to be public officials unless they got the citizenship more than 10 years. For another, "equal citizenship" must be the basic spirit in a modern democratic country; to treat a category of citizens disadvantageously simply because they are not born here is thus very offensive to the idea of constitutionalism. Accordingly, this sort of national origin discrimination is legally equivalence of race discrimination, which is prohibited by the ROC Constitution and the International Convention on the Elimination of All Forms of Racial Discrimination simultaneously. Although the constitutional court had never shown sympathy to aliens and Mainland Chinese people yet, we (including Ms Hsieh, two practicing attorneys, and I) determined to file a constitutional lawsuit against this second-class legislation for we all consider that "naturalized citizens" must be treated as "born citizens."

Nonetheless, the constitutional court rendered a horrendous decision. In its Interpretation No. 618, it upheld the law on the ground that the judiciary must defer to the political branches' decision because foreign or cross-strait relation is involved. Worse, the court explained that the substantive reason for this sort of second-citizenship legislation is that Mainland Chinese have been exposed to Communist indoctrination over the years; therefore, they need more time to understand Taiwan's liberal democratic constitutional order.

What an insulting decision to Ms Hsieh!! Note how Ms Hsieh pursues her goal of life and faces the countless challenges—to migrate to a foreign land, to take and pass the civil service examination, and to file constitutional litigation. Can you grand justices sitting in the court find another native-born Taiwanese more active, courageous, independent, and law-abiding to be a citizen in a democracy? To me, this second-class citizenship ruling is as notorious as the U.S. Supreme Court's *Dred Scott v. Scott* decision[5] holding black slaves not as persons but as the property of the slave owner. The endorsement effect of Interpretation No. 618 is devastating in that the final arbiter of our legal system confirmed the national origin discrimination's legitimacy. That might further alienate every pre–Mainland Chinese citizens—since this country treats us like this, why should I love this country?

F. Summary

The laws mentioned above embody racism with respect to nationalism, nativism, and cultural superiority. The reason is partly due to the tension between the emerging Taiwan identity and the newly infused marital immigrants. Those harsh, exclusionary laws demonstrated that Taiwan is a sovereign nation; therefore, "we the people" have the power to exclude outsiders and to subordinate noncitizens. When politicians and law enforcement officials said that "every sovereign state is doing the same thing," they also sent a message that "Taiwan" is like other "sovereign states."

Moreover, most marital immigrants must tolerate these harsh laws in that their status is vulnerable. No nation would treat multinational corporations or global businesses this way in that every "sovereign nation" is competing for investment. In general, nationalism or nativism does not choose foreign capital as target. Nonetheless, marital immigrants in Taiwan could be the cheap object of "Taiwanese supremacy" because they don't have such leverages, despite their enormous contribution to this society.

III. CHANGE

In response to these nativist laws and policies, marital immigrants decided not to keep silent. They gradually understood that they should not wait for politicians' mercy. As long as Taiwan is a democracy, anyone caring about his/her own destiny must stand up for his/her rights. Many immigrants and NGOs organized to change the social perception and the laws. Only when they proved that they can live like Taiwanese, work like Taiwanese, and fight like Taiwanese, the Taiwan society would just accept them as real Taiwanese. Through a variety of public advocacy efforts, including lobbying the legislators, staging street protests, and writing op-ed articles and academic papers, Taiwanese increasingly appreciate that immigrants could operate democratic processes so well. It turns out that both social attitude and laws changed.

The efforts of "the Alliance for Human Rights Legislation for Immigrants and Migrants" (AHRLIM) may be worth mentioning. AHRLIM was created in 2003, which consisted of various immigrants' organizations, social advocacy groups, labor organizations, women's rights groups, scholars, and lawyers who paid attention to immigration issues.

AHRLIM and its member groups initiated a lot of actions to make the Taiwan society aware of the significance of immigrants' rights. The most remarkable is to lobby the government (including the legislature, the executive, and the courts) in revising the notorious Immigration Act and other laws. As Taiwan's nativist racism was so fashionable then, it is naïve to expect that the discriminatory system can have sudden change. The change must be gradual and piecemeal. Furthermore, social change and legal change would be mutually reinforcing, so that reformers have to challenge social attitude and laws simultaneously.

In the beginning, AHRLIM's effort was deemed "mission impossible" in that few legislators concerned with what immigrants wanted. After all, most of the marital immigrants were not voters yet. Through years, however, the public increasingly sympathized with marital immigrants. It's harder and harder to regard them as pure "outsiders." Rather, more and more Taiwanese admitted that marital immigrants, no matter where they were from, regardless of their nationalities, have been the members of the "Taiwan family."

As a result, a number of laws mentioned above changed. For instance, in 2007, the Immigration Act was amended:

- to give the potential deportee certain "right to be heard" before NIA enforces removal process[6]
- to recognize lawful resident aliens' right to peaceful assembly[7]
- to allow certain kinds of marital immigrants to stay, notwithstanding their matrimonial relationship has been terminated[8]

Also, the Cross-Strait Relations Act was amended in 2009 to shorten the mainland spouses' citizenship waiting period, from 8 to 6 years. In addition, the 2009 amendments conferred the mainland spouses general right to work; they didn't have to worry about being removed because of "unauthorized working." This transformation not only showed the Ma administration's friendlier attitude over immigrants from Mainland China, but also likely revealed that the Taiwan society has been more willing to separate "mainland immigrants residing in Taiwan" and "pure Mainland Chinese."

Since 2013, Taiwan's constitutional court has changed previous unfriendly attitude over aliens and Mainland Chinese; it delivered a number of decisions in favor of immigrants. In two watershed cases, the grand justices cited due process spirit and then held that immigration detention must provide judicial remedies similar to habeas corpus.[9] In the other one, the ruling emphasized the interest of family reunion are protected by the ROC Constitution, even though cross-strait relations are involved.[10]

IV. CONCLUDING REMARKS

Coincidentally (or unfortunately), the wave of marital immigrant in 1990s met the Taiwan nation-building movement then. Therefore, the lawmakers, government officials, and the general populace just exploit the vulnerable "race" to satisfy the pride of Taiwan nationalism.

This sort of nativist racism is even more dangerous than pure domestic one[11] in the sense that it could be masked by sovereignty, border control, citizenship, and other nationalist vocabularies so as to make it harder to detect the existence of racism. Even Taiwan's constitutional democracy was so achievable, it cannot resist the nationalist racism in the 1990s because it may justify racial discrimination in the name of national sovereignty—"we" exclude and subordinate "them" in order to maintain the national boundary. In this vein, immigration law could be the best example demonstrating how a nation-state defines itself. And Taiwan's experience shows that a democracy could be very harsh, discriminatory, and exclusionary, as long as it defines immigrants as "outsiders" and the inferior kind of people. Law, as the most expressive and enforcing mechanism of state apparatus, constructed a race called immigrants; it also implements and justifies racial discrimination against immigrants.

In challenging and transforming such nativist racism, marital immigrants in Taiwan successfully changed certain laws. Though the current situation is still far from ideal, it is far better than 1990s or even pre-2008 stage. It suggests that even the nationalist or nativist racism could be changed by the "victims." The legal system was a suppressive mechanism to most immigrants before;

however, it could be transformed to be a liberating weapon! From Taiwan's experience, we know that the law may construct (or distort) people's meaning, but the immigrants, as well as other oppressed people, could redefine the meaning of law and turn out redefining their own life accordingly.

NOTES

1. The official name of Taiwan is the Republic of China (aka ROC). Therefore, ROC and Taiwan are interchangeable in this chapter.

2. Migrant workers in Taiwan have been facing the worse treatment than marital immigrants. Though I agree that economic immigrants and marital immigrants are not exclusionary genre, I will primarily focus upon marital immigrants in this article.

3. KMT means Kuomintang, aka the Nationalist Party. See the Kuomintang official website, available at http://www.kmt.org.tw/english/index.aspx (last visited February 15, 2015).

4. The official statistics regarding "foreign spouses" started from 1987; the "mainland spouses" statistics is from 1990. See the website of the National Immigration Agency, available at http://www.immigration.gov.tw/ct.asp?xItem=1291286&ct Node=29699&mp=1 (last visited February 15, 2015).

5. 60 U.S. 393 (1857). This decision ruled that African Americans may not turn into citizens, even though they obtained "free person" status.

6. Section 3 of the article 36 of the current Immigration Act provides: "The National Immigration Agency shall convene a review committee meeting and provide the alien, who has already acquired a residence permit or a permanent residence permit, an opportunity to submit claims before deportation is enforced in accordance with the preceding paragraph."

7. Article 29 of the current Immigration Act provides: "Aliens who are visiting or residing in the State may not engage in activities or employment that is different from the purposes of their visits or residence. The acts of filing petitions or imitating lawful assembly and procession by those aliens who reside legally shall not be subject to the foresaid restriction."

8. In accordance with Article 31 of the Immigration Act, the circumstances under which the immigrants may still reside without regard to the fact that the marriage was terminated:

> *1. His/Her dependent relative is deceased. 2. Is a spouse of a national with registered permanent residence in the Taiwan Area and is physically or mentally abused by his/her spouse. He/She is protected by the protection order issued by the court. 3. An alien acquires the guardianship of his/her own children with registered permanent residence in the Taiwan Area after his/her divorce. 4. Is suffered from family violence and divorced after the judgment of the court. The alien also has his/her own minor children with registered permanent residence in the Taiwan Area. Subject to court divorce. 5. Is deported from the State forcibly due to the revocation of his/her residence permit and is believed to have*

caused severe and irrecoverable damage to his/her own minor children with registered permanent residence in the Taiwan Area. 6. Has a labor dispute with the domestic employer and the lawsuit procedure is in the process.

9. Interpretation No. 708: Article 38, Paragraph 1, of the Immigration Act (as amended on December 26, 2007; hereinafter the "Act") provides,

"The National Immigration Agency may temporarily detain a foreign national under any of the following circumstances. . ." (this provision is the same as the provision promulgated on November 23, 2011, which provides, "The National Immigration Agency may temporarily detain a foreign national under any of the following circumstances. . ."). Under this provision, the temporary detention of a foreign national for a reasonable period in order to complete repatriation does not provide the detainee with prompt judicial relief. Moreover, an extension of the aforementioned temporary detention also is not subject to judicial review. These two aspects of the provision are both in violation of the meaning and purpose of physical freedom protection guaranteed under Article 8 of the Constitution, and shall be null and void no later than two years from the issuance of this Interpretation."

Interpretation No. 710 in furtherance struck down some provisions of the Cross-Strait Relations Act on the ground that they are inconsistent with due process requirement.

10. Interpretation No. 712:

"Article 65 Paragraph 1 of the Act Governing the Relations Between People of the Taiwan Area and the Mainland Area states that "the court shall not approve People of the Taiwan Area adopting children of the Mainland Area under any one of the following circumstances: 1. where any one of the adoptive parents already has a child or adopted child. . . ." The section of the clause pertaining to the restriction of people of the Taiwan area adopting children of a spouse from the Mainland Area violates Articles 22 and 23 of the Constitution of the Republic of China and the principle of proportionality. It is to be held invalid from the date of issuance date of this Interpretation."

11. "Domestic racism" has nothing to do with xenophobia. For instance, White supremacy makes White Americans demean African Americans; Taiwanese Han People discriminate against Indigenous Peoples.

REFERENCES

Chavez, Leo R. 2013. *The Latino Threat: Constructing Immigrants, Citizens, and the Nation*, 21–69. Stanford, California: Stanford University Press.

Hing, Bill Ong. 2004. *Defining America Through Immigration Policy*. Philadelphia, Pennsylvania: Temple University Press.

Hsia, Hsiao-Chuan and Huang, Lola Chih-Hsien. 2010. "Taiwan," in *For Better or for Worse: Comparative Research on Equity & Access for Marriage Migrants,* edited by Hsiao-Chuan Hsia, 27–73. Hong Kong, China: Asia Pacific Mission for Migrants.

Johnson, Kevin R. 2004. *The Huddled Masses Myth: Immigration and Civil Rights*, 13–54. Philadelphia, Pennsylvania: Temple University Press.

Karst, Kenneth L. 1995. *Law's Expression: Visions of Power in the Politics of Race, Gender, and Religion*. New Haven, Connecticut: Yale University Press.

Chapter 7

Intersecting Japanese Nationalism and Racism as Everyday Practices

Toward Constructing a Multiculturalist Japanese Society

Yuko Kawai

Racism has been downplayed as a foreign issue in Japan. However, Japanese society is now confronting racism because of a recent increase in publicly expressed verbal and behavioral aggression against Koreans and Chinese by ultraright groups such as *Zaitokukai* (citizens against the special privileges of ethnic Koreans).[1] Although antiracist groups and protests have drawn more attention than ever, public discussions of racism have been far from sufficient, and there is a tendency to regard racist violence as exceptional. This is demonstrated in the number and the popularity of books and magazine articles that denigrate Koreans and Chinese.[2] Often published in trade paperbacks and some becoming bestsellers, such books and articles have now become a literary genre known as "*kenkan kenchū* (hate-Korean, hate-Chinese)."[3]

This limited public awareness of racism in Japan is closely connected to the two Japanese concepts of race—*jinshu* and *minzoku*—and to Japanese nationalism, or more specifically, how Japan and the Japanese are dominantly imagined: Japan as a single-racial/ethnic nation (*tan'itsu minzoku kokka*) and the Japanese as a racialized ethnic/national group.[4] Moreover, the racism against Koreans and Chinese is linked to the increasing significance of Asia as a discursive Other for the construction of Japaneseness.[5] The rise of Asia as a significant Other is inseparable from the ascendance of China, Korea, Taiwan, and other Asian countries as economic and cultural powers, which coincides with the so-called "lost two decades" of Japan after the burst of the bubble economy in the early 1990s.

Nationalism and racism pose serious challenges to multiculturalism. While difference and equality are central multicultural issues,[6] nationalism often suppresses difference by homogenizing "us" and racism rejects equality by

exaggerating difference between "us" and "them." Despite the dominant ideology of Japan as a homogenous nation, Japanese society has always been
multiracial/ethnic[7] and thus is multicultural in a descriptive sense. However,
it is *not* "multiculturalist" in the sense that cultural difference is positively
recognized without being essentialized, and at the same time, pursuing
social equality between Japanese and non-Japanese is treated as an important
agenda.

Racism is an integral part of nationalism,[8] yet not only the two are often
seen as separate, but also racism—an "excessive" ideology—is usually
viewed as far more negative than nationalism—a "normal" ideology.[9] In
addition, repeatedly practiced and normalized, everyday nationalism and racism are often taken for granted.[10] However, such practices are problematic,
reinforcing fixed boundaries between Japanese and non-Japanese and unwit-
tingly perpetuating inequality. Therefore, viewing Japanese nationalism and
racism as interconnected and examining how they are so in everyday contexts
are indispensable to elucidate critical issues for making a multiculturalist
Japanese society.

This chapter explores the interrelationship between Japanese nationalism and racism by focusing on everyday practices in order to scrutinize the
exclusion of people of Korean and Chinese descent who constitute about half
of foreign nationals in Japan.[11] In the following sections, I engage in three
conceptual discussions: the relationship between nationalism and racism; the
Japanese concepts of race that impact the relationship in Japan; nationalism
and racism as everyday practices. Then using examples from the interviews
that I conducted in the course of multiple research projects, I examine how
Japanese nationalism and racism are interconnected in everyday situations.

NATIONALISM AND RACISM

Nationalisms have been popularly categorized as "ethnic" or "Eastern" and
"civic" or "Western" nationalism.[12] "Ethnic" nationalism takes more cultural
and exclusive or "blood-and-soil" forms of national membership, whereas
"civic" nationalism is more political and inclusive by viewing the nation as
an association of individuals, not as a group of people with common ancestry.
However, the distinction between the two is not so clear. "Civic" nationalism
is equally cultural and exclusive, privileging and protecting the culture of the
majority group over minority cultures.[13] For example, in the United States,
which is often cited as a leading example of the "civic" nation, the majority
"white" culture and people constitute the American nation or American-ness.

Modern nations have striven to match not only national and state boundaries but also national and ethnic or racial boundaries even though they usually

do not possess a particular ethnic basis.[14] Étienne Balibar postulates that "fictive ethnicity" or the production of the people is indispensable to concretize and substantiate the nation.[15] Both racial (e.g., the whites in the United States) and ethnic groups (e.g., the Japanese in Japan) are fictive ethnicities.

Language and race are two central elements in the construction of fictive ethnicity.[16] Language makes the nation look real because of its immediacy: language is visible in written materials and audible as spoken words; people use it in everyday communication and to construct their sense of the self. However, language alone is not sufficient because anyone can learn any language, and therefore national membership is open to anybody. In short, "it [language] 'assimilates' anyone, but holds no one."[17] Thus, the construction of fictive ethnicity requires another key element—the idea of race. Race limits and fixes national membership since its conceptual core lies in the "schema of genealogy" or the idea that "the filiation of individuals transmits from generation to generation a substance both biological and spiritual and thereby inscribes them in a temporal community known as 'kinship.'"[18] With the idea of race, people of one nation are imagined members of one big family, sharing something biological and spiritual passed down for generations. While language stresses the present and the inclusiveness of ethnicity, race provides ethnicity with both continuity to past and future as well as exclusivity.

Furthermore, Balibar argues that nationalism and racism as ideologies are in a complicit and conflicted relationship.[19] Racism is "a supplement internal to nationalism, always in excess of it, but always indispensable to its constitution and yet always still insufficient to achieve its project."[20] Racism serves nationalism in two ways: as supernationalism and as supranationalism.[21] On the one hand, racism reinforces nationalism by insisting upon the cultural and racial "purity" of the nation and thereby distinguishing one nation from others. On the other hand, racism undermines nationalism because "the 'superior' race [. . .] can never, by definition, coincide with the whole of the national population, nor be restricted to it."[22] For example, the racial category "white," which Balibar seems to focus on, accommodates multiple peoples and nations in the West, transcending and betraying national boundaries, and thus "the gap subsists between the representations and practices of nationalism and racism."[23]

The gap noted by Balibar is narrower between Japanese nationalism and racism. Such a gap persists in the West because peoples of the white race wish to maintain their status as the "superior" race and Western (i.e., white) values—which are often equated with "universal" values—in addition to their own national boundaries. However, the Japanese, a people of an "inferior" race (i.e., yellow), desire to discard this "inferior" racial category, driving them to differentiate themselves from other Asians and equate Japan's national boundaries more strictly with its racial boundaries.

JAPANESE CONCEPTS OF RACE AND JAPANESENESS

One of the two Japanese concepts of race, *minzoku*, has played a key role in the production of the fictive Japanese ethnicity. *Minzoku*, consisting of two Chinese characters, *min* (民 people) and *zoku* (族 group), is Japan's counter-concept to the Western concept of race, which was translated as *jinshu* by using two Chinese characters, *jin* (人 human) and *shu* (種 species).[24] In the Western concept of race or *jinshu*, the Japanese, along with other Asians, were depicted as the yellow race and placed in a subordinate position to the white race in the Western racial hierarchy. Creating a new concept of race, *minzoku*, Japanese elites tried to leave the Western racial order and build a Japanese version so as to retain their own racialized notion of Japaneseness as well as to subjugate other Asians and thereby justify Japan's colonization of Asia. The term *minzoku* came into use between the late 1880s and the early 1890s and was popularized in the subsequent two decades.[25] In prewar Japan, the concept of *minzoku* characterized the Japanese as "a group of people who are related to each other, sharing the same blood from the same ancestors" as well as "children" of the emperor, their symbolic father, and descendants of the imperial family.[26]

This idea of Japaneseness was tied to the prewar dominant Japanese nationalist ideology "*kazoku kokka*" or Japan as a family nation in which Japanese language, Japanese culture, and the Japanese nation were viewed as indivisible.[27] Race, nation, and gender intersect in this ideology of Japan as a family nation—a nation comprised of Japanese family units tied in blood (i.e., race) through and headed by the emperor or the "fictive patriarch" (i.e., gender). In the concept of *minzoku*—a notion influenced by the German concept of *Volk*[28]—lineage, language, culture, and environment were regarded as fixed determinants of Japaneseness.[29] For example, Ueda Kazutoshi, a scholar and bureaucrat prominent in constructing *kokugo* or Japan's national language, called the Japanese language "spiritual blood" indispensable for the Japanese national character (*kokutai*).[30] The Japanese as a *minzoku* were racialized by treating Japanese culture and language not as what is to be learned socially but as what is to be transmitted "biologically" from parent to child as well as from the emperor to the Japanese (i.e., the emperor's children). The two elements of fictive ethnicity, language and race, are clearly embedded in the idea of *minzoku*.

As Japan expanded its colonial territories and intensified its assimilation policies to further exploit the colonial population as laborers and soldiers in the late 1930s and early 1940s, the racialized idea of Japaneseness encountered a dilemma: while the Japanese ruling elites were attempting to assimilate the colonized Asians, the Japanese needed to remain distinct from those Asians. Assimilation policies that Japan imposed in Korea and

Taiwan included Japanese language education, Japanizing their names, and encouraging intermarriage specifically between Japanese men and Korean or Taiwanese women. However, the colonized Asians were never fully accepted as Japanese since the Japanese government distinguished Japan's colonial territories from mainland Japan by calling the former "*gaichi*" (outer territories) and the latter "*naichi*" (inner territories) and separated family registries (戸籍 *koseki*) into external (*gaichi*) and domestic (*naichi*) ones. As an embodiment of the ideology of Japan as a family state, the *koseki* system was deployed to prevent the colonized Asians from becoming fully Japanese and to justify their treatment as less than equal.[31]

In postwar Japan, due to its close association with prewar militaristic and imperialistic nationalism, both the dominant and popular discourses avoided the term *minzoku* and used the word "*jin*" (人 human) in self-reference to the Japanese. However, calling themselves *nihon-jin* (日本人 Japanese human) did not erase the idea of the Japanese as a *minzoku* or a racialized and cultural-national group but sustained it in a more obscured manner.

Nihonjin is a depoliticized version of the Japanese *minzoku*. As Japan shifted its self-representation from a multi-*minzoku* empire to a single (*tan'itsu*) *minzoku* nation-state in the 1960s,[32] Japanese cultural nationalist discourse known as *nihonjinron* ("discussions on the Japanese") defined Japaneseness similarly to the prewar idea of the Japanese *minzoku* that postulated "equivalency and mutual implications among land, people (i.e., race), culture, and language,"[33] but depoliticized them.[34] *Nihonjinron* was popularized along with the rise of Japan's economic power and internationalization (*kokusaika*) discourses in the 1970s and 1980s, which necessarily intensified Japan's identity construction. Under the strong influence of Ruth Benedict's 1946 work *The Chrysanthemum and the Sword*,[35] *nihonjinron* writers defined Japaneseness, contrasting Japanese cultural characteristics with those seen as prevalent in the West, especially the United States. They essentialized the Japanese language as fully mastered and understood only by the Japanese and depicted Japanese culture as, for example, collectivistic, hierarchical, and high contextual as opposed to Western cultures, which were depicted as individualistic, egalitarian, and low contextual.[36]

In the 1990s as internalization discourses have shifted to globalization discourses, significant discursive Others for the construction of Japaneseness have expanded by incorporating other parts of the world[37] and especially Korea and China in the 2000s. However, the racialized notion of the Japanese, which is inseparable from the idea of Japan as a single (*tan'itsu*) *minzoku* nation, has not been eliminated despite some modifications exemplified by more positive views toward *hafu* ("mixed" Japanese), especially those who were born to a "white" and a Japanese parent. In more recent years, the depoliticized notion of the Japanese has become repoliticized as seen in the intensification of publicly expressed racial violence against Koreans and Chinese.

NATIONALISM AND RACISM AS EVERYDAY PRACTICES

Michael Billig introduces the notion of banal nationalism, criticizing the tendency to associate nationalism with emerging nations, right-wing ideologies, and extreme nationalist movements. For Billig, nationalism is "the ideology by which the world of nations has come to seem the natural world—as if there could not possibly be a world without nations."[38] Banal nationalism, observed in established nations, consists of "a whole complex of beliefs, assumptions, habits, representations and practices," which is "reproduced in a banal mundane way."[39] Examples of banal nationalism include "unwaved, unsaluted and unnoticed"[40] flags on flagpoles by the street, national symbols on coins and bank notes, weather forecasts containing a national map and weather information limited to a single country, and the unspoken presumption of the nation in political speeches and news reports.

In a comparative study of black women's encounters with racism in the Netherlands and the United States, Philomena Essed proposes a concept of racism that is closely related to banal nationalism—everyday racism.[41] The "everyday" in everyday racism is "a familiar world, a world of practical interest, a world of practices with which we are socialized in order to manage in the system."[42] Everyday practices are racist "only when they activate existing structural racial inequality in the system."[43] Thus, everyday racism is "a process in which socialized racist notions are integrated into everyday practices and thereby actualize and reinforce underlying racial and ethnic relations."[44] Put differently, everyday racism involves practicing cultural norms taken for granted by the majority group, which simultaneously perpetuates hierarchical relationships with ethnic and racial minority groups.

Everyday racism consists of three interlocking processes: marginalization, problematization, and repression.[45] Marginalization is a process in which people of ethnic and racial minority groups may be tolerated but not fully accepted as members of a community. Examples include comments and actions based on Euro/white-centrism such as a hospital cleaner mistaking a black female doctor for a cleaner and a white male patient for a doctor.[46] Problematization is a process in which ethnic and racial minorities and their cultures are viewed as "inferior" to the majority group. It is exemplified by cultural denigration such as a white Dutch person saying to a black Dutch person, "Your Dutch is excellent" or "Your Dutch is different."[47] Repression is the trivialization of racism and thereby discouraging potential counteractions from the victim. Its major form is the denial of racism in which a victim is accused of being "paranoid" or "oversensitive" about discrimination.[48] Another example is assimilation or not acknowledging cultural difference so that the majority group does not have to deal with it.[49]

Both concepts similarly problematize what is often seen as "natural" or "common," but differ in how each concept is constructed and what it explains, not to mention that each deals with either nationalism or racism. As Billig pays more attention to mundane practices of nationalism than visible and intense practices often observed in political movements, Essed attends to "routine and familiar" practices of racism, differentiating them from "incidental and uncommon expressions of racism."[50] However, Billig's focus is on macro-level or public discourses such as policymakers' remarks and media representations, whereas Essed's target is micro-level discursive practices or racialized minority people's experience in interpersonal interactions, which Essed argues are informed by the macrolevel discourses.[51] Moreover, banal nationalism is mainly concerned with drawing national boundaries, whereas everyday racism is primarily about making inegalitarian meanings or evaluations (i.e., superior or inferior, positive or negative, and normal or abnormal) about peoples inside and outside of racial boundaries.

Neither Billig nor Essed explicitly connect nationalism and racism. However, as Stephen Castles contends, "the nexus between racism and nationalism is central to modern nation-states."[52] Moreover, as there is not one racism but racisms,[53] there is not one concept of race (i.e., the Western concept of race) but localized concepts of race such as *jinshu* and *minzoku*.[54] In addition, Stuart Hall advocates the importance of "analyz[ing] and deconstruct[ing] language and behavior in order to decipher the patterns of ideological thinking which are inscribed in them."[55] Then it is crucial to look into how the two ideologies, Japanese nationalism and racism—which are inseparable from the Japanese concepts of race—intersect and are practiced in microlevel or everyday situations. Hereafter, providing examples from the interviews that I conducted in multiple research projects between 2010 and 2015 with people of Chinese and Korean descent living in Japan,[56] I discuss examples of Japanese nationalism and racism as everyday practices, focusing on language and race, the two pillars of Balibar's notion of fictive ethnicity.[57]

INTERSECTION OF JAPANESE NATIONALISM AND RACISM IN EVERYDAY PRACTICES

Language

The first example concerning language is the assumption that the Japanese language is only for the Japanese, which is tied to the prewar notion of *minzoku* as well as Japaneseness constructed in *nihonjinron*. Interviewee A, a third-generation *zainichi* Korean[58] (female, age 24), received most of her education in Korean schools operated by the General Association of Korean Residents in Japan that has close ties with North Korea. She worked full-time for a few years at a private company before coming to study at a Japanese university. She does not have Japanese nationality and uses her Korean name in everyday life. She recalled looking for a part-time job:

> When I signed a labor contract, the manager asked me, "Is your visa all right?" I said to him, "I have a valid foreign resident registration card." He was not satisfied and then asked me, "Is your Japanese all right [*nihongo wa daijōbu*]?" I felt like saying "Give me a break." I am asked these questions many times and every time I look for a job. So now I say I was born in Japan.

Interviewee B (female, age 47), a naturalized Japanese citizen, came from Taiwan when she was eight years old. Since then she has attended Japanese schools and spent most of her life in Japan. She has working experience in both business and academic settings. Using her Chinese name at work, she has been often asked, "Is your Japanese all right [*nihongo wa daijōbu nano*]?" When she exchanges name cards, Japanese people often look surprised upon seeing her name. Recalling this experience, she said: "I often feel I have to say up-front that I am from Taiwan but my Japanese is all right [*nihongo wa daijōbu desu*]."

The question "Is your Japanese all right?" demonstrates how one of the two key elements of fictive ethnicity (i.e., language) meets the other (i.e., race) in the nexus of nationalism and racism. This question was posed to the interviewees even though they were speaking Japanese. Having grown up in Japan, the two interviewees are comfortable speaking in Japanese, although they also speak their heritage language. The question means not simply asking whether they can communicate in Japanese but whether they speak Japanese like the Japanese do, or literally "all right-ly." It *problematizes* their cultural characteristic and thereby *marginalizes* them—two of the three processes of everyday racism. Anybody can learn Japanese but will never be recognized as fully belonging to this linguistic community when the language is racialized or essentialized as what is to be learned properly only by the Japanese. The Japanese language turns into a racial characteristic inaccessible to non-Japanese peoples and is used to exclude or justify excluding them.

A tightly related example is Japanese people's antipathy to people speaking Asian languages in public. Interviewee C (female, age 25) was born to Chinese parents in China and came to live in Japan for her parents' jobs when she was six years old. She is a naturalized citizen of Japan with a Japanese-style family name and working at a company. She said: "When I am speaking in Chinese on the train, I can sometimes tell from people's facial expressions that they think it is noisy [*urusai*]." Her mother sometimes told her on the train to move to other seats, telling her that "people in front of us seem to be very annoyed [*sugoi meiwaku gatte iru*] because we are speaking in Chinese." Interviewee B also talked about receiving disapproving glances from other passengers on the train when she speaks in Chinese. She said: "When I was a child, I remember I often talked to my mother in Japanese when we were outside." Her mother's Japanese was not as fluent as that of Interviewee C, so "I often didn't understand what my mother said. We couldn't understand each other so later I had to ask her again what she said."

Such disapproval of Asian languages is expressed not only nonverbally but also in the form of physical aggression. Interviewee A said that being glared at by Japanese people when she was speaking in Korean has become so "normal [*atarimae*]" that she does not think about it much. In 2002, when the media frequently reported North Korea's involvement in abducting Japanese citizens, she said: "Teachers told us not to speak Korean on public transportation. It was really dangerous because someone called our school and threatened us by saying, 'I will kill one of you by any means.'" She remembered that the school received many similar phone calls. When this "routine and familiar" practice escalates, it can incite physical violence. In 2011, a 45-year-old Japanese man was arrested for kicking Korean children at a subway station near Tokyo South Korean School. It was reported that the suspect hated hearing Korean children speaking Korean on the train.[59]

These attitudes toward Korean and Chinese are contrasted to Japanese people's more favorable attitudes toward Western languages, especially English. Interviewee D (female, age 50), who came to Japan from China more than 20 years ago and married a Japanese man, said: "I have never seen Japanese people say 'stop it' to Americans speaking very loudly [in English] on the train, but I have seen some Japanese say it to people speaking in Chinese." Interviewee B also mentioned that disapproving glances were not usually directed at people speaking in English in public. According to B, this is because while Chinese sounds "noisy [*sōzōshii*]," English or European languages sound "sophisticated [*senrensareta*]" to the Japanese. She added: "I strongly feel the West and Westerners are treated far better in Japanese society. Japanese people don't have positive images about not only Chinese but also Asian languages and peoples in general because they are from developing countries and former colonies."

The three views on Japanese, Asian languages, and English are interconnected with the two Japanese concepts of race—*jinshu* and *minzoku*. The resentment of people speaking in non-Japanese languages is tied to the myth of Japan as a single (*tan'itsu*) *minzoku* nation that only Japanese people who speak the Japanese language live in Japan. However, the concept of *minzoku* does not explain why English does not elicit the same disapproval. English is not as resented as Korean and Chinese are because in the concept of *jinshu*, the whites are a "superior" race to the yellows and so is English, the most powerful language of the whites. Balibar argued that the gap between nationalism and racism arises from the two roles of racism in nationalism: as supernationalism and as supranationalism. Japanese racism based on *minzoku* is super-nationalist. However, when it is based also on *jinshu*, it functions not as a supra-nationalism but a de- (i.e., reducing or negating) nationalism, which exempts English from being subject to the "supremacy" of the Japanese language. This also explains why the Japanese government and schools often spend more of their financial and human resources on English education than Japanese education or why Japanese people themselves often perceive English as more "sophisticated" than Japanese.[60]

Race

One example of race is the pressure placed on people of Asian descent to use a Japanese-style name. Interviewee E (female, age 23), a university student from South Korea, talked about working part-time as a waitress. All of the Chinese and Korean students working there were required to wear a name badge with a Japanese name. She recalled: "The manager said that some customers would feel uncomfortable about the [Korean] name so I had to have a Japanese name." Her Japanese coworkers told her: "It will be good because if customers recognized your accents, they would think you are a Japanese who grew up in Korea." A customer once wrote a comment card: "Why does a Korean have a Japanese name? It is disgusting [*kimochi warui*]." The customers for whom she served food were friendly when she told them that she was actually Korean.

When Interviewee A was working for a company, she also had to use a Japanese-style name when she had Japanese clients. At that time, she rationalized it by thinking that "the name was only to Japanese people and just a formality [*keisikiteki*]" so "it was useless [*shōganai*] to think about it much." She knew that her friends and other graduates of her Korean school also used a Japanese-style name at work.

Interviewee F (female, age 21), a university student, was born to a *zainichi* Korean father and a Korean mother in Japan and grew up attending Japanese schools. All of her family members use a Japanese surname in public. She said:

> My parents believe if we think we are Korean and have a strong will to be Korean, the fact does not change even though we keep that identity inside ourselves. They thought I didn't have to use my Korean name at the risk of being bullied. They still think like that. So I have been told to use my Japanese name that will not cause me a problem [*bunnana*].

Not fully agreeing with this idea, she often told her classmates that she was Korean: "When I told my parents, 'At school, I said I am Korean,' they got so angry by saying, 'Why do you ask for trouble? You will be bullied!'" Although she has not been harassed because she is Korean, she often heard Japanese people, who assumed that she was Japanese, express their "true feelings [*honne*]" about Koreans. When she heard such "true feelings," she admitted: "I am angry but don't show it. I just remain silent. I am a minority. If I said I am not Japanese, it would be pointless. I keep my anger inside."

Using a Japanese-style name is so common to the extent that counteractions are repressed as seen in Interviewee A's remark (that "it is useless to think about it much"). Although there have not been many recent surveys on this issue, according to the 2000 Korean Residents Union in Japan (Mindan) survey, only 13.4% of the respondents always used a Korean name.[61] In the 2007 Kyoto municipal government survey, 23.2% of the *zainichi* Korean respondents did at work and school.[62] It should be noted, however, that the problem is not the use of a Japanese-style name itself: people of Korean descent use it for a variety of reasons, which reflect their diverse sense of belonging.[63] The central issue here is *not* their everyday practices as an ethnic minority in Japan *but* Japanese people's everyday practices that push them to "choose" using a Japanese-style name.

This is an everyday practice of Japanese nationalism and racism in the sense that it racially realizes Japanese nationalism or the idea that Japan is the place where only the Japanese people live. This practice erases their existence (i.e., racism) to secure the boundaries of the Japanese nation (i.e., nationalism). People of Korean and Chinese descent are phenotypically indistinguishable from the Japanese. A Japanese-style name renders them invisible to the Japanese and thereby the racial homogeneity of Japanese society appears to be real.

The three processes of everyday racism can be used to explain this practice. Making them invisible *marginalizes* their existence and, more importantly, *represses* their resistance to Japanese racism. As Interviewee F described, she could not say anything when a Japanese person made a negative comment about Koreans in front of her, not knowing that she was Korean. In short, making their existence invisible also makes Japanese racism invisible and thereby enables Japanese people to be racist with impunity. Moreover, this practice does not simply assimilate people of Korean descent but erases them by *problematizing* them as different *minzoku*. As Interviewee E reported, for her Japanese coworkers, a Japanese raised in Korea and thus speaking in accented Japanese is "better" than a Japanese-speaking Korean living in Japan. Language matters less than race here; being Japanese is "better" than being Korean. In addition, the Japanese customer's comment that a Korean person using a Japanese-style name is "disgusting" indicates the fear of the boundaries between the Koreans and the Japanese becoming blurred. A Japanese-style name does not lead to incorporating them as Japanese; it just obliterates their existence facially while the boundaries remain intact.

A closely related example is the phrase "go back to your country [*jibun no kuni ni kaere*]." Interviewee G is a first-year university student who was born to a Chinese mother and a Japanese father (female; age 18). She said that not only bullies but also her classmates often threw this phrase at her as a way of teasing. According to Interviewee G, this is "the abusive phrase most frequently thrown at us [Japanese of multiracial/ethnic/national background]." She added: "That is the most damaging phrase. I think that hurts us most."

Interviewee A also heard this phrase frequently. When she wore her Korean school uniform in the train station near the school, "ordinary" middle-aged men and women often asked: "What kind of education are you receiving? Why don't you go back now [*hayaku kaeri nasai yo*]?" Interviewee A added: "I would like Japanese people to know why we are here. I feel hurt the most when they tell us not to live here because we are anti-Japanese [*han nichi*]." In addition, Interviewee B's experience at job interviews exemplifies a "milder" version of this attitude. She said: "Interviewers were often surprised to find me, a foreigner, at job interviews. The first question to me was usually 'Why are you in Japan [*nande nihon ni iru no*]?'" Some of them even asked her: "Even though you are a foreigner, are you going to keep living in Japan forever [*nihon ni zutto sumu ki aru no*]?"

The phrase "go back to your country" is an everyday practice of Japanese nationalism and racism. Calling a fear of race mixing "mixophobia" and defining it as "racism fused with nationalism," Pierre-André Taguieff argues that "xenophobia is fundamentally mixophobic because it opposes race mixing, which is said to cause the disappearance of what is pure."[64] This phrase implies the desire to reserve Japan for the Japanese by removing non-Japanese and not-fully Japanese people whose existence contaminates the racial "purity" of the Japanese nation. Interviewees A and G were born in Japan and all of the three (Interviewees A, B, and G) grew up in Japan, and thus they are full members of the Japanese linguistic community. Yet the dominant Japanese view is that they are not entitled to be in Japan because according to the concept of *minzoku*, they are of a different race or a mixed race.

It is crucial to understand this phrase as a practice in which Japanese nationalism and racism are interconnected. Referring to the phrase, Ghassan Hage claims:

> It has become part of an anti-racist common sense to consider "go home" statements as mere "racism." Yet, surely, the expressed wish to send undesirable others to their "home" is as clear a nationalist desire as can be, even if it involves a racial categorization of those one wishes to see "go home."[65]

The phrase is considered racist in Australia on which his study is based, probably because it is usually directed at nonwhite peoples. Hage contends that practices often labeled as racist, such as the phrase "go home," should be better understood as nationalism[66] because "the classification of these practices as 'racist' has often helped to construct them as if they belonged to a minority mode of thinking totally alien from that held by the majority."[67] However, in the context of Japan, there is a danger that if designated primarily as nationalism, the phrase "go back to your country" would be far less problematized because unlike racism, nationalism is an ideology validated under the nation-state framework—the default system of the world today. In Japan, this phrase is seen not as an expression of racism but rather as that of nationalism, although it is certainly perceived as discriminatory. When defined as a nationalist practice, the desire of expelling non-Japanese from Japan can be legitimized as an act of protecting the sovereign territory, an integral element of the right to national self-determination. What is needed is not to stress one over the other but rather to see them as intersected in order to highlight the role of racism in Japanese nationalism and thus problematize the nationalism itself.

TOWARD CONSTRUCTING A
MULTICULTURALIST JAPANESE SOCIETY

These examples of language and race are "common" practices that are repeated in everyday situations, and therefore tend to be overlooked or minimized. Normalizing and trivializing these practices reproduce and perpetuate the dominant ideology of Japan as a single (*tan'itsu*) *minzoku* nation by demarcating Japanese from people of Chinese and Korean descent and relegating their languages and existence to inferior status (i.e., marginalizing and problematizing) and invisible (i.e., repressing counteractions). Exploring an alternative form of multiculturalism in Britain, Stuart Hall suggests that "rather than a strategy for improving the lot of the so-called "ethnic" or racialized minorities alone, it [the commitment to expose and confront racism] would have to be a strategy which broke with [the] majoritarian logic and attempted to reconfigure or reimagine the nation as a whole in a radical post-national form."[68] A multiculturalist Japan is not possible without Japanese people, the majority group in Japan, becoming critically aware of these everyday practices of Japanese nationalism and racism as well as challenging the dominant way in which they imagine the Japanese nation.

Scrutinizing everyday Japanese nationalism and racism practices directed at people of Korean and Chinese descent is particularly important. This is not simply because more than half of Japan's foreign nationals are people of Chinese and Korean descent, probably more if naturalized citizens and *hafu* (mixed) Japanese people are included, but more importantly because Japanese nationalism and racism often affect them more intensely than it does other peoples because of Japan's imperil and colonial relationship with them. Stephen Castles argues that "many forms of racism are part of the legacy of colonialism."[69] Graham Day and Andrew Thompson also postulate that "the most fundamental consequence of imperialism and colonialism is its contribution to 'nation building.'"[70] Put simply, Japanese nationalism and racism intersect not only with each other but also with Japanese imperialism and colonialism. This explains why ultraright groups such as *Zaitokukai* and the popular literary genre "*kenkan kenchū* (hate-Korean, hate-Chinese)" target people of Chinese and Korean descent. In addition, these "excessive" practices are linked to the "normal" or everyday practices in the sense that both construct Japaneseness by racializing and hierarchically distinguishing the Japanese from these people, although the two practices rely on different modalities.

Furthermore, interrogating the nexus of nationalism and racism in Japan, a nonwhite nation, requires a different approach from those in the white nations of the West. It cannot be conducted properly without looking into both Western and Japanese imperialisms and colonialisms, from which the Western concept of race (i.e., *jinshu*) and the Japanese concept of *mizoku* are inseparable. And *jinshu* and *minzoku* were key concepts in the construction of modern Japan's national identity.[71] Thus, such an interrogation requires unlearning the Western racial (*jinshu*) order that hierarchizes the whites and the nonwhites as well as the Japanese racial (*minzoku*) order that places Japanese and non-Japanese Asians within a hierarchy.

A trans-East Asian perspective is indispensable to unlearn both Western and Japanese racial orders and to debunk the dominant ideology of Japanese homogeneity. It must be not simply transnational but be trans-East Asian because the *jinshu* category "yellow" cuts across peoples in East Asia, and differentiating the yellows lies in the core of *minzoku*, which has a pivotal position in the dominant idea of Japaneseness. This perspective involves reviewing and re-narrating historical and contemporary interrelationships among peoples in East Asia as well as between East Asia and the West. It includes reimagining Japan as a milieu where East Asian and other peoples and cultures have always coexisted and mingled, without neglecting the power relations entailed in the transnational hybridity. Highlighting trans-East Asian hybridities is especially important in Japan because such hybridities tend to be overlooked or embraced less positively than Japan-West hybridities, and also because it will challenge essentialized and hierarchical views toward East Asian peoples that are assumed in everyday practices of Japanese nationalism and racism. The myth of homogeneity is a common majoritarian logic in Korea, Taiwan, and Japan.[72] The majoritarian ideologies in Korea and Taiwan are probably tied to both Western and Japanese imperial and colonial remnants. Ways of displacing the logic would vary in each socio-historical context, yet further inter-East Asian dialogue will be necessary to make a more multiculturalist East Asian society.

NOTES

1. *Zaitokukai* is an ultraright group established in 2006. As of November 2015, the group has 15,682 members and chapters in 36 of the 47 prefectures in Japan (see the *Zaitokukai* website: http://www.zaitokukai.info/). In 2009 and 2010, *Zaitokukai* vandalized a Korean elementary school in Kyoto, calling the children "cockroaches" and "spies" (see for example, Martin Fackler, "Japanese Court Fines Rightist Group over Protests at a School in Kyoto," *New York Times*, October 7, 2013, http://www.nytimes.com/2013/10/08/world/asia/japanese-court-fines-rightist-group-in-elementary-school-protest.html). Since 2012, *Zaitokukai* and other similar groups have held anti-Korean demonstrations numerous times, carrying placards that included comments such as "Good or Bad Koreans: Kill Them All" (see for example, Hideaki Ishibashi, "Anti-Korean Protests Trigger Counter-Protests against Hatemongers," *Asahi Shimbun*, March 26, 2013, http://ajw.asahi.com/article/behind_news/social_affairs/AJ201303260097 and Eric Johnston, "Politicians Silent on Curbing Hate Speech," *The Japan Times*, July 10, 2014, http://www.japantimes.co.jp/news/2013/07/10/national/social-issues/politicians-silent-on-curbing-hate-speech/#.U3Pw4vmKWm4).

2. *"Nihon wa naze? Kenchū hankan shoseki ne'pū* [The drastic increase and popularity of anti-Korean books in Japan]," *The Hangyoreh*, Feb. 12, 2014, http://japan.hani.co.kr/arti/international/16680.html.

3. More than 200,000 copies of the trade paperback *"Bōkanron* [A treatise on stupid Korea]" written by a journalist have sold since its publication in December 2013. As of April 1, 2015 the book *"Dai kenkan jidai* [The great anti-Korean era]" by *Zaitokukai*'s former chairperson Sakurai Makoto published in September 2014 was ranked as the top-selling book in the Asian and African area studies category of the Amazon Japan online bookstore.

4. Yuko Kawai, "Deracialized Race, Obscured Racism: Japaneseness, Western and Japanese Concepts of Race, and Modalities of Racism," *Japanese Studies*, 35, no. 1 (2015): 23–47.

5. See for example, Yuko Kawai, "Neoliberalism, Nationalism, and Intercultural Communication: A Critical Analysis of a Japan's Neoliberal Nationalism Discourse under Globalization," *Journal of Intercultural and International Communication*, 2, no. 1 (2009): 16–43.

6. See for example, Stuart Hall, "Conclusion: The Multicultural Question," in *Un/Settled Multiculturalisms: Diasporas, Entanglements, Transruptions*. Barnor Hesse (ed.), (London and New York: Zed Books, 2000), 232; Tariq Modood, *Multiculturalism* (Cambridge: Polity, 2007), 37–62.

7. See for example, John Lie, *Multi-ethnic Japan* (Cambridge, MA: Harvard University Press, 2001) and Tessa Morris-Suzuki, *Re-inventing Japan: Time, Space, Nation* (New York: M.E. Sharpe, 1998).

8. See for example, Étienne Balibar, "Racism and Nationalism," in *Race, Nation, Class*. Étienne Balibar and Immanuel Wallerstein (ed.), (London: Verso, 1991a), 37–67 and Stephen Castles, *Ethnicity and Globalization* (Thousand Oaks, CA: Sage, 2000).

9. Balibar, "Racism and Nationalism," 47.

10. Michael Billig, *Banal Nationalism* (Newbury Park, CA: Sage, 1995); Philomena Essed, *Everyday Racism*, (Newbury Park, CA: Sage, 1991) and "Everyday Racism," in *Race Critical Theories*. Philomena Essed and David Theo Goldberged (ed.), (Malden, MA: Blackwell, 2002), 176–94.

11. As of the year 2014, among the total of 2,121,831 residents with foreign nationality, 654,777 residents are Chinese (30.9%), 501,230 are Korean (23.6%), and 40,197 are Taiwanese (1.9%). See Ministry of Justice, *"Heisei 26 nen matsu ni okeru zairyū gaikokujin kazu ni tsuite* [The Number of Foreign Residents in 2014]," last modified March 20, 2015, http://www.moj.go.jp/nyuukokukanri/kouhou/nyuukoku-kanri04_00050.html.

12. See, for example, Hans Kohn, *Nationalism: Its Meaning and History* (Malabar, FL: Krieger, 1965), John Plamenatz, "Two Types of Nationalism," in *Nationalism: The Nature of Evolution of an Idea*. Eugene Kamenka (ed.), (London: Edward Arnold, 1976), 23–36, and Anthony Smith, *National Identity* (Reno, NV: University of Nevada Press, 1991).

13. For example, Kymlicka Will, *Politics in the Vernacular* (Oxford: Oxford University Press, 2001), chapter 12.

14. Étienne Balibar, "The Nation Form: History and Ideology," in *Race, Nation, Class*. Étienne Balibar and Immanuel Wallerstein (ed.), (London: Verso, 1991b), 96–100.

15. Balibar, "The Nation Form," 86–106.

16. Ibid., 96.

17. Ibid., 99.

18. Ibid., 100.

19. Balibar, "Racism and Nationalism," 37–67.

20. Balibar, "The Nation Form," 54.

21. Ibid., 59–61.

22. Ibid., 61.

23. Ibid., 54.

24. Shin'ichi Yamamuro, *Shisō kadai to shite no ajia* [Asia as a Conceptual Issue] (Tokyo: Iwanami Shoten, 2000), 9.

25. Hiroshi Yasuda, "Kindai nihon ni okeru minzoku kan'nen no keisei [Construction of the Concept of *Minzoku* in Modern Japan]," *Shisō to gendai* [Philosophy and Society] 31, (1992): 66.

26. Ibid., 69.

27. Naoki Sakai, *Shizan sareru nihongo nihonjin* [The Stillborn of the Japanese as Language and as Ethnos] (Tokyo: Shin'yōsha, 1996), 131–145.

28. See for example, Junzo Kawata, "Minzoku gainen ni tuite no memo [On the Concept of *Minzoku*]." *Minzokugaku kenkyū* [Japanese Journal of Ethnology] 63, (1999): 457–58, and Morris-Suzuki, *Re-inventing Japan*, 87.

29. Yasuda, "Kindai," 72.

30. Kazutoshi Ueda, "Kokugo to kokka to [The National Language and the State]," in *Meiji bungaku zenshū 44 kan* [The Meiji Era corpus vol. 44]. Sen'ichi Hisamatsu (ed.), (Tokyo: Chikuma Shobō, 1968 [1894]), 110.

31. For example, Masataka Endo, *Kindai nihon no syokuminchi tōchi ni okeru kokuseki to koseki* [Nationality and Family Registry in Modern Japanese Colonial Rule] (Tokyo: Akashi Shoten, 2009).

32. Eiji Oguma, *Tan'itsu minzoku shinwa no kigen* [The Origin of the Myth of Ethnic Homogeneity] (Tokyo: Shin'yōsha, 1995) and *"Nihonjin" no kyōkai* [The Boundaries of the Japanese] (Tokyo: Shin'yōsha, 1998).

33. Harumi Befu, "Nationalism and *Nihonjinron*," in *Cultural Nationalism in East Asia: Representation and Identity*. Harumi Befu (ed.), (Berkeley, CA: Institute of East Asian Studies, University of California at Berkeley, 1993), 116.

34. For example, Peter N. Dale, *The Myth of Japanese Uniqueness* (New York: Routledge, 2001 [1986]), 38–39.

35. Aoki Tamotsu, *Nihonbunkaron no hen'yō* [Transformation of the studies of Japanese culture] (Tokyo: Chūō Kōron Sha, 1991), 29.

36. For example, Kosaku Yoshino, *Cultural Nationalism in Contemporary Japan* (London: Routledge, 1992), 10–22.

37. Koichi Iwabuchi, *Bunka no taiwaryoku* [The Power of Cultural Dialogue] (Tokyo: Nihon keizai shuppan sha, 2007), 198–223.

38. Billig, *Banal Nationalism*, 37.

39. Ibid., 6.

40. Ibid., 40.

41. Essed, *Everyday Racism* and "Everyday Racism."

42. Essed, "Everyday Racism," 205.

43. Essed, *Everyday Racism*, 39.

44. Ibid., 145.

45. Ibid., 180–181 and Essed, "Everyday Racism," 207–8.

46. Essed, *Everyday Racism*, 155.

47. Ibid., 202.

48. Ibid., 115 and Essed, "Everyday Racism," 207.

49. Essed, *Everyday Racism*, 173 and 207–8.

50. Ibid., 53.

51. Ibid., 50–53. Essed posits that everyday racism includes not only direct interactions between people but also "indirect" practices of everyday racism such as policymakers' remarks and media discourses. However, these public discourses are not analyzed but treated as informing microlevel practices.

52. Castles, *Ethnicity and Globalization*, 169.

53. David Theo Goldberg, Introduction to *Anatomy of Racism*. David Theo Goldgerg (ed.), (Minneapolis, MN: University of Minnesota Press, 1990), p. xiii; Stuart Hall, "Gramsci's Relevance for the Study of Race and Ethnicity," in *Stuart Hall: Critical Dialogues in Cultural Studies*. Kuan-Hsing Chen and David Morley (ed.), (London and New York: Routledge, 1996 [1987]), 435.

54. Yasuko Takezawa, "Jinshu gainen no hōkatsuteki rikai ni mukete [Toward a Comprehensive Understanding of the Concept of Race]," in *Jinshugainen no fuhensei*

o tou [Is Race a Universal Idea?]. Yasuko Takezawa (ed.), (Kyoto: Jinbun Shoin, 2005), 9–109.

55. Stuart Hall, "Signification, Representation, Ideology: Althusser and the Post-Structuralist Debates," *Critical Studies in Mass Communication* 2, no. 2 (1985): 99–100.

56. Interviews were conducted in research projects on Korean newcomers' life stories funded by The Toyota Foundation (Grant Number: D09-R-0422), *hafu* (mixed) Japanese, and multiculturalism in Japan funded by Japan Society for the Promotion of Science (Grants-in-Aid for Scientific Research Grant Number: 24530657). Most interviewees were students and teachers.

57. Balibar, "The Nation Form."

58. *Zainichi* Koreans are descendants of Koreans who were brought or migrated to Japan during the colonial era. *Zai-nichi* literarily means staying (*zai*) in Japan (*nichi*).

59. "*Tōkōchū no Tokyo kankoku gakko jidō ni bōkō, nihonjin dansei* [Japanese Man Assaulted Korean Children on Their Way to Tokyo Korean School]," *Yonhap News Agency*, September 14, 2011, http://japanese.yonhapnews.co.kr/headline/2011/09/14/0200000000AJP20110914003300882.HTML.

60. For example, Philip Seargeant, *The Idea of English in Japan* (Bristol, UK: Multilingual Matters, 2009).

61. "Kika hitsuyō nai ga nanawari [Seventy Percent of *Zainichi* Koreans Say Naturalization is not Necessary]," *Shimbun Mindan*, April 4, 2001, http://www.mindan.org/shinbun/010404/topic/topic_h.htm. The number of respondents was 1,295 (817 men and 478 women) of the total 2,924 *zainichi* Koreans between the ages of 15 and 64 selected by the random sampling method.

62. Kyoto Municipal Government, "*Kyoto shi gaikokuseki shiminishiki ji'tai chōsa hōkokusho dai4shō* [Survey Report: Kyoto Citizens with Foreign Nationality Chapter 4]," last modified August 28, 2008, http://www.city.kyoto.lg.jp/sogo/cms-files/contents/0000031/31528/4.pdf. The number of respondents was 979 (594 "old comers" and 385 "new comers") of the total 3700 foreign nationals selected by the random sampling method. The "old comers" are *zainichi* Koreans.

63. Kohei Kawabata, *Jimoto wo aruku* [Walking the Local] (Tokyo: Ochanomizu Shobo, 2013).

64. Pierre-André Taguieff, "National Identity Framed in the Logics of Racialization: Aspects, Figures, and Problems of Differentialist Racism," in *Racism*. Leonard Harris (ed.), (New York: Humanity, 1999), 310.

65. Ghassan Hage, *White Nation* (London and New York: Routledge, 2000), 39–40.

66. Hage argues that "there is more than an analytical issue at stake in the understanding of these practices as primarily nationalist rather than racist. There is also a political dimension." Ibid., 76.

67. Hage, *White Nation*, 76.

68. Hall, "Conclusion," 232.

69. Castles, *Ethnicity and Globalization*, 176.

70. Graham Day and Andrew Thompson, *Theorizing Nationalism* (New York: Palgrave Macmillan, 2005), 138.

71. Yamamuro, *Shisō kadai*, 9–10.

72. Rhacel Salazar Parreñas and Joon K. Kim, "Multicultural East Asia: An introduction," *Journal of Ethnic and Migration Studies* 37, no. 10 (2011): 1555–6.

REFERENCES

Aoki, Tamotsu. 1991. *Nihonbunkaron no hen'yō [Transformation of the studies of Japanese culture]*. Tokyo: Chūō Kōron Sha.

Balibar, Étienne. 1991a. "Racism and Nationalism," in *Race, Nation, Class*, edited by Étienne Balibar and Immanuel Wallerstein, 37–67. London: Verso.

Balibar, Étienne. 1991b. "The Nation Form: History and Ideology," in *Race, Nation, Class*, edited by Étienne Balibar and Immanuel Wallerstein, 86–106. London: Verso.

Befu, Harumi. 1993. "Nationalism and *Nihonjinron*," in *Cultural Nationalism in East Asia: Representation and Identity*, edited by Harumi Befu, 107–35. Berkeley, CA: Institute of East Asian Studies, University of California at Berkeley.

Billig, Michael. 1995. *Banal Nationalism*. Newbury Park, CA: Sage.

Castles, Stephen. 2000. *Ethnicity and Globalization*. Thousand Oaks, CA: Sage.

Dale, Peter, N. 2001. *The Myth of Japanese Uniqueness*. New York: Routledge, [1986].

Day, Graham and Thompson, Andrew. 2005. *Theorizing Nationalism*. New York: Palgrave Macmillan.

Endo, Masataka. 2009. *Kindai nihon no syokuminchi tōchi ni okeru kokuseki to koseki [Nationality and Family Registry in Modern Japanese Colonial Rule]*. Tokyo: Akashi Shoten.

Essed, Philomena. 1991. *Everyday Racism*. Newbury Park, CA: Sage.

Essed, Philomena. 2002. "Everyday Racism," in *Race Critical Theories*, edited by Philomena Essed and David Theo Goldberg, 176–94. Malden, MA: Blackwell.

Fackler, Martin. 2013. "Japanese Court Fines Rightist Group Over Protests at a School in Kyoto," *New York Times*. Accessed May 31, 2014. http://www.nytimes.com/2013/10/08/world/asia/japanese-court-fines-rightist-group-in-elementary-school-protest.html.

Goldberg, David Theo. 1990. "Introduction," in *Anatomy of Racism*, edited by David Theo Goldgerg, xi–xxiii. Minneapolis, MN: University of Minnesota Press.

Hage, Ghassan. 2000. *White Nation*. London and New York: Routledge.

Hall, Stuart. 1985. "Signification, Representation, Ideology: Althusser and the Post-Structuralist Debates." *Critical Studies in Mass Communication*, 2(2): 91–114.

Hall, Stuart. 1996. "Gramsci's Relevance for the Study of Race and Ethnicity," in *Stuart Hall: Critical Dialogues in Cultural Studies*, edited by Kuan-Hsing Chen and David Morley, 411–40. London and New York: Routledge, [1987].

Hall, Stuart. 2000. "Conclusion: The Multicultural Question," in *Un/Settled Multiculturalisms: Diasporas, Entanglements, Transruptions,* edited by Barnor Hesse, 209–41. London and New York: Zed Books.

Ishibashi, Hideaki. 2013. "Anti-Korean Protests Trigger Counter-Protests against Hatemongers," *Asahi Shimbun*. Accessed January 30, 2015. http://ajw.asahi.com/article/behind_news/social_affairs/AJ201303260097.

Iwabuchi, Koichi. 2007. *Bunka no taiwaryoku [The Power of Cultural Dialogue]*. Tokyo: Nihon keizai shuppan sha.

Johnston, Eric. 2014. "Politicians Silent on Curbing Hate Speech," *The Japan Times*. Accessed January 30, 2015. http://www.japantimes.co.jp/news/2013/07/10/national/social-issues/politicians-silent-on-curbing-hate-speech/#.U3Pw4vmKWm4.

Kawabata, Kohei. 2013. *Jimoto wo aruku [Walking the Local]*. Tokyo: Ochanomizu Shobo.

Kawai, Yuko. 2009. "Neoliberalism, Nationalism, and Intercultural Communication: A Critical Analysis of a Japan's Neoliberal Nationalism Discourse under Globalization." *Journal of Intercultural and International Communication*, 2(1): 16–43.

Kawai, Yuko. 2015. "Deracialized Race, Obscured Racism: Japaneseness, Western and Japanese Concepts of Race, and Modalities of Racism." *Japanese Studies*, 35(1): 23–47.

Kawata, Junzo. 1999. "Minzoku gainen ni tuite no memo [On the Concept of *Minzoku*]." *Minzokugaku kenkyū [Japanese Journal of Ethnology]*, 63: 451–61.

"Kika hitsuyō nai ga nanawari [Seventy Percent of *Zainichi* Koreans Say Naturalization is not Necessary]." 2001. *Shimbun Mindan*. Accessed Jan. 28, 2014. http://www.mindan.org/shinbun/010404/topic/topic_h.htm.

Kohn, Hans. 1965. *Nationalism: Its Meaning and History*. Malabar, FL: Krieger.

Kymlicka, Will. 2001. *Politics in the Vernacular*. Oxford: Oxford University Press.

Kyoto Municipal Government. "*Kyoto shi gaikokuseki shiminishiki ji'tai chōsa hōkokusho [Survey Report: Kyoto Citizens with Foreign Nationality]*." Last modified August 28, 2008. http://www.city.kyoto.lg.jp/sogo/cmsfiles/contents/0000031/31528/4.pdf.

Lie, John. 2001. *Multi-ethnic Japan*. Cambridge, MA: Harvard University Press.

Ministry of Justice. 2014. "*Heisei 26 nen matsu ni okeru zairyū gaikokujin kazu ni tsuite [The Number of Foreign Residents in 2014]*." Last modified March 20, 2015. Accessed November 14, 2015. http://www.moj.go.jp/nyuukokukanri/kouhou/nyuu-kokukanri04_00050.html

Modood, Tariq. 2007. *Multiculturalism*. Cambridge: Polity.

Morris-Suzuki, Tessa. 1998. *Re-inventing Japan: Time, Space, Nation*. New York: ME Sharpe.

"Nihon wa naze? Kenchū hankan shoseki ne'pū [The Drastic Increase and Popularity of Anti-Korean Books in Japan]." 2014. *The Hangyoreh*, February 12, 2014. Accessed November 6, 2014. http://japan.hani.co.kr/arti/international/16680.html.

Oguma, Eiji. 1995. *Tan'itsu minzoku shinwa no kigen [The Origin of the Myth of Ethnic Homogeneity]*. Tokyo: Shin'yōsha.

Oguma, Eiji. 1998. *"Nihonjin" no kyōkai [The Boundaries of the Japanese]*. Tokyo: Shin'yōsha.

Parreñas, Rhacel Salazar and Kim, Joon K. 2011. "Multicultural East Asia: An Introduction." *Journal of Ethnic and Migration Studies*, 37(10): 1555–61.

Plamenatz, John. 1967. "Two Types of Nationalism," in *Nationalism: The Nature of Evolution of an Idea*, edited by Eugene Kamenka, 23–36. London: Edward Arnold.

Renan, Ernest. 2001. "What is a Nation?," in *Nations and Identities*, edited by Vincent P. Pecora, 162–76. Malden, MA: Blackwell, [1882].

Sakai, Naoki. *Shizan sareru nihongo nihonjin [The Stillborn of the Japanese as Language and as Ethnos]*. Tokyo: Shin'yōsha, 1996.

Seargeant, Philip. 2009. *The Idea of English in Japan.* Bristol, UK: Multilingual Matters.

Smith, Anthony. 1991. *National Identity.* Reno, NV: University of Nevada Press.

Taguieff, Pierre-André. 1999. "National Identity Framed in the Logics of Racialization: Aspects, Figures, and Problems of Differentialist Racism," in *Racism,* edited by Leonard Harris, 297–313. New York: Humanity.

Takezawa, Yasuko. 2005. "Jinshu gainen no hōkatsuteki rikai ni mukete [Toward a Comprehensive Understanding of the Concept of Race]," in *Jinshugainen no fuhensei o tou [Is Race a Universal Idea?],* edited by Yasuko Takezawa, 9–109. Kyoto: Jinbun Shoin.

"*Tōkōchū no Tokyo kankoku gakko jidō ni bōkō, nihonjin dansei [Japanese Man Assaulted Korean Children on Their Way to Tokyo Korean School].*" 2011. *Yonhap News Agency.* Accessed September 15, 2011. http://japanese.yonhapnews.co.kr/headline/2011/09/14/0200000000AJP20110914003300882.HTML.

Ueda, Kazutoshi. 1968. "Kokugo to kokka to [The National Language and the State]," in *Meiji bungaku zenshū 44 kan [The Meiji Era corpus vol. 44],* edited by Sen'ichi Hisamatsu, 108–13. Tokyo: Chikuma Shobō, [1894].

Yamamuro, Shin'ichi. 2000. *Shisō kadai to shite no Ajia [Asia as a Conceptual Issue].* Tokyo: Iwanami Shoten.

Yasuda, Hiroshi. 1992. "Kindai nihon ni okeru *minzoku* kan'nen no keisei [Construction of the Concept of *Minzoku* in Modern Japan]." *Shisō to gendai [Philosophy and Society],* 31: 61–72.

Yoshino, Kosaku. 1992. *Cultural Nationalism in Contemporary Japan.* London: Routledge.

CULTURAL POLITICS
OF MULTICULTURAL
SUBJECT MAKINGS

Chapter 8

Can "Multicultural Soldiers" Serve the Nation? The Social Debate about the Military Service Management of Mixed-Race Draftees in South Korea

Hyun Mee Kim

INTRODUCTION

I, the undersigned, as a soldier of the Republic of Korea, solemnly swear loyalty to the state and *the Korean people*, and, observing all laws, promise to obey the commands of my superiors and to faithfully carry out the tasks given to me. (emphasis added)

New Soldier's Oath

When new soldiers begin their military service, they sign this kind of oath. In 2012, the above phrase "the Korean people" was changed to the word "citizens." Given the social trend represented by the rapid increase in the number of inductees who were the offspring of international marriages—the so-called multicultural families—this reflected public sentiment that the word "citizen," which describes the composition of a nation, was more appropriate than the word "people" (*minjok*), which carries with it the concept of a Korean "race" (Yoon 2012).

Korea's long-cherished cultural concept of the nation based on a homogenous Korean essence is being challenged by the rapid increase in migrant workers, marriage migrants, and Korean returnees who previously lived abroad due to migration, work, and study. These challenges create a pressing dilemma of how to preserve a homogenous ethnic society in the face of the increasingly hybrid cultures generated by a reliance on transnational reproductive migration to maintain and reproduce the Korean family. In response, the South Korean government coined the term "multicultural family" to refer to a marriage where one spouse was of non-Korean origin and funded and implemented a variety of programs to help migrant women take on the role of Korean wives and settle down in South Korea. The notion of such multicultural families as a vulnerable social group is deepening and the occurrence of expressions such as "the second generation multicultural family," "multicultural children," "multicultural adolescents," and so on heard in day-to-day life mark such families with a social stigma. Young men beginning military service who are the children of multicultural families have been labeled "multicultural soldiers."

The Korean military was for a very long time an exclusively male social institution founded on the principle of Korean ethnic purity. Against the backdrop of Korean racial purism, the homogeneity of the soldiers came to be seen as protecting the loyalty, solidarity, as well as the system of hierarchy between men, and so the military banned the inscription of men of "mixed race" who might upset the status quo. Men of mixed race were waived the responsibility of military service until 2009 when the regulation was abolished as anti-constitutional. Despite the fact that male citizens of mixed descent—half-Korean or mixed ethnicity—have been drafted since 2012 as a result of the revision of the Military Service Act, there are growing social concerns and debates about the direction that the management of such mixed-race service members should take. This chapter analyzes the nature of the social debates about conscription and management of these "multicultural soldiers" in the military in regard to issues of combat capabilities, allegiance, and loyalty.

"MULTICULTURAL" AS AN IDIOM FOR
FOREIGNNESS AND MARGINALITY

The Korean migration regime parallels those found in Japan, Taiwan, and Singapore in that it promotes "migration without settlement" (Seol and Skrentny 2009: 582). Foreigners are admitted as workers and, upon completion of their employment contracts, are forbidden from settling down or seeking naturalization. These restrictions have been attributed to Korea's strong tradition of *jus sanguinis* citizenship, which, like those in neighboring countries, defines national membership on the basis of blood descent, historically through the male line. Prior to the implementation of the new nationality law in 1998, for example, only children of a Korean father were granted the right to be citizens, while the children of a Korean mother and non-Korean father were not. The 1998 revisions to the law removed the systemic discrimination against the children of Korean women.

Foreign women who came to Korea as the first "settler-type" immigrants under the prevailing anti-immigration regime generated a wide range of discourses on multiethnicity and multiculturalism. Korea's marriage migration policy was implemented to alleviate the crisis of low birth rates and an aging population, as well to restore a balanced ratio between men and women in the marriage market. Women of China's ethnic Korean minority, called *Chosonjok*, were initially preferred as brides because they were perceived as perpetuating the ethnic and linguistic homogeneity of the Korean nation (Freeman 2005, 2011; Lee 2005). Local agricultural associations and the government-funded associations for the "welfare of farm and fishing villages" recruited rural bachelors to join in marriage tours to China's northeast in search of ethnic Korean brides from China's *Joseonjok* minority community. Local governments quickly found it more convenient to rely on marriage brokers to secure a constant supply of women from other Asian countries. As a result, the new millennium witnessed a "marriage boom" as matchmaking businesses prospered, protected by Korean law that treated the mediation of international marriage as a legitimate business. With this growth in broker-age came an expansion in the type of men targeted by brokers, with lower class urban men and divorcees joining their rural counterparts in the search for foreign wives. The nationalities of foreign women recruited for marriage became more diverse as well due to a sharp increase in market-oriented, transnational brokerage and increasingly specialized advertising as a result of brokers' focus on certain Southeast Asian countries such as Vietnam, the Philippines, and Cambodia.

The presence of foreign wives in Korea, especially those from Southeast Asia, has resulted in diverse discourses about the emergence of a multicul-tural society. The shift from co-ethnic international marriages to multieth-nic and interracial ones sparked national fears and anxieties about racial and cultural purity. Marriage migrants were accepted as (potential) Korean citizens because of their reproductive roles as bearers of Korean children, thus legitimizing their membership in Korean families. The South Korean government has traditionally regarded the reproductive sphere of family and marriage as the core of its national culture and ethnic identity. The state often mobilizes family to support a strong sense of national sovereignty, linguistic homogeneity, and the ideology of a "pure blood," mono-racial nation. But the domains of home and family are now facing critical challenges from their growing dependence on foreign women to resolve the country's social repro-duction crisis due to declining fertility rates and the rapid marketization of welfare benefits for child and elderly care. These challenges create a pressing dilemma of how to preserve a homogenous ethnic society in the face of the increasingly hybrid cultures generated by a reliance on transnational repro-ductive migration to maintain and reproduce the Korean family. In response, the South Korean government termed a family formed through cross-border marriage a "multicultural family" and funded and implemented a variety of programs to help migrant wives settle down in South Korea. The South Korean government proclaimed its "transformation towards a multiracial, multicultural society" in April 2006, and then enacted laws such as the Act Concerning the Treatment of Foreigners in Korea in 2007 and the Multicultural Families Support Act in 2008. Since 2006, the state has emphasized a strong assimilationist model to quickly "Koreanize" these ethnically diverse marriage migrants. Also, the term "multicultural" has begun to replace "mono-ethnic," which has been long cherished by the society as an idiom for national success. The term "multicultural society" is now used commonly in day-to-day language. Though the notion of *multicultural society* was generally welcomed by many in South Korea, given its novelty, "multicultural" became an idiom denoting "foreignness," "a family member of international marriage," or "mixed-bloodedness," failing to incorporate the ethical stand of multiculturalism, which is based on mutual recognition of different cultures and the development of equitable relationships between Korean society and migrants (Kim 2011: 216).The sole aim of fast assimilation, instead of considering heterogeneity, differences, classes, and cultural pride within the boundary of the multicultural family, identified all multicultural families as members of a "vulnerable social group" and committed the cultural violence of permanently fixing them as belonging to the marginalized class. Multicultural families, especially the migrant members, are targets of the government's disorganized welfare strategy and are easily selected as objects for intervention under the guise of corporate social responsibility. Ironically, the notion of multicultural families as a vulnerable social group is deepening and the occurrence of the expressions such as "the second generation multicultural family," "multicultural children," "multicultural adolescents," and "multicultural military personnel" marks families with a social stigma. South Korea has yet to possess the vision of coexistence that is desirable in a real multicultural society, that is, to accept and respect cultural differences vital for individuals in order to avoid discrimination in both the public and private spheres, and to create an atmosphere conducive for democratic participation.

THE KOREAN MILITARY'S INSTITUTIONAL RACISM

Institutions serve as a site where race and racism are constructed and maintained yet simultaneously obscured and normalized (Joseph et al. 2012; Fleras 2014: 146). The Korean military has been the foremost site in reinforcing and reflecting racism as an institution. Institutional racism refers to both overt and covert processes by which organizational practices and standard operating procedures adversely penalize minority women and men through rules, procedures, rewards, and practices that have the intent or effect of excluding or exploiting (Scheurich and Young 1997; Fleras 2014, 145). The Korean military's racism, which kept in place the principles of racial purity for such a long time, prohibited the induction of mixed-race soldiers themselves. Exactly who was deemed a proper man and who was fit to be a soldier was decided by the Korean military's institutional racism.

The Korean Constitution declared military service to be a basic duty of citizenship, and a system of universal conscription was adopted. The earliest law regarding military service was adopted in 1949, and, after the Korean War in 1957, the system of universal conscription was introduced (Hong 2010: 51–52). According to Article 39 of the Constitution concerning military service, male citizens of the Republic of Korea must faithfully serve and women citizens may be called to active duty to support them. Furthermore, men upon reaching the age of 18 must take a physical examination to determine their fitness to serve (Hong 2010: 52–53). Prior to the 1970s and the advent of military rule, the system of universal conscription was not applied strictly, and for various reasons, many men did not continue on to military service. For example, firstborn sons who were responsible for the livelihood of the family or those men who found ways to benefit from special privilege were exempt from the draft. Men of mixed parentage were also exempt from military service, even in the event that they were drafted or signed up to serve voluntarily. From the 1950s onward, through the Korean War and later during US military occupation, many "mixed-race" children were born to American servicemen and Korean women, but through state-run adoption programs, they disappeared from the South Korean landscape. Under the banner of "One Nation, One People" (the principle that in one country, only one ethnic group should exist), the mixed-race children born to American soldiers and Korean women during the Korean War era were sent abroad for adoption. During the period 1955–1961, out of 4,190 children sent abroad for adoption, 2,691 were of mixed race, or about 62% (cited from Lee 2008: 35).

However, after the 1970s when the system of universal conscription was put in place, severe discrimination between males subject to the draft and those who were exempt began to arise. In the 1970s and 1980s when the active troop levels exceeded 200,000, the Korean government kept its elite troops on active duty while instituting an "alternative service program" for the remaining manpower, assigning them to such tasks as public service work, or serving as riot police, prison staff, special research assistants, skilled industrial workers, and the like (Hong 2010: 58). When the Korean military considers Korean males from the point of view of military service, they are roughly grouped into two large categories: "usable resources" and "not usable" resources, the latter including men exempt for medical reasons, men exempt on special grounds such as economic difficulties, low levels of education, prisoners, orphans, men of mixed race, overseas permanent residents, and those whose whereabouts are unknown, among others. Prisoners, orphans, and those of mixed race, without regard to any physical defect, were singled out as being essentially "exempt" from service (Hong 2010: 2). With the romanticization of the army as a place where soldiers share a "deep understanding and friendship" with one another through their training and communal life in characteristically 24-hours-a-day contact, prisoners, orphans, and individuals of mixed-race backgrounds were regarded as posing a possible threat to this male bonding. In the Military Service Act, Article 136 reads: "In the case of clearly, externally identifiable persons of mixed race, they are included in disqualified conscription status." That is, they cannot participate in barracks life. Not only can mixed-race people not receive the induction physical but, regardless of their physical fitness level, they cannot participate in the military. The external appearance of the mixed-race men was not asserted to be a type of "defect" preventing them from serving, but nevertheless, the problem of why such men could not serve on active duty was not concretely explained. They were just defined as possessing a distinct appearance of otherness that prevented them from being included in the category of the "elite forces" that the military desired.

In Korea, the concept of mixed race is extremely unclear. Generally, it denotes all people, born to a Korean ethnic parent and an "immigrant" parent, who are not of full-blooded Korean ethnicity. When considering the historical record, beginning with the Mongol invaders who took up residence in Korea, through the "Japan and Korea Are One" policy that led to Japanese-Korean intermarriage, to the sexual union of US troops and Korean women during the US military occupation, it is not easy to establish who is of "pure blood" and who is of "mixed blood" in Korea. Nevertheless, on the basis of being "clearly and externally identifiable," such children—especially those whose non-Korean parent was black or white—were barred from conscription.

In Korean society, where the people (*minjok*) and Korean national (*kukmin*) have long been one and the same, a Korean national (*kukmin*) whose father or mother is of a different race does not conform to the ideal type. The mixed-race soldier is imagined as a disturbing presence in whom obedience to the demands of the state and the hierarchical solidarity between males cannot be reconciled. The Korean military, which has influenced Korean organizational culture by treating the solidification of "identity" and male solidarity and hierarchy as its most important values, has contributed to the strengthening and reproduction of racism. In that respect, the military in Korean society has fortified its inbred-edness, rather than serving as an organization that represents the whole of civil society. Multicultural men, instead of being exempt from military life, have been entirely excluded from it. The possibility of choosing the military as a career has been completely shut off from them. More than anything, the fact that without having completed military service, one cannot satisfy one of the basic demands employers make of job seekers.

Because of this, mixed-race men who were not allowed to serve in the military were not given a proper chance and were consequently subject to poverty.

THE ADVENT OF MULTICULTURAL SOLDIERS

The discourse surrounding the "multicultural society" that appeared after 2006 had an effect on the military as well. As the ethnically homogenous state gave way to multicultural society, the debate intensified about whether it was time for the military too to make some changes. As the reduction in the population due to the decline in the birth rate after the 1990s cut available military manpower, the number of men available for active duty became insufficient. This situation was not simply due to the low birth rate as the result of an absolute reduction in the population but rather resulted from the fluid situation of young Korean men in their 20s. From the 1990s onward, "global mobility" rapidly increased within Korean society, stimulating the desires of Korea's rising transnational class. Starting in the 1990s, the number of children sent by their parents for education in English-speaking countries—the United States, Canada, Australia, etc.—climbed rapidly, and by 2010, the number of elementary, middle, and high school students being educated abroad had reached 410,000 (Cha 2012: 2). Some of the students who had spent their youth in foreign countries continued to reside there after obtaining permanent residency, and as multiple paths arose as alternatives to returning to Korea for military service, the number of potential male army recruits grew unpredictable.

It was not only the children of marriage migrants but also those of foreign workers and new settlers from North Korea that needed to be introduced into the military. More than anything, this logic benefited from the fact that the economically productive sector of the population is aging rapidly and the shortage of a labor supply of good quality is adversely affecting the growth potential of the nation. In order to achieve "sustainable growth and a sustainable society," it was emphasized that the Korean society needed to integrate a variety of human resources to address this problem, ranging from the admission of immigrants into the country to enticing well-educated young Korean living abroad to return. In 2004, a system was even introduced to encourage Koreans holding foreign passports to sign up for the military (Hong 2010: 62).

After 2007 when calculations showed that future military manpower would fall short, discussions began to take place about revisions to the military service law concerning the qualifications for new recruits. At the time, it was estimated that the available military manpower would quickly begin to drop starting in 2017 and that there would be a shortfall of 160,000 troops by the year 2023 (Hong 2010: 60). Thus, the need arose to convert existing "non usable" manpower into "usable" manpower, and so the Military Service Act was revised. The act, amended in 2005, called for the induction of only those mixed-race individuals born after January 1, 1987, and allowed them to choose whether to be assigned to active service or as public service personnel (Hong 2010: 56).

Additionally, in December 2007, the clause in the military service law that instituted discrimination on the basis of race and skin color was declared unconstitutional on the grounds that the Constitution promised equal treatment to all regardless of race or skin color, and so the law was revised. However, at the same time, the previous provision specifying that "clearly, externally identifiable" mixed-race persons, that is, mixed-race individuals with a black or white parent, were disqualified from military service was not stricken from the law. Finally in 2009, the discriminatory character of this law that viewed those of mixed Asian and mixed black or white parentage differently was recognized as racist and was struck down, allowing any male citizen regardless of appearance to serve in the military (Lee TY 2009). In Korea, military services is a duty of all male citizen, but, at the same time, participation requires that the citizen in question be physically, mentally, and socially "normal," which we can understand as a type of qualification or competence; as a result, because mixed-race individuals were seen as abnormal and as second-class citizens, this became problematic (Lee 2009: 50). The exemption of mixed-race individuals from military service provided them no advantage and was criticized rather for being essentially a policy to segregate them, and so a forward-thinking policy was proposed to accept such men into the military to form a new, advanced, "multicultural" fighting force. Thereafter, the terms "multicultural military" and "multicultural soldier" came into formal use in the Korean military. Finally, in 2011, the amendment to the military service law that specified that, regardless of race or skin color, the duties of military service were incumbent on all came into effect and the "multicultural soldier" was thus born. In their publication "The Multicultural Era and the Advanced, Powerful Army" (2010), the Korean Ministry of Defense divided multicultural families into three types—"international marriage families, foreign worker families, [and] North Korean refugees" (14)—and called children from these types of families "multicultural military personnel." In the case of North Korean refugee families, young people born while their parents were resident in South Korea were then able to join the armed forces, but young people who left North Korea themselves were exempt from service (9).

The Korean military was pushed toward "multiculturalism," but the individuals who contributed to this change were the so-called second generation multicultural families. In broad terms, the children of multicultural families are of "mixed blood" as they were born to couples brought together through the rapid introduction of international marriages in the 1990s, but since most of the mothers are of Asian provenance, the children are largely indistinguishable in terms of appearance. For this reason, military conscription was justified. In Korea, the expression "multicultural soldier" to signify a child born to a multicultural family who had entered the military soon became a stock phrase.

AMBIGUOUS INTERPELLATION OF MULTICULTURAL SOLDIERS IN THE KOREAN MILITARY

In these three countries in East Asia—Japan, South Korea, and Taiwan—the ethnic homogeneity was quite strong and the birth of children of mixed heritage began to cause some concern in society. This phenomenon challenges the traditional view of ethnic homogeneity in these East Asian countries and the idea that citizenship itself was an ethnically based concept. The military in South Korea was, for a very long time, an exclusively male social institution that enforced ideas of Korean ethnic purity—playing a pivotal role in the state's formation of a specific male national subject through mandatory military service. Starting in 2011 when "multicultural soldiers" began to serve, about 1,000 men have been inducted each year. By 2016, this should rise to a yearly average of 2,456, then to 4,651 annually in 2022, and exceed 12,000 in 2030 at which time multicultural soldiers will make up 4.6% of the military's manpower (Kukbang Ilbo 2012.7.8). With this shift to a multicultural military, various worries have arisen. A social debate has begun between military officials and scholars concerning the way that "mixed race" or second-generation children from multicultural families should be treated and managed. Early on, the Ministry of Defense, which had announced the change in direction toward a multicultural military, also changed the wording of the soldier's oath from "Korean people" to "nation," saying that according to policy, multicultural soldiers should not be discriminated against and instead must receive "equal treatment." As well, they declared that soldiers from multicultural families should be protected from exposure insofar as it was possible and so they would not be releasing a tally of the number of such soldiers who had joined the ranks, advancing the opinion that releasing such information would discriminate against personnel (Hong 2012). Furthermore, they announced that they had developed training materials for the multicultural soldiers entitled "The Strong, Advanced Army in the Era of Multiculturalism" and that they intended to provide such training to all soldiers on a regular basis (Bae 2010).

Nevertheless, at the same time, there continues to be debate about the pros and cons of including the multicultural soldiers in the program of compulsory military service. Various policy suggestions have been put forward to solve the problems of the introduction of the multicultural soldiers into the ranks of the military (Park 2010; Choi 2010). The concerns about the multicultural military and the multicultural soldiers and the policy recommendations follow.

First, due to the heterogeneity arising from the military's shift toward multiculturalism, there is a concern that the solidarity between soldiers will weaken. If one defines sharing not only the same values but also the same standards of behavior, discipline, cooperation, loyalty, devotion, and traditions and holding all to the same standard as "military culture," there was concern that with the introduction of the multicultural military, cultural conflicts would be amplified because of increased heterogeneity within the same military organization (Hong 2010: 67–68). The idea of cultural heterogeneity was soon reduced to that of the intensification of conflict, and so as a result, the final conclusion was that pains had to be taken to strengthen feelings of brotherhood (*dongjilgam*) and a common sense of purpose (*dongnyo uishik*).

Second, there remain concerns about the loyalty of the multicultural soldiers. On the basis that a good soldier shows a high degree of attachment toward the state, the so-called children of multicultural families will establish loyalty, patriotism, and a shared view of the enemy, but the opinion is that they will inevitably have difficulties doing so and that there will be a clear difference in identity between themselves and ordinary soldiers (Kim 2013: 24). The second-generation multicultural families think that "I grew up in a multicultural family and I am an outsider who doesn't belong to any country," and consequently as a soldier, it is difficult for them to have a clear-cut view of the state that is making demands upon them. To counter this, education on Korean society and history must be provided to children of multicultural families on the proper views of history, the state, and who the enemy is (North Korea,) so that they gain clear consciousness prior to their induction to reduce the maladaptive triggers that may arise during job seeking or on personality tests (Jeong 2013: 45). The interesting thing is the constant insistence on the necessity for "security [anti-communist] education" for migrant wives and multicultural families (Lee JH 2012). Trips to visit the area around the DMZ were even organized. One police chief from Daegu organized an event he called the "'Year of the Rat' multicultural family field visit to the DMZ and cultural tour," where they visited Yeoncheon in Gyeongi-do and Cheolweon in Ganghwa-do. When South Korean media conducted interviews with participants, the resulting article was headlined "Hopes that the divided Korean peninsula can soon be reunited" (Lee JH 2012).

Third, there is concern about multicultural soldiers' maladjustment to military life and possible resulting problems. This involves psychological aversion toward them as well as their sense of being discriminated against by their fellow soldiers inside the military. Multicultural children "have been put in difficult educational circumstances, lagging in linguistic development as a result of being raised by mothers with insufficient Korean language skills and experiencing cultural maladjustment." Consequently, due to insufficient linguistic abilities, children of multicultural families often suffer in their studies, face crises of identity, and in the growing-up process, experience emotional stress due to their ostracization from the larger group, and so on, and these factors lead to concerns that such individuals pose a possible threat to the safety in the barracks. It is said that because of the "barracks stress" they experience, multicultural soldiers become the target of incidents and crimes while in the army. For instance, a multicultural soldier may become the victim of ostracization by regular soldiers and, due to their maladaptation, attack someone with a gun (Park 2010). Following the surge in international marriages in Korea, concerns and stigmatization connected with the "multicultural family" and multicultural teens and young adults have naturally extended to concerns about multicultural troops. Because the children of multicultural families have not adapted well to Korean society, it is predicted that their adaptation to military life will also be difficult. Children of multicultural families "in the process of growing up cannot adapt to school education, and this is connected to various social problems such as suicide, murder, arson, etc. When these kinds of problems are directly introduced into barracks life, disputes within the troops arise and consequently there are social and economic costs for the state and its citizens and the degradation of trust in the military results in anxiety" (Kim 2013: 29). As well, because of racial discrimination, regular soldiers were worried about the possibility that soldiers who had not adjusted properly to military life due to being bullied or ostracized by the group would end up provoking violent incidents. As a result of these concerns that multicultural soldiers would not be able to adapt to life within the military, they became the object of various types of special "care." For example, they were encouraged to enlist with friends or brothers or given the right to select where they wished to be deployed (Hong 2012).

However, at the same time, there is an emerging discourse by the academic writings and the media about the possible "usefulness" of multicultural soldiers. It has been said that the presence of multicultural soldiers can contribute to the transnational efforts of the Korean military. When one considers that, as of September 2012, a total of 1,451 individuals from 15 countries had been dispatched as peacekeepers or as medical personnel, multicultural soldiers from Korea stationed abroad could demonstrate Korea's "multicultural capacity" in overseas activities (Cha 2012: 7).

The interesting thing was that, while permitting multicultural soldiers to serve in the military put an end to the institutional racism of the military, the micromanagement of surveillance of multicultural soldiers within the military itself was expanded upon. While continuing to perpetuate Korean society's racial discrimination toward multicultural families and their off-spring, in the end multicultural soldiers became the targets of screening that saw them as potentially dangerous and warranting special attention. In the first place, the Ministry of Defense, which had said it wouldn't keep statistics on or do surveys of the multicultural soldiers, modified its position and introduced an "Integrated Management System" to keep track of them. The Korean military established a policy that prohibited "discrimination" based on appearance or ethnicity, but at the same time introduced a system that was able to distinguish who was a multicultural soldier and who was not (Hong 2010: 65; Kim 2013: 52), thus demonstrating the power of management and control. Starting in 2010, as each multicultural soldier entered training camp, he began to be tracked in a continuously updated computer system that could single him out. When a soldier from a multicultural family joins the forces and it is noted that the new recruit asked for special attention, he is put on a list of "soldiers of special attention." In order to help these soldiers adapt to military service, a "buddy enlistment" system between second-generation multicultural soldiers was implemented. Multicultural troops remain under restriction and under the supervision of a service member called the "security officer" (Lee 2013). Currently, the army excludes multicultural soldiers from serving near the DMZ, and the "relatively straight-forward tasks they are assigned" are considered somewhat plum jobs. One officer said that to avoid any "accidents" or "psychological problems," multicultural soldiers are often granted leave or given permission for overnight stays because they need "soothing." These measures have resulted in the complaints from ordinary soldiers, giving rise to the complaint that they are the victims of "reverse discrimination."

CONCLUSION

The emergence of multicultural soldiers within the army is still a matter of dispute. Their ambiguous position clearly reveals the governmental character of "multicultural society" within Korean society.

To improve the security of the active forces and with the view toward creating an "advanced military" of global stature, mixed-race men were allowed to serve in the military but, as in the past when multicultural people were singled out based on particular characteristics, they are still stigmatized as soldiers on the basis of their "inferiority," be it appearance, past background, cultural heterogeneity, linguistic abilities, or so on. While on the surface it appears that the Korean military's institutional racism has come to an end, the reality is that identifying multicultural troops as different from regular troops, managing and deploying them differently, classifying them as potential threats, and so on have just put into place a new set of day-to-day dimensions of racism. This kind of governmentality, while giving agency to the multicultural soldiers in a particular way, tends to racialize them as the ambiguous subject who cannot acquire the full membership in the Korean society.

REFERENCES

Bae, Minuk. 2010. "Seouldae, gun jangbyeong damunhwagyoyug gyojae gaebal [Seoul National University writes the Coursebook on Multicultural Education for the soldiers]." *Newsis.* Accessed May 6, 2014. http://news.naver.com/main/read. nhn?mode=LSD&mid=sec&sid1=102&oid=003&aid=0003051068.

Cha, Yongkuk. 2013. "Damunhwasahoeui hanguggunui gwajewa yeoghale gwanhan yeongu [The Korean military's roles and missions in the multi-cultural Korean society]." Unpublished Master's Thesis, Yonsei University.

Choe, Seon-Ae. 2010. "Damunhwagundaeleul daebihan mingwa gunui junbibanghyange gwanhan jeon [Suggestions to the Civil Society and the Military the Preparation of the Future Multicultural Army]." *Korean Academy of Military Social Welfare,* 3(1): 93–113.

Fleras, Augie. 2014. *Racism in a Multicultural Canada: Paradoxes, Politics, and Resistance.* Ontario, Canada: Wilfrid Laurier University Press.

Freeman, Caren. 2011. *Making and Faking Kinship: Marriage and Labor Migration between China and South Korea.* Ithaca, NY: Cornell University Press.

Hong, Seok-Cho. 2010. "Hanguggun damunhwa gundaeloui jeonhwane gwanhanyeongu [Research on Conversion to Korean Army Multiculturalism Army]." Unpublished Master's Thesis, Sangji University.

Hong, Sangji. 2012. "Damunhwa jangbyeong ttalo gwanlihaneun ge chabyeol, ttoggati daeuhal geos"—gugbangbu gimjeongsu byeongyeongjeongchaeggwajang inteobyu ["Multicultural Soldiers would be treated equally, not separately" An Interview with Kim Jeongsu, Army life Policy manager of the Ministry of National Defence]." *JoongAng Sunday* 280. Accessed May 6, 2014. http://sunday.joins.com/article/view.asp?aid=26877.

Joseph, J., Darnell, S., and Nakamura, Y. 2012. *Race and Sport in Canada: Intersecting Inequalities.* Toronto: Canadian Scholars' Press.

Jung, Myung-Ho. 2014. "Damunhwahwangyeong daebi hanguggun daeeunge gwanhan yeongu [Study on ROK military response for a multicultural environment]." Unpublished Master's Thesis, Kookmin University.

Kim, Gwi-geun. 2009. "Gun, 'damunhwa gundae'e daebihaeya [The Military should prepare for the 'Multicultural Army']." *Yonhap News Agency,* June 24. Accessed May 6, 2014. http://news.naver.com/main/read.nhn?mode=LSD&mid=sec&sid1=102&oid=001&aid=0002730592.

Kim, Hyun Mee. 2011. "The Emergence of the 'Multicultural Family' and the Genderized Citizenship in South Korea," in *Contested Citizenship in East Asia: Developmental Politics, National Unity, and Globalization*, edited by K. S. Chang and B. S. Turner, 203–17. New York: Routledge.

Kim, Yong-ki. 2014. "Hanguggunui damunhwa janyeo ibyeonge ttaleun daebibangane gwanhan yeongu [A Study on the Preparation for Multicultural Enlistment to the Korean Army Focusing on the Army life]." Unpublished Master's Thesis, Chosun University.

Lee, Hye-Kyung. 2005. "Honinijuwa honiniju gajeongui munjewa daeeung [Marriage Migration to South Korea: Issues, Problems, and Responses]." *Korean Journal of Population Studies*, 28(1): 73–106.

Lee, Ji-hyeon. 2012. "'Bundandoen hangug ppalli pyeonghwatongil dwaesseumyeon . . .' - hyeonyeog ibyeong apdun damunhwagajog janyeodeul ['Hope the Peaceful Unification on the divided Korea arrives soon. . .' Multicultural children who have Conscrption ahead]." *The Maeil Shinmun*, August 30. Accessed May 6, 2014. http://www.imaeil.com/sub_news/sub_news_view.php?news_id=49261&yy=2012.

Lee, Kwang Seok. 2013. "Damunhwagajeong janyeoui byeongyeongsaenghwaleseo yesangdoeneun munjewa geu daeeunge gwanhan yeongu [A Study on the anticipated problems of multi-cultural family children in military camp life and on their alternatives]." *Korean Public Administration Quarterly*, 25(4): 1003–22.

Lee, Yewon. 2008. "Gwihwan haeoe ibyangin jojighwawa diaseupola undong [Returning Overseas Adoptees' Organizations and Diaspora Movement]." Master's Thesis, Yonsei University. Ministry of National Defense.

Park, An-seo. 2011. "Damunhwajangbyeong ibyeonge ttaleun byeongyeonghwangyeong joseongbangan [A Study on the Preparations for Enlistment of Multicultural Youths]." *The Quarterly Journal of Defense Policy Studies*, 90: 177–207.

Scheurich, J. J. and Young, M. D. 1997. "Coloring Epistemologies: Are Our Research Epistemologies Racially Biased?" *Educational Researcher*, 26(4): 4–16.

Seol, Dong-Hoon and John D. Skrentny. 2009. "Why Is There So Little Migrant Settlement in East Asia?" *International Migration Review*, 43(3): 578–620.

Yi, Zoon-Il. 2009. "Honhyeolin byeongyeogmyeonjeui pyeongdeunggwon chimhaeseong [Constitutional Issues on the Exemption of the Mixed Blood from Military Service]." *Korea Law Review*, 52: 41–64.

Yoon, Sangho. 2012. "Gugbangbu 'damunhwa gundae' majchwo talbug cheongsonyeon ibdaeheoyong chujin [The Ministry of Notional Defense promotes the legislative work for the young north korean refugee's military accession, catching up with the 'Multicultural Army']." *The Dong-A Ilbo*, May 14. Accessed May 6, 2014. http://news.donga.com/3/all/20120514/46219752/1.

Chapter 9

The Making of Multiculturalistic Subjectivity

The Case of Marriage Migrants' Empowerment in Taiwan

Hsiao-Chuan Hsia

A phenomenon of marriage migration in East Asia has generated concerns and discussion about "multiculturalism" in those host countries where citizenship is based on blood. Much discussion and critiques have been focused on how these host societies deal with the influx of im/migrants with different cultural backgrounds. For instance, Japanese government has been criticized for not making immigration issues and multiculturalism a national policy agenda (Iwabuchi 2014), while South Korea's national "multicultural family" policy has been criticized as only appropriating the name of multicultural and actually intending to assimilate marriage migrant women into the Korean society (Kim 2007). The implication of such discussion is that only the citizens of the host countries have to learn to be multiculturalistic whereas the im/migrants automatically embrace multiculturalism.

However, based on the author's long-term research on marriage migrant issues, this chapter argues that im/migrants also have prejudices against other ethnicities and nationalities. It is in the process of being transformed from an isolated "foreign bride" to an active "immigrant activist" that the marriage migrant's sense of "self" broadens and become multiculturalistic subjects, who endeavor to put the ideals of multiculturalism into praxis by being reflexive of their attitudes and behaviors towards other nationalities and ethnicities.

PROSPECTS AND CHALLENGES OF MULTICULTURAL CITIZENSHIP UNDER GLOBALIZATION

Taiwan has become a host country for many im/migrants from neighboring countries since the mid-1980s. Consequently, an increasing number

of women from Mainland China and Southeast Asian countries, including Vietnam, Indonesia, Thailand, Philippines, and Cambodia, immigrate
to Taiwan through transnational marriages. Most women decide to marry
Taiwanese men to escape poverty and turbulence in their home countries.
However, their Taiwanese husbands are mostly small farmers and working
class, who are also marginalized in Taiwanese societies (Hsia 2004). When
these women began to catch the media's attention in the late 1980s, they
were called "foreign brides," which reflects the discrimination they face as
women from the poorer countries (Hsia 2007). In addition to social discrimination, these women are constrained by stressed economic conditions, lack
of social networks and support, and discriminatory policies and laws (Hsia
and Huang 2010).

Since Taiwan is a newly emerging host country of immigrants, the laws
and policies regarding immigrants are not comprehensive and reflect the
traditional ideology of incorporation based on the principle of *jus sanguinis*,
inclusive of people who can claim a common ancestral origin and exclusive
of people who do not share that commonality (Cheng 2002). Despite recent
changes in the immigration and nationality laws, it remains extremely difficult for those excluded from nationality to become citizens of Taiwan, except
for spouses and children of Taiwanese citizens

The Taiwanese government did not develop an immigration policy until
2003. Since then, the government quickly initiated programs and revisions to
immigration-related laws aiming to control the inflow of marriage migrants,
increasing barriers for them to acquire citizenship, and assimilating them into
Taiwanese culture (Hsia 2012). The main purposes of these laws and policies were to ensure effective measures to "govern" immigrants by including
"high quality" immigrants while excluding those deemed of "low quality,"
the policing of immigrants as part of crime prevention, and the education of
those "low quality" immigrants already living in Taiwan in order to assimilate them (Hsia 2013).

Taiwan is not an isolated case. As the world becomes increasingly globalized, discussion of citizenship has been critical of the traditional concept that
associates citizenship with the nation-state, which is assumed to be culturally
and morally homogenous.

Multicultural citizenship is an alternative proposed by scholars who recognize both the importance and limits of political citizenship, and is based
on the idea that the nation-state contains a degree of plurality that allows
migrants to retain their cultural identity provided they adhere to political
norms (e.g., Kymlicka 1995). Multiculturalism, however, is not always an
entirely positive development. The problems with the conception of citizenship centered on group rights include: leading to tension between groups
competing for special status of additional entitlements and funds, and thus

weakening the solidarity among them to combat common problems (Faulks 2000; Alund 1991); essentializing cultural differences and migrant identities (Bissoondath 1994); and neglecting oppression within the group, particularly women in the male-dominant cultures (Yuval-Davis 1997).

Despite various problems, multicultural citizenship can still be empowering and liberating in Taiwan and other East Asian countries, whose traditional citizenship is based on blood. Previously, I illustrated how the meaning of multiculturalism is a field of contestation, wherein both state actors and social movement actors actively engage themselves and each other to advance their agendas (Hsia 2013). Moreover, my study shows that by radicalizing the rhetoric of multiculturalism, the Alliance for Human Rights Legislation for Immigrants and Migrants (AHRLIM) has successfully employed the concept of multiculturalism to advance the campaigns to challenge and reform the exclusionary practices of citizenship in Taiwan. I therefore argue that from the perspectives of social movements, though the concept of multicultural citizenship can be easily co-opted, it can still be used as an effective framing strategy to make the traditionally exclusionary model of citizenship more inclusive (Hsia 2009).

Moreover, as Werbner and Yuval-Davis (1999) point out, despite its gendered history, the language of citizenship provides women with a valuable weapon in the fight for human, democratic, civil, and social rights. Moreover, community-level women's activism is not only a way of raising consciousness and self-confidence; it also opens up new spaces for women's voices to be heard. In other words, the concept of multicultural citizenship can be a political field where the discourses of governing and empowering immigrants are constantly contested. By engaging immigrants in this contestation starting from community level, it can serve as the pre-political base for social movements where immigrants and locals are politicized to gradually achieve the power to affect long-term changes in mainstream politics (Hsia 2013).

Marriage migrant women in Taiwan have indeed demonstrated their agency. Many marriage migrants organized by TASAT (TransAsia Sisters Association, Taiwan) have been active in AHRLIM's campaigns since 2003. They have gone to protests against unfair treatment by governmental agencies. In 2007, hundreds of marriage migrant women from Southeast Asia and Mainland China joined a rally protesting against the financial requirements for applying citizenship. This rally caught much media attention because it was the first time in Taiwan's history that hundreds of marriage migrants held a street demonstration.

In the following, this chapter aims to illustrate how marriage migrants are not necessarily multiculturalistic and analyze how some marriage migrants involved in the immigrant movement have been changed and their sense of "we"-ness have been broadened and become more inclusive of others.

IMMIGRANTS ARE NOT AUTOMATICALLY
MULTICULTURALISTIC

Much of the discussion on multicultural citizenship or multiculturalism focuses on the relationship between the natives and the im/migrants, particularly about how the natives should learn to be inclusive of im/migrants. For instance, Houser (1996) argues that multicultural self-development of dominant-culture students is essential in education to achieve the goal of narrowing the opportunity gap between the dominant and dominated groups. The underlying assumption appears to be that the im/migrants are automatically multiculturalistic and treat fellow im/migrants as equals. However, my previous studies show that im/migrants from different nationalities also have prejudices against each other, even though they face common problems such as discriminatory policies and racism in their host societies. For instance, migrant workers in Hong Kong have predispositions against migrants from other nationalities (Hsia 2009a); marriage migrants in Taiwan construct themselves as the "exception" of what discriminatory public rhetoric portrays rather than fundamentally negate the dominant construction (Hsia 1997). Similarly, Pyke and Dang (2003) show that racial beliefs, meanings, and stereotypes of the mainstream society shape how children of Korean and Vietnamese immigrants think about co-ethnics. Moreover, the system of "intraethnic othering" serves as a basis of sub-ethnic identities, intraethnic social boundaries, and the monitoring and control of social behavior. This kind of internalization needs to be understood as the oppressive conditions that migrants live in the host societies. For instance, McIlwaine et al. (2006) finds that low-paid migrant workers in London perceive migrants of their own ethnic groups as especially hardworking and thus superior to other migrant groups to rationalize their labor market experiences and validate their position in low-paid and low-status jobs.

My long years of working with im/migrants show that though im/migrants are victims of discrimination by the host countries, they are not automatically united. In the Chinese programs I initiated in 1995 for marriage migrant women, we often encountered tension among marriage migrants from different nationalities and ethnic groups, such as English-speaking Filipinos versus non-English-speaking Southeast Asians, Southern Vietnamese versus Northern Vietnamese, Chinese Indonesians versus non-Chinese Indonesians. Women from the same nationalities but who enter Taiwan with different types of visas may also have prejudices against each other. For instance, when AHRLIM was first established, one Vietnamese marriage migrant, who was outspoken about discrimination against marriage migrants, told me that AHRLIM should be careful about migrant workers because they may deceive and use us. When I asked her how the migrant workers and marriage migrants were different given that they were both considered "foreigners" in Taiwan, she replied, "We are here to become real Taiwanese, but they are here only to make money."

Class background is another factor. A highly educated Vietnamese marriage migrant Ms. Chen has assumed the role of spokesperson for marriage migrants in Taiwan, particularly for the Vietnamese. In 2005, marriage migrants from Kaohsiung, the Southern county in Taiwan, went to Taipei, the Capital city, to join the protest action held by AHRLIM. At that time, she published a newspaper article to criticize this protest as "using marriage migrants," because in her eyes, these marriage migrants were not educated and from rural areas, so they could not possibly speak for themselves.

> We (marriage migrants) simply hope for good health, happiness and being ourselves quietly. Especially for those foreign spouses whose lives are mostly confined to the boundary given by the husband's families, this is really the only simple and practical wish for them. . . . But the newspapers reported that a group of so-called foreign brides took to the streets to protest against the Ministry of Education. These simple and innocent sisters probably could not have even entered the Ministry of Education in their home countries, and could not have even gone outside the front doors of the husband's family, how could they possibly travel from Kaohsiung to protest the Ministry of Education in Taipei? . . . I experienced the worst pain and sorrow since I moved to Taiwan, not only because of the feeling of humiliation by the fact that foreign spouses are manipulated, but also because of my witnessing of the craziness of the Taiwanese. (Chen 2005)

Ms. Chen has been very actively promoting Vietnamese languages and cultures in Taiwan and gained much financial support from different sources, including the media, universities, and governmental agencies. As the activities promoting multiculturalism of the im/migrants became more popular, Ms. Chen (2014) published another newspaper article to differentiate the "genuine" Vietnamese from the "fake" Vietnamese.

> It is not simply like whoever can speak Vietnamese and put on Vietnamese costume are genuine Vietnamese. Because ethnic identity concerns much about blood and cultural nurturing, which can be felt in the subtle gestures and cannot be pretended. The formal ethnic name of we Vietnamese people is the Kinh. The traditional Vietnamese long gown is specifically designed for we Kinh sisters' special slim figures, so other peoples wearing it could not show its ethnic characteristics. Therefore, all the ethnic promotion activities must watch for these details.

Ms. Chen's argument in the midst of the increasingly popular promotion of multiculturalism of im/migrants in Taiwan is very revealing. It not only falls into the trap of essentializing cultures, as many critics of multicultural citizenship have pointed out, but also demonstrates the irony of immigrants' tendency to become more exclusionary while demanding the host societies to be more inclusive of the immigrants' cultures.

To combat discrimination and exclusion, im/migrants have to be united. However, as illustrated, im/migrants are not automatically united and inclusive of others. It is therefore crucial to engage with im/migrants of different backgrounds and to create a space for them to recognize and respect their differences while forging a united force for their common goals.

Moreover, marriage migrants' "group identities" are not fixed. They change over time during their participation in the campaigns for the immigrants' rights. While my previous studies demonstrated how the concept of multicultural citizenship can impact the immigration policies and the Taiwanese citizens (Hsia 2009), this chapter aims to analyze how the subjectivity of marriage migrants involved in the immigrant movement have been changed.

To deepen the analysis of this change of subjectivity, Alaine Touraine's concept of *subjectivation* will be employed. Unlike dominant social movement theories, such as political opportunity, mobilization structures, and framing processes, Touraine pays more attention to issues of "subjectivation." To be distinguished from the commonly used term of social movement, Touraine (1988) introduced the concept of "societal movement," where "historicity" and "subject" are two key components. The concept of historicity means how society "acts upon itself" to remake social relations and cultural models by which we represent ourselves and act. Societal movements are not merely groups of actors with specific grievances within institutions, but are marked by the degree to which they act upon the prevailing cultural model. Touraine is concerned about the struggle of social actors (the subject) over historicity, that is, who controls the terms of the cultural model upon which action is based. Moreover, the development of a societal movement is a process of transforming the "personal subject" to "historical subject," who makes the mark on history by remaking the social relations and the cultural model that determine our identity. This process of subjectivation is the social action that challenges the existing social orders (Beckford 1998).

This study is based on my long-term ongoing praxis-oriented research since 1994, which I directly involve myself in the empowerment of marriage migrants from Southeast Asia (Hsia 2006) and the development of the immigrant movement in Taiwan (Hsia 2008). In 1995, I initiated a Chinese literacy program based on the "pedagogy of the oppressed" (Freire 1970) aiming to empower marriage migrants, which led to the formal establishment of the first national organization of marriage migrants, TASAT, in 2003. TASAT is a grassroots organization where marriage migrants are deeply involved in decision-making, program implementation, and daily organizational operations. In 2003, I cofounded AHRLIM to spearhead a movement to promote the rights of immigrants and migrant workers in Taiwan, of which TASAT is one of the founding and active members. Marriage migrants organized by TASAT have been at the frontlines of the activities and protest action organized by AHRLIM.

To understand how the marriage migrants involved in the immigrant movement transform their views about themselves and their relationship with others, I conducted a focus-group study where the active marriage migrants shared drawings to reflect on their experiences at different stages of lives: before they migrated to Taiwan, early years of migration before they joined TASAT's programs, and after they became leaders of TASAT. Five marriage migrants were selected for the focus group because their involvement with TASAT were long (from five to nine years in early 2011, when the focus group was conducted) and have been active in campaigns for immigrants' rights. After the focus group, a follow-up in-depth interview was conducted with each participant regarding their views about other nationalities and how those have changed over time.

DIFFERENT BACKGROUNDS, SAME DESPAIRS IN EARLY YEARS OF IMMIGRATION

To understand the experiences of the marriage migrants actively involved in the immigrant movement, I requested them to draw pictures depicting themselves at different stages. After drawing, they were requested to share their pictures and explain why they used those pictures to depict their lives. This drawing method was not meant to be therapeutic to diagnose their psychological problems. Rather, it was used as a medium by which the five long-term immigrant activists can have some time to reflect on their experiences and later collectively share and discuss those experiences. Therefore, the marriage migrants are the ones explaining their own drawings, rather than me interpreting the drawings as art therapists would normally do.

The five marriage migrants selected to participate in the project included two Thai (Yao and Yadrung), two Vietnamese (Manchi and Jean), and one Cambodian (Pei) women. All of them had been elected as officers of TASAT (Yao and Yadrung as chairpersons, Manchi as vice chairperson), and three of them (Yadrung, Pei, and Manchi) became TASAT's staff after serving as elected officers.

The life experiences of the marriage migrants in their home countries before migration were quite diverse. Their narratives ranged from being joyful to being desperate.

Yao first came from Thailand as a factory worker and met her husband in Taiwan. Her picture of a house in a rice field surrounded by mountains and three persons with big smiles represents her reminiscence of happiness before becoming a marriage migrant. Contrarily, some marriage migrants had difficult lives and their migrations to Taiwan were seen as a way out of desperation and resentment. For instance, Pei, from Cambodia, felt hopeless in her life before she came to Taiwan. She drew a sapling almost fallen by a boisterous wind.

> I felt I almost fell before I came to Taiwan, hit by a lot of storms . . . I actually had thought of giving myself up. But I also worried about my father. So I decide to go to Taiwan, thinking that if anything happens to me, so be it. I also hoped that if I die abroad, it's better because he will not see me.

Despite the different frames of narratives about lives before migration, all five marriage migrants shared similar feelings of being isolated, helpless, worthless, and suppressed in the early stage of migration as the result of the common structural constraints as previously mentioned.

Isolated and Helpless

In contrast to her life full of love and joy in Vietnam, Manchi recalled her life after she arrived in Taiwan as empty and isolated as she described in her drawing.

Figure 9.1 Pei's Image of Life before Migrating to Taiwan. *Source*: courtesy of Pei-Hsiang Lee.

I was isolated in the house every day, not happy and no smiles. All I knew was the house and the next door neighbors. . . . There was only person in the house, who was me. . . . I cried in the room, missing my home [in Vietnam].

Similarly, Yao's life after arriving in Taiwan as a marriage migrant was in great contrast to her reminiscence in Thailand.

I did not know Chinese when we got married. I was like a fish in the river, struggling to find her direction but in vain. . . . It was like the bean buried in soil, not knowing which direction to go.

Pei drew another sapling to depict her life in the early years of immigration, which was still under strong wind but was standing upright while the sun was out, though not completely.

Since we could not communicate due to language barriers, there was also strong wind. But I felt they treated me well so there was sunlight. . . . The sun was only half because I also encountered many frustrations. . . . There was still strong wind, but no more rain. . . . Gradually, some problems happened at home and there were something sour and uncomfortable. . . . One day my mother-in-law told me: "You did not make money so you just did the housework." I was happy to do housework for them because we were a family but what she said made me feel like I was doing the labor just to exchange for food and accommodation. . . . Then I recalled that I never did anything for my father and brother. I felt pity about myself.

Figure 9.2 Pei's Image of Life in Early Years of Immigration. *Source*: courtesy of Pei-Hsiang Lee.

Worthless and Self-abased

In contrast to her life full of passion, energy, and dreams in Vietnam, Jean's life in the early stage after migration was narrated as being worthless and self-abased, as she explained why she drew a snail within a half moon.

> This is a moon but only half moon. . . . It was very difficult to adjust when I first came to the new environment. . . . I saw myself as being inadequate, being deficient. . . . I did not know how to face it and I even despised myself. . . . So the snail is me, because I felt I was very slow and could not follow my own thoughts and hopes. The moon means that I could only slowly and silently walk in the dark alone.

Suppressed and Stifled

Yadrung, from Thailand, described her early years of migration as being a "chick," dramatically changed from being a wild cat before she became a marriage migrant.

> I used to be very independent and could do whatever I wanted. But after I came to Taiwan, I suddenly became a chick, meaning that I had a big head with many things in mind but I could not move. I wanted to fly but I could not, even though I have wings. . . . My family in Taiwan thought I did not know anything. . . . It made me suppress myself. I was a wild cat in my home country, but suddenly they treated me like a child.

STORIES OF TRANSFORMATION THROUGH ORGANIZATION AND MOVEMENT

After these marriage migrants joined TASAT and became active in the advocacy and campaigns for immigrants' rights, they described their lives as being transformed to being self-confident, finding fulfillment and direction for life, and inspired to help others.

Yao drew a picture of a small pea growing up to a tree to illustrate her growth in self-confidence. A house with many people inside and many more walking toward it represented the growing organization she has been involved in.

Pei drew plants to systematically represent her life at different stages, from a sapling almost fallen from a storm to another sapling standing upright with half sun, and then to a big tree with sunlight and nurturing rain drops.

> There is sunshine and rain, which is not like the storm before. This rain nurtures the tree and the sun gives it light and there is still wind. I have grown a lot because of the nutrition and sunlight. Though there is still some wind meaning

that I am still encountering frustration while learning and doing things. . . . The wind sometimes feels like a typhoon, sometimes like a breeze. . . . Whether a strong wind or not, I can still see things I have learnt and therefore have more strength and energy to move forward.

Being active in TASAT and the immigrant movement, these women have experienced transformation of their lives. Manchi has changed from feeling isolated and empty to feeling fulfilled and abundant in her life.

The present is like a big circle, very abundant and colorful. In the circle, there are trees, sun, moon, flowers, fruits and grass, meaning that my life becomes colorful with many things.

Similarly, Jean, who felt inadequate in early years of immigration, drew a carabao head to show how she has found her direction in life after joining TASAT.

Carabao is a solid animal that put her feet on the ground, using her determination and strength to realize what she wants. . . . This carabao is supposed to have her body and stand in the field, but she has not yet found her body. Before I joined TASAT, I despised myself, felt lost and saw my inadequacy, so I could not even find the head. . . . But after I joined TASAT, I found my head. Now because at least I know that my inadequacy will not affect what I want to do. I can learn what I am inadequate of. So my head appears. Now I am continuing to search for my body and my own field. So I still have to work hard and move forward.

Figure 9.3 Pei's Image of Life after Her Involvement in TASAT. *Source*: courtesy of Pei-Hsiang Lee.

These women not only become more self-confident and fulfilled, but also more inspired to help others; that is, their scopes of concerns have gone beyond their immediate needs and reached out to the needs of others. As Yadrung pointed out,

> I have found the wild cat I originally was. I want to learn more and do more. I want to use what I have learnt to help others. . . . I must do something to change unfair things. . . . Now I have this opportunity and capacity, I feel I can do something to help others.

Dialectical Process of Growth

While being involved in the organization and immigrant movement has helped these women overcome isolation and made their lives more fulfilling, this process is not always smooth. To understand the marriage migrants' experiences in the organization, I requested them to draw the curves of their experiences with high and low points, share what happened during the highest and lowest points, and explain what helped them out of the lowest points.

Yadrung is a witness of TASAT's organizational development. As one of the few leaders in the beginning, she experienced much frustration and almost left the organization. From an organizational crisis, TASAT managed to get out of the bottom and leap forward. Yadrung's drawing of the curve of her experiences in the organization illustrates this dynamic process.

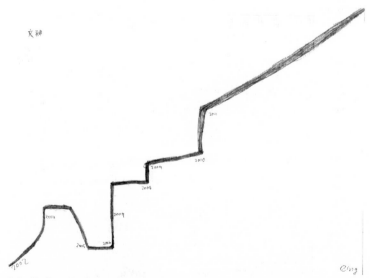

Figure 9.4 Yadrung's Curve of Involvement in TASAT. *Source*: courtesy of Pei-Hsiang Lee.

The lowest points of the experiences were like hitting walls, when one feels that everything goes wrong. The reasons of these low points included pressure from family and work, not knowing what to do and how to run an organization, and sour feelings toward others when working as a group.

First of all, marriage migrants are expected to give priority to family. When their involvement in the organization increases, they often feel pressured by the family. Moreover, since many of them need to work to support their family's finance, they have limited time and energy for the organization.

> Yao: It's the high point when I started to attend the Chinese classes. . . . But because I was outside often, there was some tension in the family. Also, I started to work again and began to feel tired. . . . I really felt like giving up. . . . I became active again after 2007 and joined protests a lot. But my mother-in-law reacted negatively. She said, "It's not your business. Why do you go?!" In late 2010, because of work and family, especially my mother-in-law's nagging, I felt very tired, and became less active.

Since none of these women had experiences of being involved in an organization before, it can be frustrating to start working as a group, especially for those who are elected as leaders.

> Yadrung: It is the lowest point in 2005. . . . I was TASAT's Chairperson, so I felt the tasks and responsibilities very heavy. . . . I felt like to forge ahead but did not know what to do. . . . I felt like leaving TASAT. I did not want to give myself too much pressure. . . . But the other side of me felt it was a pity if I gave up. . . . I was inspired but still could not grasp it.

The lack of experience in working collectively in the organization often leads to tension and conflicts among the members. It is particularly difficult for a group like TASAT whose members are from different nationalities with various cultural and language barriers, not to mention preexisting stereotypes against other ethnicities and nationalities. The leaders are often blamed for the problems arising in the organization, but the criticism often appeared as gossiping and backstabbing rather than issues open for discussion, which would worsen the tension and conflicts.

> Yadrung: Some people criticized me behind my back. . . . I felt like giving it up, leaving TASAT.
> Manchi: When we learnt to work as a group, we had some problems but we did not know how to express, or were afraid to express it, worrying that if we did not express properly we might got into fights. So it turned out that we did not openly discuss problems.

Contextualizing Discontent in the Broader Scope of "We"-ness

Like all organizations, TASAT has experienced a lot of ups and downs since its establishment. Every time TASAT hits the bottom, we try to transform the organizational crisis into opportunities and eventually leap forward. Through discussion and various trainings, one key method to overcome crisis is to reflect on and reassess the goals of TASAT by looking at the history of the organization and reevaluating everyone's development in the organization.

> Yadrung: When I hit the bottom, Hsiao-Chuan asked us: "What is it that you feel a pity if you give it up? What is it that you feel angry about? What do you think that TASAT has brought you?" So we started discussing about what would happen if we give it up and we realize it would be a big pity. . . . Hsiao-Chuan invited a Filipino organizer to give us trainings, which helped us rethink the original point where we started. . . . I realize that it is not easy to take the route of grassroots organization. . . . I felt we should be more united. No one should let go so we can beat all troubles.

In addition to trainings to broaden perspectives, TASAT often arrange for the leaders to be exposed to grassroots organizations in other countries. These exposures help marriage migrants learn from other organizations and realize their struggles are not alone.

> Yadrung: In 2008, we went to Philippines to attend the Cordillera Day, the big event of the indigenous peoples movement. . . . Because of the exposure and sharing with organizations abroad, we learnt that these organizations are doing similar things and they also have problems. When we visited the organizations, I asked them: What do you do when some officers' families are against what they are doing? How does the organization help overcome that? She said that this problem, though personal, should be brought to the organization and the organization is responsible to help handle it. After hearing her reply, I immediately cried, because I was facing great tension with my family then. . . . The exposure helped me realize that I was not the only one having problems and learn from others about how to deal with it.

Through trainings and exposure to other organizations and movements, these marriage migrants gradually developed perspectives beyond their personal problems. They began to see members of the organization as part of the bigger "we" with the same goals, and the moments of feeling discontent are perceived only as temporary emotions and should not get in the way of achieving larger goals of the organization and the movement.

Jean joined TASAT as the most recent of the five marriage migrants, and when she became active, TASAT already overcame the organizational crisis and began the process of restructuring and implementing systematic trainings and evaluation. Therefore, the curve of her experience in the organization has been steadily going upward, since she learned to contextualize discontent in a broader perspective.

> I did not have low points because I feel it's only temporary point in the growing process. . . . I felt that everyone has some emotions. . . . So it's nothing after it is released. . . . We live in the society where everyone is unique with her own ideas. . . . If there is only my idea in the organization, this organization is in danger and not moving forward, not learning things. . . . Sometimes when we have different ideas, tension and argument, I just try to accept it and see things from different positions, so that we can make progress collectively. . . . So we cannot see differences as conflicts or obstacles that prevent us from moving forward. So I simply see it as a temporary emotion.

EXPANSION OF LIFE WORLD: FROM PERSONAL, COMMUNAL TO HISTORICAL SUBJECTIVITY

To understand how their perspectives have broadened, I requested the marriage migrants to draw the people appearing in the horizon of their lives when they reflect on their lives at different stages they depicted in the drawings, and show the distance between themselves and these people. All of the five marriage migrants showed their life worlds expanding dramatically after joining the organization, from having only primary groups (family and friends), to more peoples and communities they do not know personally, including the other marginalized and disadvantaged groups nationally and internationally. In the following, I will use Pei's drawings to illustrate the expansion of the life worlds.

Before migrating to Taiwan, Pei's life was quite simple with family and friends closest to her and the match-maker and coworkers in the factory a bit farther.

In the early years of immigration, her life world expanded a little bit by adding her husband's family and people she did not know personally but saw while walking between home and the market. Her husband's family became the closest to her, while her father and sister in Cambodia became farther away.

After joining the organization, her life world dramatically expanded and became "very colorful!!" she exclaimed as. She has expanded her circle of friends to outside of her neighborhood. The friends she made in the organization became the closest to her life, while her husband's family became farther away. More importantly, she included the abstract concept of immigrants in other countries in her life world since she is able to "see politics and environments for immigrants in other countries."

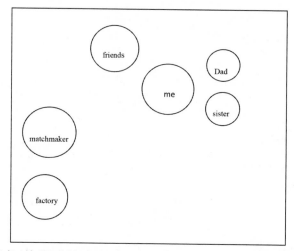

Figure 9.5 Pei's Life World before Migration. *Source*: courtesy of Pei-Hsiang Lee.

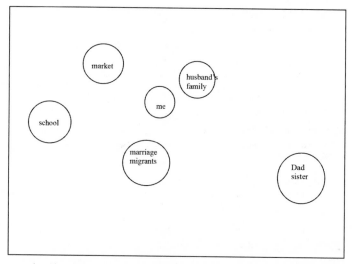

Figure 9.6 Pei's Life World in Early Stage of Migration. *Source*: courtesy of Pei-Hsiang Lee.

It became very colorful!! After joining TASAT, aside from my son, there are teachers, sisters, friends of TASAT around me. . . . There are also school and the house of my mother-in-law and my father and sister, a bit farther. There are also friends that live far away from me. . . . To expand further, after joining TASAT, I am able to see politics and environments for immigrants in other countries. I got to see them, but I only begin to know a little, not too much. So I just drew a bit to show that it begins to appear, though not clear yet.

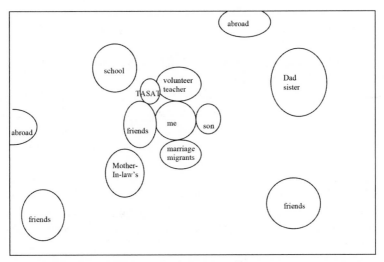

Figure 9.7   Pei's Life World after Joining TASAT. *Source:* courtesy of Pei-Hsiang Lee.

From the narratives these marriage migrants shared through their drawings, we can see how their sense of "self" broadens as their social world expands from their nuclear family to the community of marriage migrants in Taiwan, to the global community of im/migrants and the general marginalized mass. This process of transformation coincides with Touraine's (1988) discussion of "subjectivation," which depicts the process where the social actors (subject) are struggling over who controls the terms of the cultural model while their subjectivity is being transformed from "personal subject" to "historical subject," who make their mark on history by remaking the social relations and the cultural model that determine our identity. Moreover, Touraine stressed the process of subjectivation is the social action that challenges the existing social orders (Beckford 1998). In other words, the personal subject or historical subject does not evolve naturally. Rather, it can only be developed in the process of struggling against the existing values and structures.

While echoing Touraine's concept of subjectivation, elsewhere I have argued that in between the "personal subject" and "historical subject," a "communal subject" needs to be developed in the process of subjectivation (Hsia 2006a). As the result of their social, economic, cultural, and political disadvantages, "foreign brides" are isolated and silenced. A space must be created to help them break away from isolation, build self-confidence, and become a "subject," which is achieved through "an individual's will to act and to be recognized as an actor" (Touraine 1995: 207)

Despite common issues, these marriage migrants did not immediately develop a sense of "community," due to the barriers of differences in personalities, countries of origins, class, ethnicity, educational levels, and so on. These barriers often result in tension and conflicts, which hinders them from working collectively.

Since the beginning of empowering marriage migrants via the Chinese program, TASAT has emphasized the importance of dialog and encouraged marriage migrants to express their subjectivity. When encountering conflicts among individuals, TASAT upholds this principle and creates a space to help them reflect upon themselves and collectively come up with resolution, that is, to move further from personal subjectivity to a sense of community-communal subjectivity. Without a sense of community, they cannot work collectively toward advancing their welfare and rights.

As TASAT becomes more established, marriage migrants develop a stronger identity with TASAT. However, some members fell into the trap of identity politics, which Touraine (1988) criticized for not being able to transform the historicity. For instance, some felt that migrant workers should be blamed for the social stigma against marriage migrants because the former misbehave and come to Taiwan only to make money.

Being part of the same movement helps im/migrants change their stereotypes against others. My study of the grassroots migrant movement in Hong Kong shows migrant workers involved in the Asian Migrants Coordinating Body (AMCB) began to criticize their previous prejudices against other nationalities (Hsia 2009a). Similarly, to transcend the politics of identity solely based on their own ethnicities, gender, and class, TASAT has made efforts to help marriage migrants see the link between themselves and the so-called "others." Two crucial methods of moving toward the "others" include the creation of an environment where marriage migrants develop empathy with the other disadvantaged and build alliances with them. For instance, since TASAT is an active member of AHRLIM, which is composed of organizations from different sectors including those of migrant workers, TASAT members are often requested to serve as interpreters to help cases of migrant workers, which help marriage migrants develop empathy with migrant workers. By joining AHRLIM, TASAT members learn about issues that migrant workers face and thus see the commonalities between migrant workers and themselves and the importance of collaboration. As Manchi reflected on her learning in the process,

> I also had stereotypes against migrant workers, feeling that it's because of them that the Taiwanese have negative images about we Vietnamese. . . . After I went abroad to attend activities, I realized that migrants and immigrants from different countries are facing the same problems.

When the oppressed build self-confidence and begin to stand up for themselves, it is common for them to neglect their tendency to look down upon others, the "oppressor-consciousness of the oppressed" as Freire (1970) pointed out. This lack of reflexivity becomes a barrier for the marginalized people to build bridges and be united. Therefore, TASAT makes efforts to help members develop reflexivity and critique their own ignorance, stereotypes, and discrimination against others.

> Yadrung: I learnt self-reflection. We had a training . . . about how to do critique and self-critique. . . . We learnt that critique is not saying bad things about you, but to remind you what you do not see. . . . I used to be feeling too good about myself, not being able to see my own weakness in the organization. . . . In TASAT, we have many opportunities to attend activities organized by others. Being integrated and collaborated with the indigenous peoples here in Taiwan, I began to reflect on the ethnic relations in Thailand. I was from the city and did not know much about the indigenous peoples in Thailand. I realized that we also have stereotypes against them.

In addition to encouraging marriage migrants to join activities organized by other organizations in Taiwan, TASAT often sends delegates to participate in activities like rallies in other countries to expose them to other issues and ways of organizations and mobilization. TASAT has gradually broadened their perspectives and expanded international networking while becoming active members of several regional and international alliances and platforms. Through increasing international networking, marriage migrants of TASAT have begun to understand capitalist globalization as a root cause of their escape from their home countries and see the importance of transnational collaboration (Hsia 2009). They also expressed appreciation of learning from and working in solidarity with organizations in different countries. The marriage migrants began to see themselves and TASAT as part of the broader, global movement of im/migrants and realized the importance of linking the social movements in the home countries of im/migrants. As Pei put it,

> I did not know much about the Filipino peoples. After I went to the Philippines and learnt about their organizations, I am very impressed by them and feel we can learn a lot from them. . . . I learnt that the Filipino people are fighting, including old and young. . . . I was inspired to see that though they are in danger and some were even murdered by the military, they are still continuing to fight bravely. . . . They are so united and committed, and that's why no one is afraid. . . . It's the feeling of solidarity that makes people not afraid. . . . I feel happy doing these things because I feel meaningful and therefore happy. . . . Some people might ask, "Is what you are doing making any differences?" My answer is: Of course! Or else, why would we do it? . . . If things are not changed yet, we will work harder to make it change!

In sum, marriage migrants, like other minority groups, are not automatically multiculturalistic because of their minority status in the host country.

On the contrary, they also have stereotypes and prejudices against others because of their own nationality, ethnicity, class, and gender backgrounds. In fact, it is very natural for them to become exclusionary against other minorities because must survive in a hostile environment which pit them against each other and fight over very limited resources. Through joining organizations and being involved in the movement, the marriage migrants learn to work collectively with others, broaden their worldviews, and transform their subjectivity. These activist marriage migrants have begun to perceive their efforts as not only for their own immediate welfare and rights but also for the justice for other marginalized people and the betterment of the world; that is, they have become the "historical subjects" who collectively struggle to transform the "historicity."

The process of subjectivation is not linear and smooth, with many ups and downs. It is in this dialectical process of struggling and participating in organizations and the movement that they gradually broaden their scopes of "we"-ness, from the immediate family to organization, and then international communities of im/migrants, and even all marginalized people. It is in the same process that these marriage migrants develop and deepen their sense of a critical version of multiculturalism, which is not only inclusive of others but also willing to collaborate with others to further transform the societies for equalities.

REFERENCES

Alund, A. 1991. "The Power of Definitions: Immigrant Women and Problem Ideologies," in *Paradoxes of Multiculturalism: Essays on Swedish Society*, edited by A. Alund and C.-U. Schierup, 47–68. Aldershot: Avebury.

Basch, L., Glick Schiller, N., and Szanton Blanc, C. 1994. *Nations Unbound: Transnational Projects, Postcolonial Predicaments and Deterritorialized Nation-States*. Langhorne, PA: Gordon and Breach.

Beckford, James. A. 1998. "Re-Enchantment and Demodernization: The Recent Writings of Alain Touraine." *European Journal of Social Theory*, 1(2): 195.

Bissoondath, N. 1994. *Selling Illusions: The Cult of Multiculturalism in Canada*. Toronto: Penguin.

Cheng, Lucie. 2002. "Transnational Labor, Citizenship and the Taiwan State," in *East Asian Law—Universal Norms and Local Cultures*, edited by A. Rosett, L. Cheng, and M. Y. K. Woo, 85–105. London and New York: RoutledgeCurzon.

Faulks, K. 2000. *Citizenship*. London and New York: Routledge.

Freire, Paulo. 1970. *Pedagogy of the Oppressed*. New York: Continuum.

Houser, Neil O. 1996. "Multicultural Education for the Dominant Culture Toward the Development of a Multicultural Sense of Self." *Urban Education*, 31(2): 125–48.

Hsia, Hsiao-Chuan. 2004. "Internationalization of Capital and Trade in Asian Women— the Case of 'Foreign Brides' in Taiwan," in *Women and Globalization*, edited by D. Aguilar and A. Lacsamana, 181–229. Amherst, New York: Humanity Press.

Hsia, Hsiao-Chuan. 2006. "Empowering Foreign Brides and Community through Praxis-Oriented Research." *Societies Without Borders*, 1: 89–108.

Hsia, Hsiao-Chuan. 2006a. "Xin yi min yun dong de xing cheng: cha yi zheng zhi, zhu ti hua yu she hui xing yun dong [The Making of Immigrant Movement: Politics of Differences, Subjectivation and Social Movement]." *Taiwan she hui yan jiu ji kan [Taiwan: A Radical Quarterly in Social Studies]*, 61: 71. (in Chinese).

Hsia, Hsiao-Chuan. 2007. "Imaged and Imagined Threat to the Nation: The Media Construction of 'Foreign Brides' Phenomenon as Social Problems in Taiwan." *Inter-Asia Cultural Studies*, 8(1): 55–85.

Hsia, Hsiao-Chuan. 2008. "The Development of Immigrant Movement in Taiwan—the Case of Alliance of Human Rights Legislation for Immigrants and Migrants." *Development and Society*, 37(2): 187–217.

Hsia, Hsiao-Chuan. 2009. "Foreign Brides, Multiple Citizenship and Immigrant Movement in Taiwan." *Asia and the Pacific Migration Journal*, 18(1): 17–46.

Hsia, Hsiao-Chuan. 2009a. "The Making of a Transnational Grassroots Migrant Movement—A Case Study of Hong Kong's Asian Migrants' Coordinating Body." *Critical Asian Studies*, 41(1): 113–41.

Hsia, Hsiao-Chuan. 2013. "The Tug of War Over Multiculturalism: Contestation between Governing and Empowering Immigrants in Taiwan," in *Migration and Diversity in Asian Contexts*, edited by Lai Ah Eng, Francis Leo Collins and Brenda Yeoh, 130–49, Institute of Southeast Asian Studies Publishing, Singapore.

Hsia, Hsiao-Chuan and Lola Huang. 2010. *"Taiwan,"* in *For Better or for Worse: Comparative Research on Equity and Access for Marriage Migrants*, edited by Hsiao-Chuan Hsia, 27–73. Hong Kong: Asia Pacific Mission for Migrants.

Iwabuchi, Koichi. 2014. "Cultural Citizenship and Prospects for Japan as a Multicultural Nation," in *Transnational Trajectories in East Asia: Nation, Citizenship, and Region*, edited by Yasemin Soysal, 23–253. London: Routledge.

Kim, Hyun Mee. 2007. "The Sate of Migrant Women: Divergent Hopes in the Making of 'Multicultural Families' in Contemporary Korea." *Korea Journal*, 47(4): 100–122.

Kymlicka, W. 1995. *Multicultural Citizenship*. Oxford: Oxford University Press.

McIlwaine, C., Datta, K., Evans, Y., Herbert, J., May, J., and Wills, J. 2006. *Gender and Ethnic Identities among Low-Paid Migrant Workers in London*. London: Queen Mary, University of London.

Pyke, Karen and Tran Dang. 2003. "'FOB' and 'Whitewashed': Identity and Internalized Racism among Second Generation Asian Americans." *Qualitative Sociology*, 26(2): 147–72.

Touraine, Alain. 1988. *Return of the Actor*. Minneapolis: University of Minnesota Press.

Yuval-Davis, N. 1997. "Citizenship and Difference," in *Gender and Nation*, 68–88. London: Sage.

Werbner, P. and Yuval-Davis, N. 1999. "Women and the New Discourse of Citizenship," in *Women, Citizenship and Difference*, edited by N. Yuval-Davis and P. Werbner, 1–38. London and New York: Zed Book.

Chapter 10

Historicizing Mixed-Race Representations in Japan

From Politicization to Identity Formation

Sachiko Horiguchi and Yuki Imoto

In the context of emerging multiculturalism in contemporary Japan, persons of mixed race—popularly called *hafu*—have become one symbol of hybridity, internationalism, as well as an emergent third space for the communal expression of subjectivities. But its meaning is contested, variable, and attached to related historical concepts and memories. What are the various categories that represent mixed race in Japan? Who defines those categories, who resists them or uses them to their interest or consumes them? Who are the actors involved in the process of constructing realities of mixed race, and more generally of what it means to be "Japanese"? Paralleling the cases of Korea and Taiwan as discussed in other parts of this book, Japanese national identity has been tightly entwined with notions of "blood." As Takezawa points out, "Race as a category has played a key role in domestic and foreign policy alike; Japan's bumpy road to modernization, its so-called 'Leaving Asia, Entering Europe' (*datsu-a nyu-ō*) program, and its subsequent empire-building in Asia" (2015: 5). This chapter will trace the representations of mixed race in Japan since its modernization and thus delineate the contested and conflated boundaries of "Japanese blood/race/ethnicity."[1]

Contemporary popular media representations of mixed race are filled with images of *hafu* youth, a category primarily referring to half-Caucasian half-Japanese (Iwabuchi 2014b: 623). Although *hafu* largely has positive connotations, as Storrs points out, racial mixing has historically been a site of stigmatization (Storrs 1999), or problematization (Burkhardt 1983), and Japan's case is no exception. In order to question and destabilize the popular media representation of *hafu*, we examine the period *before* these positive appraisals of *hafu* emerged. Mixed race has been accorded multiple meanings in Japan from before the term *hafu* emerged, and these can be examined by tracing the different keywords, or labels that are used to refer to the group being signified—children and youth born to families of international/ethnic/racial family backgrounds—and by unpacking their meanings historically.

In the first part of this chapter, we will describe the representation, commodification and consumption of the term *hafu* in contemporary discourse through a number of symbolic, contested examples. We will then trace how the term *hafu* came into circulation in the 1970s, bringing a new positive, but stereotyped meaning to the public perception surrounding mixed race. We then go back in time and bring our focus to the term *konketsu*—which literally means "mixed blood"—the most popularized term used in prewar and postwar Japan. We will examine: who have been labeled as *konketsu* by whom, what have been seen as problems associated with *konketsu,* and how its meanings have shifted over time especially in public discourse.

In order to discuss when certain terms emerged as social problems and when those terms may have shifted onto other terms, we have traced articles on Asahi Shinbun—one of the major national daily newspapers in Japan that started its publication in 1879. We will examine the use of the term *konketsu* in the Asahi between 1882 (when the term first appeared) until 2011 in an attempt to discern the historical context in which the word *konketsu* was used in governmental policies as well as scholarly research. We will then examine how in the postwar period, *konketsu* began to be discussed as a social problem. In doing so, we note the historical context and the conceptions of race, ethnicity, gender, and "Japanese-ness" reflected in the public discourse as well as scholarly research at each period in time.

We will then discuss ways in which issues of Japanese-Filipino children labeled *kokusai-ji* (international children) and Amerasian children—primarily in Okinawa—were problematized from the 1990s through activist movements led by parents and scholars directly concerned with these issues. Finally, we examine how this category has more recently become a site for identity formations and a new expression of cultural politics among mixed-racial youth.

HAFU AS A SYMBOL OF MULTICULTURAL JAPAN?

To consider the multiple and contested meanings of *hafu* in the contemporary context, we begin with an excerpt from the *New York Times* article by Martin Fackler that features the winner of the Miss Universe Japan 2015 beauty contest—Ariana Miyamoto.

Ms. Miyamoto is one of only a tiny handful of "hafu," or Japanese of mixed race, to win a major beauty pageant in proudly homogeneous Japan. And she is the first half-black woman ever to do so. Ms. Miyamoto's victory wins her the right to represent Japan on the global stage at the international Miss Universe pageant expected in January. She said she hoped that her appearance—and better yet, a victory—would push more Japanese to accept hafu. However, she said, Japan may have a long way to go. . . .

The child of a short-lived marriage between an African-American sailor in the United States Navy and a local Japanese woman, Ms. Miyamoto grew up in Japan, where she says other children often shunned her because of her darker skin and tightly curled hair. That experience has driven her to use her pageant victory as a soapbox for raising awareness about the difficulties faced by mixed-race citizens in a country that still regards itself as mono-ethnic. (Fackler 2015)

It is questionable to what extent Miyamoto's intention of "raising awareness," or the problematization by foreign journalists and Japan-critics of Japan's mono-ethnic myth in Anglophone media, such as the one cited here, reached the majority Japanese readership, considering that domestic media attention to her victory seems limited. We can nonetheless consider discussions such as the above as one example of the complex levels of identity politics surrounding *hafu*—and the changing, diversifying nature of its discussion. The 2013 documentary film *Hafu: The Mixed Race Experience in Japan*, directed by Megumi Nishikura, is another example of how *hafu* is being represented as a symbol and potential agent of change in the conceptions of Japan's ethnic identity/ies.

A number of young mixed-race individuals have voiced their own views, questioning or alleviating the *hafu* category and its meanings. The publication *"Why Hafu Exhibit Their Talent: The Future of a Multicultural Multiracial Japan"* by Yamashita Maya (2009) introduces voices of young *hafu* and depicts *hafu* as positive agents with transnational/global skills, while Sandra Haefelin's publication *"Hafu is Beautiful is a Fantasy! My Daily Battle with the 'Pure Japanese'"* (2012) voices resistance against stereotyped, aestheticized, or commodified images of *hafu*. We the authors are not identifiable as *hafu* ourselves and are not actively involved in the emerging communities and social movements of such young *hafu*. However, our intention is to add another small voice to the discussion of Japanese ethnicity, through directing attention to both its history and connection to contemporary media discourse and youth identities.

THE COMMODIFICATION AND CONSUMPTION OF MIXED RACE AND *HAFU*

An article in the Asahi from July 23, 1967, begins with the caption "*Konketsu-Singers Are All the Rage.*" As this suggests, mixed race—referring mainly to Caucasian-Japanese hybrid—was a desirable, marketable identity in the entertainment industry from the late 60s to 70s. While the term *konketsu* was also still in currency, the term *hafu* emerged and came to be nationally recognized in Japan from around the 1970s, due in part to the popularity of the *Golden Hafu,* a female idol singing group where all its members promoted themselves as Caucasian-Japanese (Murphy-Shigematsu 2000: 212–13). Following their success, Japan's entertainment industry actively recruited "half-white and half-black" Japanese teenagers as pop singers, musicians, and fashion models (Koshiro 2003: 76). The entertainment scene was one liminal space within Japanese society where representations of mixed-race youth were appropriated for commercial consumption, with positive, desirable meanings accorded to them albeit with ambivalence and unequal distribution of symbolic capital. Particularly in the early stages, *hafu* images continued to overlap or intertwine with the images and representations of *konketsu* and Amerasians.

The Actor's School in Okinawa was established in 1983 by Makino Masayuki, who in the 1990s made his success in the entertainment industry through raising stars, many of them being mixed race. Makino explained that he was charmed by the "exotic" beauty of mixed race, Okinawan women (Shimabukuro 2002: 92). Shimabukuro points out that the mixed-race stars from Okinawa tended to mobilize orientalized images of exotic *konketsu* Okinawans, rather than the *hafu* image linked to the West (Shimabukuro 2002).[2] *Hafu* celebrities meanwhile—to various degrees—have continued to be seen as embodying positive ideals of English language skills, cosmopolitan experience as well as physical attractiveness (Murphy-Shigematsu 2000: 212–13).

An online article written in 2007 begins with the caption "*Hafu* Girls Sweep over the Entertainment Industry!" While as we have seen, mixed-race stars have been popular in the entertainment industry since the late 60s, a marked *hafu boom* emerged in the late 2000s, which is explained as follows:

> The *hafu tarento* (celebrity) boom comes and goes at regular intervals, but one analyst presents an explanation for this latest boom.
> The bubble years of around 20 years ago meant that many foreign workers entered Japan, and many Japanese went abroad as business expats. What I mean is that the fruits of intercultural communication that took place in the bubble years is now blossoming as *hafu* youth. These young girls take advantage of their high quality looks to become fashion magazine models, which paves the way for their entering the entertainment industry. (Shima Miruwo, February 14, 2012)

As in the above excerpt, sweeping generalizations are found in popular, everyday discourse about the backgrounds and experiences of international marriage, and of *hafu* youth. While most international marriages that increased during the bubble years would have been among Asians, the dominant image of *hafu* is a young female with Western-looking features. Another case of how the feminized and exotified *hafu* image is explained and thus reinforced is found in the following excerpt from a magazine article.

> *Yamatonadeshiko*—in other words, young women with a Japanese-looking face— are contrasted with girls with "*bata-kusai*" faces (butter-smelling faces) who have strong facial features (this was used both in positive and in negative ways). These days, real *hafu* are appearing, and they are really very cool and exotic. They gave something that pure Japanese do not have—a particular kind of confident but friendly communication style, and a certain awkwardness about their Japanese language which makes you want to support them—something that really clicks for the island Japanese. These *hafu* are increasing at quite a rate. (Endo Hiro, May 30th, 2007)

Endo's remarks represent and reinforce the essentialized notion of "island Japanese" with pure-blood—and stereotypically male, juxtaposed against *hafu*, who are stereotypically female. *Hafu* are prized for their good looks, exoticism, and their ambivalent position as being foreign (read as Western) but not "too" Other to the extent that they become threatening and powerful. Rather, they are friendly and somewhat vulnerable—needing "support" as Endo explains above. This vulnerability connotes "cuteness"—or the aesthetic of *kawaii*—in Japan. As Kinsella explains, "Kawaii or 'cute' essentially means childlike; it celebrates sweet, adorable, innocent, pure, simple, genuine, gentle, vulnerable, weak and inexperienced social behavior and physical appearance." (Kinsella 1995, 220). *Hafu,* from the dominant male gaze (that largely defines popular media discourse and the entertainment industry), thus embodies both cuteness and exoticism.

MEDIA REPRESENTATIONS OF *KONKETSU* (MIXED-BLOOD) FROM MEIJI TO PREWAR JAPAN: SYMBOLS OF CRIME AND BEAUTY

As we have discussed thus far, the emergence and popularization of the *hafu* category has been largely associated with popular culture. This section will examine the more politicized category of *konketsu* (mixed-blood) which precedes the emergence of the word *hafu*. Figure 10.1 shows the number of articles that include the word *konketsu* in their headlines on Asahi Shinbun. It was in 1903 that the word *konketsu* first appeared in the headline of an Asahi article, and in 1882 that the term appeared in an Asahi article for the first time. From Meiji (1868–1912) to the prewar period, there were reportings of problems or crimes associated with *konketsu-ji* or mixed-blood children, but also

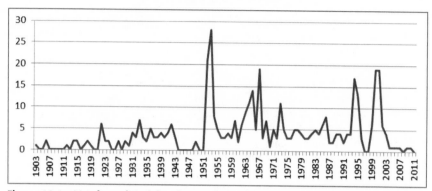

Figure 10.1 Number of Articles that Include *Konketsu* in Asahi Shinbun Headlines (1903–2011). *Source*: courtesy of the author.

articles which focused on the beauty of *konketsu*. An article on July 16, 1906 reports on the "big escape of *konketsu-ji* (mixed-blood child)," the headline of another article on January 27, 1906, reports on a "*konketsu* German deported," and the headline of an article on July 14, 1922, reads "Massage therapist murder—in search for *konketsuji*." These articles represent images of *konketsu* tied to crimes.

At the same time, a column on "beautiful men and women" that appeared on October 23, 1909, focused on the beauty of the "*konketsu-kei* (mixed-blood type)." This column goes as far as to suggest that interracial marriages should be encouraged and the Japanese men should get married to white women from the West to create "a more beautiful Japanese nation." This represents images of mixed race—of only "whites" in this case—as symbols of desirable "Japanese modernity" wherein the Western and Japanese are mixed and Japan can enjoy its status as a Westernized nation. As Iwabuchi notes,

> Significant in the Japanese experience is Japan's dual positioning of subordination vis-à-vis the western imperial power and other Asian countries, which highlights the twofold process of racialisation. Japan emulated the west-centered racial hierarchy in pushing forward with becoming a colonial power; and the clear-cut acceptance of white supremacy overshadowed and interplayed with Japan's colonial discourse of its supposed superiority to other parts of Asia. (Iwabuchi 2014b: 622)

What we find in the prewar reportings on *konketsu* therefore is that although the number of articles taking up mixed race was low, both positive and negative images coexist—which resonate with the later images of *konketsu* or *hafu*, as we will discuss below.[3]

ACADEMIC DEBATES ON *KONKETSU* IN
PREWAR AND WARTIME JAPAN

As we have seen, ambivalent images of beauty and crime were found in prewar newspaper reportings of *konketsu*. Another level of public discourse to note is the academic discourse; this section will discuss the debates on *konketsu* and the varying meanings this category has entailed. Eugenic studies played a key role in these scholarly discussions. Historian Sakano (2009: 189) writes that it was in the 1880s that mixed-race phenomenon was brought under academic attention in Japan. One of the first studies on mixed race was led by Erwin von Baelz who taught physiology and internal medicine at the Tokyo Imperial University Medical School. Baelz conducted an anthropological study of *konketsu-ji* (mixed-blood children) born to Japanese and Western parents, through examining Mongolian spots, color of the skin, or eye shapes. Backed by the inferiority complex of Japan against the West (see Majima 2014), journalist Takahashi Yoshio (1884) at the time also claimed that intermarriages between Japanese men and the "superior white" women should be promoted as a way to "improve the Japanese race." "Pure blood" proponents later took the lead, but the topic of intermarriages remained a hot issue until 1945, as symbolized in an article on *The Journal of Tokyo Anthropological Society* in 1908 written by then president of the Society Tsuboi Shogoro. As anthropologist Robertson (2007: 94–95) suggests, Japanese eugenic discourses in the prewar period concentrated on promotion of either pure-blood (*junketsu*) *or* mixed-blood (*konketsu*), and proponents for mixed race drew on theories that relied on eugenic colonialism. And as Kawai (2015) notes, these scholarly debates were ambivalent as they drew on Western imperialist conceptions of race, while denying Japan's subjugation to the West and justifying Japan's unique positionality distinct from that of the Asian others that were colonized by the West (see also Iwabuchi 2014: 622). The concept of race (*jinshu*) came to be replaced by nation (*minzoku*) in later academic discourses, yet remained to be influenced by eugenic and colonialist discourses of blood (*chi*) (Robertson 2007).

The boundaries of the Japanese race were heavily debated as Japan's colonies expanded in the war period. Japanese historian Oguma Eiji (1995: 235) suggests that the proponents of assimilationist policy for the "Asian others" drew on mixed ethnicity theory, and their assumption was that the colonized group would be eradicated through promoting mixed marriages. On the other hand, those opposing this assimilationist policy, such as Kawakami Hajime, drew on eugenic ideas and feared that the "superior" Japanese "blood" would be "contaminated" and hence its purity degraded through mixing with the "inferior" groups. The 1930s saw a rise of interest in genetics in Japanese academia, and empirical studies of mixed race, such as research on the Japanese and the Ainu, came to be conducted by Japanese scholars (Sakano 2009: 190). As Japan entered the Pacific War and started invading different parts of Asia in the 1940s, more and more studies of mixed race came to be conducted with a focus on the mixing of Japanese race with not only Westerners, but also with the Chinese, Koreans, Indians, Indonesians, and Micronesians among others.

During the 1930s and 1940s, as part of Japan's imperialization policy, intermarriages in colonized Korea and Taiwan were promoted. There emerged studies that pointed to the healthy development of mixed-race children to support these imperialist agendas (Ishihara and Sato 1914), while proponents of "pure blood" like Furuya (1941) conducted research based on eugenic paradigms to help implement National Eugenics Law (1940) and formed the basis of postwar single-nation myth of the Japanese (Sakano 2009: 191)—similar to the "One Nation, One People" ideology in Korea and concerns and debates around "multicultural soldiers" examined in Kim's chapter.

KONKETSU-JI AS SYMBOLS OF AFTERMATH OF WAR

In the postwar period, there were almost no reportings of *konketsu* (mixed-blood) until April 28, 1952, when the GHQ (general headquarters) ended its postwar occupation in mainland Japan; this was due to censorship measures taken by the GHQ administration.[4] With the end of censorship, "impure" "polluted" images of mixed-blood children often called "GI babies" came to be widely reported in public discourse. *Tensei jingo* (Vox Populi, Vox Dei) daily column on the Asahi (July 11, 1952), for instance, draws attention to the issue of *koketsu-ji* (mixed-blood children) as "troublesome," claiming that many of these children were born out of prostitution rather than "a proper marriage." The negative stereotypes against these children and their mothers also reflected strong anti-US sentiments in Japanese society at the time (Burkhardt 1983: 528–29). At the same time, there were some critics who saw racial mixing to produce a "new" type of Japanese as a way to potentially supplement the postwar Americanization of Japan and postwar progress of Japanese society (Koshiro 2003: 69).

Education for the *konketsu-ji* increasingly came to be considered a social problem in the immediate postwar period (Koshiro 2003: 69).[5] Two contrasting approaches to the education of *konketsu-ji*—to place them in a normal school and socialize them as "Japanese citizens" (assimilation) or to separate them and provide different education for mixed children (segregation)—were asserted. The assimilationist approach seemed to be the general trend and was supported by the Japanese government (Koshiro 2003: 69), yet a well-known philanthropist Sawada Miki is known to have taken the latter approach due to severe racial discrimination.[6] Sawada founded an orphanage, Elizabeth Saunders Home, and an accompanying school, St. Stephano Gakuen in 1948, where mixed orphans were raised under the same environment until middle school (see Sawada 1953, Oguma 1995: 221–22; Majima 2014: 360–61). Sawada promoted adoption from Americans and in 1960 implemented a plan to migrate some children to Brazil (see Murphy-Shigematsu 2000: 202). This attempt, which was reported on Asahi Shinbun on October 21, 1952, however, ended in failure: the plantation in Brazil closed in 1975, after receiving 28 youths from Elizabeth Saunders Home (Koshiro 2003: 76, Koshiro 1999: 212–13).

Elizabeth Saunders Home became a site for large-scale research commissioned by the Health and Welfare Ministry Institute for Population Research (Sakano 2009: 198–204). These studies produced outcomes which supported the prewar eugenic ideals, pointing, for example, to the frequency of diseases among *konketsu-ji*, the unhealthy development of these children (Sakano 2009: 200, Oguma 1995: 238–39), or the children's "innate" inferior mental aptitude (Koshiro 2003: 69–70), thereby discouraging miscegenation. There are, however, anecdotal stories of Japanese mothers of *konketsu-ji* who express delight and empowerment upon their encounter with a baby with pale skin and "beautiful blue eyes" (Majima 2014: 369–370, Sawada 1953: 84–85).

Negative representations of mixed-blood children in the mass media continued until the late 1960s when reportings were made of a crime committed by a half-Japanese, half-African American boy who murdered three women in 1967. The boy was reported to have grown furious with the gaze he received from the women. This case was reported in American popular press at the time as well, drawing attention to the frustration, alienation, delinquency and self-destructive behaviors experienced by the mixed-blood adolescents and youth (Burkhardt 1983: 527). The "moral panic" (Cohen 1972) reflects stronger discrimination against "black-type *konketsu-ji*" (Okamura 2007: 13) in Japanese society (see Oguma 1995: 232–34) though it is important to note that half-white youth often were marginalized and experienced similar discrimination and frustration due to limited opportunities in education, employment, marriage, and citizenship rights (Burkhardt 1983, see also Koshiro 2003: 67–73).

CIVIL ACTIVISM: JAPANESE-FILIPINO *KOKUSAI-JI* (INTERNATIONAL CHILDREN) AND AMERASIANS

Even after the 1967 incident, media panics surrounding mixed-race could be intermittently observed. One "problem" that needs to be mentioned in particular, is that surrounding the Japanese-Filipino children. From the 1970s,

Japanese tourists and businessmen's travel to the Philippines increased, and in the 1980s, the movement of Filipino women to Japan as transnational migrants also increased—both of which led to an increasing population of Japanese-Filipinos. The 1990s was a time when the education and welfare of minority children and children of mixed-heritage background became a topic of discussion within policy and academia—a result of internationalization and accelerated labor movement. As Figure 10.2 shows, the establishment in 1994 of JFC (Japanese-Filipino Children), an advocacy group to protect and promote the rights of Japanese-Filipino children, was immediately followed by a rising visibility in the "problem" of this group of children. The critical change in the problematization process of this group of children was that the claims-makers were the parents of mixed-race children—in other words, it was a civil movement from the grassroots level rather than one initiated by media discourse and public sentiment. 1994 should also be noted as the year when the Universal Human Rights for Children was ratified by Japan, and the notion of children as legitimate holders of rights as individuals was being discussed. In a general climate more open to civil and social movements, the 1990s brought forth the mothers of *konketsu-ji* as major interested actors into the debate and the discourse.

This civil movement brought forth the question of the legitimacy of the term *konketsu-ji*. The term *kokusai-ji* (literally "international children"), which, according to Suzuki (2004) is a term first proposed in 1979, the International Year of the Child (proclaimed by UNESCO), was to be employed to replace the derogatory term and to reframe mixed-race children in a positive light, within the heightened discourse of internationalism.[7] According to Nakajima (2002, 2004), from the 2001 edition of the *Journalists' Handbook* published by Kyodo News, *konketsu-ji* began to be included in the list of discriminatory words partly thanks to lobbying by NGO Kumstaka that support foreigners in Japan. Although the word *konketsu* did not completely disappear from the media discourse (see Figure 10.1), the *konketsu-ji* came to be increasingly replaced by the term *kokusai-ji*. *Kokusai-ji* may not have become a popularized everyday term, but it continues to be used in policy papers and in educational contexts.

At the same time that the word *kokusai-ji* was being debated and promoted, the term *daburu* (double) also emerged. This was also a term that was promoted by the parents of mixed-race children (not limited to the Japanese-Filipino *kokusai-ji*), for example, the parents involved in establishing the AmerAsian School in Okinawa (see below)—as a way for overcoming the stigmatized images associated with *konketsu* and also *hafu*—an increasingly popularized terminology that had spread through entertainment media, to which we shall return in the final sections. Parents worked to resist the stereotyped and essentialized meanings of *hafu* through adopting the term *daburu*.

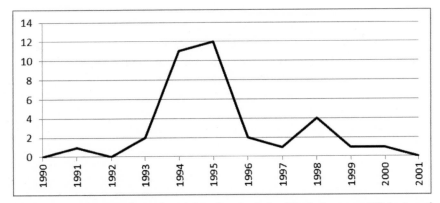

Figure 10.2 The Number of Articles that Include *Nippi* (Japanese-Filipino) and *Kokusai-ji* (International Children) in their Headlines on Asahi Shinbun (1990–2001). *Source*: courtesy of the author.

In 1995, the American-produced documentary "Doubles: Japan and Americas intercultural children" was screened and broadcast on Japanese national television. However, as interviews with mixed-race people raised in Japan (Iwabuchi 2014) have revealed, the term *daburu* has not found root either in everyday language or in the identities of mixed-race people themselves. The term *daburu*, however, has been a platform for raising the voices of the parents, bringing together shared but rarely spoken conflicts of identities.

Another important term mobilized and receiving some national media spotlight during the 90s period of civil activity, is "Amerasian"—particularly with the establishment of the AmerAsian School in 2001. The term Amerasian itself goes back to the 1960s, and was coined by novelist Pearl Buck to refer to mixed children born to American military fathers and Asian mothers. In Japan, the Amerasian issue has been primarily seen as an issue specific to Okinawa which houses 75% of the American bases in Japan. Social stigma against the Amerasian children in Okinawa due to stereotypical images of violence, prostitution or extramarital affairs, as well as lack of social welfare provisions due to their citizenship status led them to remain in socially, economically, legally, and politically disadvantaged and marginalized positions (Noiri 2011: 87–89). The revision of the Nationality Law in 1985 that enabled children of a Japanese parent (father or mother) to receive Japanese nationality was in part an achievement of the civil rights movement initially started in Okinawa (Noiri 2011: 89). While this revision meant that Amerasian children faced much less legal discrimination than previously, this also meant the decline of grassroots activism in support of Amerasian children (Noiri 2011). Noiri (2011: 90–91) brings attention to lingering social stigma against Amerasian children, apparent in the frequency of bullying in and out of schools that targeted Amerasian children in the 1980s and 1990s, fueled by strong anti-American sentiments in Okinawa.

Thirteen years on in 1998, the AmerAsian School in Okinawa was founded by five single mothers of Amerasian children as a community-based alternative school promoting bicultural and bilingual identities (Noro 2004: 10–11, Noiri 2011: 92). When a serious environmental hazard was discovered in the school grounds of Okinawa Christian School International (established 1957) where many Amerasian children were enrolled, eighty students left. Mothers of these children lobbied against both Okinawan and American authorities for support of establishment of a new alternative school, in vain. In that process, a decision was made to rely on the Amerasian category to draw attention to the globally marginalized status of these children (Noiri 2011: 93). The formation of this school has captured considerable media attention (Murphy-Shigematsu 2008: 297; Noiri 2004) as apparent in the number of Asahi Shinbun articles shown in Figure 10.3.

There is a strong emphasis on English language and an American curriculum, which is prioritized over Japanese language and curriculum (Noiri 2011: 94–95) in the newly established AmerAsian School, which leads to a conflict between the importance of an education that may strengthen the multiple ethnic identities of its students, and the costs of such an education that does not aim to prepare students for adult life in the country in which they reside (Murphy-Shigematsu 2008: 297). The AmerAsian School had "'*Daburu*' not '*Hafu*'" as slogan; the term *daburu* (double) is preferred among parents of

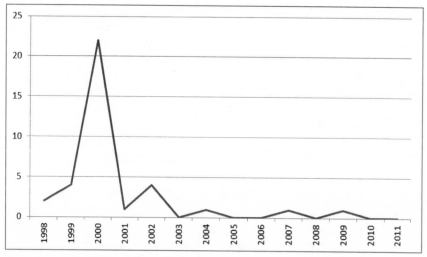

Figure 10.3   The Number of Articles that Include Amerasian in their Headlines on Asahi Shinbun (1998–2011). *Source*: courtesy of the author.

mixed race children with an aim of bringing attention to the ethnic identities of both sides of their parentage, but it has not been used by the children themselves as a self-identifying label. Mori Want (2013, see also Murphy-Shigematsu 2000) notes the importance of accepting use of hybrid names in cultivating bicultural/ multicultural identities and problematizes the Japanese family law that inhibits use of hyphenated names.

We have thus far seen how public discourse on mixed race in modern Japan has revolved around its problematization, as symbolized in the ways *konketsu* was represented. In the postwar period, such problematization has paralleled *hafu* discourse in popular media where mixed race has been celebrated as symbols of cosmopolitanism, potentially masking its problems. Media, policy makers and scholars have led these ambivalent discourses that represent the liminality of mixed race in Japan but in the last two decades, parents of mixed-race children have increasingly become involved in civil activism, successfully drawing media attention. It is worth noting that compared with Japanese scholars that led mixed-race discourses in prewar or immediate postwar periods, academic discourses in the 1990s and 2000s have been primarily led by scholars such as Stephen Murphy-Shigematsu and Annamaria Shimabuku (Shimabukuro Maria) who are themselves Amerasians and publish in both English and Japanese but have been raised in the United States. In this sense, discourses are increasingly being led by those scholars, policy makers and parents that closely associate themselves with the issue, and yet, the engagement of young scholars with mixed heritage brought up in Japan was limited until 2000s.

HAFU AS A SITE FOR IDENTITY FORMATIONS AND A NEW EXPRESSION OF CULTURAL POLITICS

While the notion of *hafu* as beautiful can be said to be engrained in the contemporary popular, everyday national imagination, they are still "marked" as ambiguous and marginal symbolic figures. The mixed youth themselves deal with experiences of discrimination and marginalization in the school context, as well as enjoying and consciously utilizing their special status and the images to which they may or may not adhere (Kamada 2010). As Yamashiro points out, many of the *hafu* celebrities have been born and raised in Japan, and "the public portrayal of mixed-race Japanese as not always bilingual or bicultural, with their phenotypes (and family histories) as the only salient markers of their foreignness, leads one to wonder about how this will affect future conceptions of Japanese-ness and the boundaries around it." (2008: 570)

Moreover, particularly from the late 2000s with the spread of social networking services and online community building, the term *hafu* which started as an external, marketing category, has come to be appropriated by the "*hafu*" (as they call) themselves for their self-identification and self-expression in the social, artistic, and grassroots media and political sphere. "Mixed Roots Japan" (http://www.mixroots.jp/) was started by a young man of mixed race in 2006 as an online community for individuals with mixed roots background in the Kansai region in 2006, and has been holding community-based events and broadcasting radio programs aimed at "creating a model for multiculturalism." In recent years, it has hosted academic forums and have increasingly made links with academics and universities. The "Hafu Project" was launched in 2008 (http://www.hafujapanese.org/index.html) by several young women based in London who all identify themselves as *hafu.* Inspired by Kip Fulbeck's "Hapa Project" as well as Walter Schels and Beate Lakotta's "Life before Death" series, this photography and interview project aims at creating a dialogue about being a *hafu* in Japan through introducing research on mixed race, narratives of young *hafu,* and running multiculturalism awareness-raising events in Japan and elsewhere. They ran exhibitions of photos and interviews in October 2008 and March 2009 in London, August 2010 in Tokyo, April 2011 in San Francisco. Two other female *hafu,* inspired by the Hafu Project, produced the aforementioned film documentary *Hafu: The Mixed Race Experience in Japan* (http://hafufilm.com/en) (2013) which features five *hafu*'s. The film aims at engaging the audience with the depth and diversity of ways in which *hafu* make sense of their personal identities and has been screened in and outside of Japan. Furthermore, in recent years, young writers and scholars with mixed backgrounds have drawn attention to the ways in which mixed-race youth make sense of their hybrid identities. For example, Yamashita (2009)'s collection of interviews with a dozen *hafu* of Western or "Asian mixes" in their 20s and 30s focus on their self-identities and represents young *hafu* as frontiers of cosmopolitanism in globalizing Japan. Murphy-Shigematsu has published works in both Japanese (2002) and English (2000, 2008, 2012) where he embeds his personal narratives of identity explorations in stories of individuals of mixed ancestry and their multicultural subject-making both at the psychological and social levels. Mitzi Uehara Carter's ethnographic study (2014) has shown that while there was a lack of empowerment for mixed Okinawans to self-identity in their recognizable difference in their militarized space and the "*hafu* hype" failed to adequately address these issues of power, the mixed Okinawans themselves, despite their transnational "in-between" positioning, have flexibly embodied their own subject-making: they have cautiously rooted themselves locally through language, fluctuating imaginaries of citizenship, and diasporic meanings of Okinawan belonging. Young mixed-race scholars raised in Japan have increasingly engaged their voices in scholarly discourses on mixed race (Okamura 2013). There has also been emerging interest in the issues with multiethnic identities of young *hafu* among academic parents of *hafu* children within the foreign language teaching community in Japan (Greer 2005, Kamada 2005, Jie 2005). Among them, Kamada (2010) examines how six adolescent *hafu* girls negotiate "othered" identities and construct hybrid identities through celebrating their cultural, symbolic, linguistic, and social capital.

Hsia (this volume) identifies three processes of "subjectivation" partly drawing upon Alain Touraine's theory of "societal movement," from the "personal subject," "communal subject," to "historical subject." We find that the grassroot *hafu* movement entails the transformation from the "personal" to the "communal," by providing psychological empowerment through a sense of belonging. But partly due to limited politicization of the term itself, the extent to which they have become "historical subjects" is only partial, though we should also note that it is too soon to evaluate their potential in this regard. This is in contrast to the Amerasian and *kokusai-ji* movements, whereby the transformation from the "personal," "communal" to the "historical" is more evident, with its success in establishing a school or changing media usage of mixed-race terminology.

FINAL REMARKS: CONSTRUCTING AND REFLECTING (ON) *HAFU* AND MULTICULTURALISM

Our examination of changing discourses on mixed race in modern Japan has illuminated its politicized nature. Focusing in particular on the categories of *konketsu* (mixed-blood) and Amerasians as they have been represented in newspapers, we have identified that there have been "peaks" of interest at certain short periods in time when they have been made subjects of "social problems" that speak to and symbolize the larger socio-political issues of the time, including issues of not only race but also Westernization, colonialization, or the challenges of globalization. The *hafu* discourses, which do not enter the newspapers, seem to be distanced from these politicized debates. Instead, attention is brought to their images as "cool" and "cosmopolitan" in popular culture—on TV, magazines, and online entertainment-related media. While the *hafu* discourses thus seem disconnected from more politicized terms such as *konketsu* and Amerasian, it is important that we examine their genealogies and contextualize contemporary stereotypes in light of their past.

It should be noted, however, that we are, in fact, seeing an increased politicization of the *hafu* category—as in the case of Ariana Miyamoto's discussion in foreign media outlets. We have furthermore seen that the main actors that construct discourses of mixed race shifted from the mass media and academics, to claims-making parents and activists that lead grassroots movements to challenge mainstream media representations and "problematizations" of mixed race and to expand the boundaries of who the "Japanese" are.

As such grassroots movements led by *hafu* themselves take hold, one of the challenges social science researchers like us face is how we should engage with activist movements. Unlike Murphy-Shigematsu, Shimabuku, or Uehara Carter who are themselves mixed race and have directly engaged in mixed-race activism, we (Horiguchi and Imoto, the authors of this chapter) are neither mixed race nor activists. We also find ourselves in an ambiguous position compared with Hsia, since despite our assuming a certain level of marginality in Japanese society due to our overseas experiences and hopes for a more multicultural Japan, we are not *hafu* ourselves and are outsiders to the *hafu* communities. This unintended process of exclusion potentially shows that ironically, race can be essentialized in the *hafu* communities, despite their attempts to problematize essentialized discourses that rely on racial stereotypes or discourses of "blood." If we align ourselves in particular collective movements, we may also risk losing sight of diversity *within* the category of mixed-race people in Japan or those that are left behind or excluded from such movements; as Hsia's chapter shows, minorities themselves may not necessarily easily unite. We may play a role in problematizing such processes of exclusion should they surface. Furthermore, at the level of everyday practice as teachers, we both work with students who are mixed race and attempt to empower them and help them explore their identities and issues in class. We feel that part of our responsibility as academics is to promote acceptance of diversity at the everyday level and continue to address remaining issues, such as those to do with the Nationality Act and the Family Law.

Our chapter has only begun to open up the histories of certain mixed-race categories for discussion, but as we write and reflect and give voice, our aim is not necessarily to overcome such dilemmas, but to continue to question and problematize both our own positionalities and identities, as well as those of the categories that we place under scrutiny, in envisaging a truly "multicultural Japan." As civil movements led by people of mixed-race backgrounds themselves expand, we hope to continue to historically contextualize changing conceptions of mixed race while noting diversities within.

NOTES

1. See Iwabuchi (2014a) for a collection of works in Japanese on mixed race in Japan. This chapter has been developed from Horiguchi and Imoto's chapter (2014) in this volume.

2. Uehara Carter (2014) shows how mixed Okinawans based in Okinawa find themselves obtusely situated along the *hafu* boom, unable to enjoy the hybrid flexibility idealized in popularized discourses.

3. Koshiro (2003: 65–66) suggests that in the late nineteenth century, scholars and politicians were discussing whether the Japanese race needed interracial marriage to

draw "superior" Western blood into their veins, yet these were met with criticisms from opponents who claimed that miscegenation between the Japanese and white Europeans would potentially lead to eventual extinction of the Japanese race and the subsequent disappearance of Japan as a nation.

4. As Murphy-Shigematsu (2000: 212) notes, the term *ainoko* that literally indicates a child of two things brought together, both human and nonhuman, was known to have been widely used in everyday discourse in Japan's immediate postwar period. Murphy-Shigematsu (2000: 212) points out that this derogatory term evokes images of poverty, illegitimacy, racial impurity, prejudice and discrimination. See Okamura (2013) for a detailed examination of semiotics and uses of mixed race categories from the Meiji Period.

5. According to Koshiro (1999: 161, cited in Ko 2014: 629), official statistical investigation into the number of mixed-race children was also banned by SCAP (Supreme Commander for Allied Powers). See also Shimabuku (2010) for a genealogical examination of miscegenation in Okinawa between 1945 and 1952.

6. Ko (2014) finds that the mixed-race children that appeared in 1950s Japanese films were primarily represented as a "social problem."

7. Majima (2014: 362–363) notes that racist prejudice against mixed-blood children shared among "Japanese" children were often influenced by their parents' contempt on the mixed-blood children and their mothers.

8. *Kokusai-ji* is in fact an ill-defined term with contested meanings. Suzuki (2004: 42) suggests that *kokusai-ji,* in its broad sense of the word, refers to children who are born to parents of different nationality, race, and/or ethnicity, while the same term, narrowly defined, means "children who are born to parents of different nationality and ethnicity." The Japanese Federation of Bar Associations, on the other hand, defines *kokusai-ji* as "children who are born with mixed characteristics taken from parents of different race in a marital relationship." (Noiri 2000, cited in Suzuki 2004).

9. A related term specific to the Okinawan context is *shima-hafu,* literally meaning island half, which refers to is an Okinawan-derived term for mixed Okinawans who primarily grew up in Okinawa, disconnected from the US military bases and primarily speak Japanese as their first or only language (Uehara Carter 2014: 650, Murphy-Shigematsu 2012: 61–79). Another term *Amerika/Amerikakei Uchinanchu* (American Okinawan) refers to the same population as *shima-hafu,* but without invoking the incomplete image associated with 'half' (Uehara Carter 2014: 650).

REFERENCES

Burkhardt, William. 1983. "Institutional Barriers, Marginality and Adaptation among Amercan-Japanese Mixed-Bloods in Japan." *Journal of Asian Studies*, 42: 519–44.

Cohen, Stanley. 1972. *Folk Devils and Moral Panics.* New York: Routledge.

Endo, Hiro. 2007. "Hafu Musume ga Gyōkai wo Sekken Suru [Hafu Girls Are Taking Over the Industry]." *All About.* May 30. Accessed February 20, 2016. http://allabout.co.jp/gm/gc/202766/all/

Fackler, Martin. 2015. "Biracial Beauty Queen Challenges Japan's Self-Image." *New York Times.* May 29th, 2015.

Furuya, Yoshio. 1941. *Kokudo/Jinkō/Ketsueki [Territory/Population/Blood]*. Tokyo: Asahi Shinbunsha.

Greer, Tim. 2005. "The Multi-ethnic Identity Paradox: Towards a Fluid Notion of being 'Hafu.'" *Japan Journal of Multilingualism and Multiculturalism*, 11(1): 1–18.

Haefelin, Sandra. 2012. *"Hafu ga Bijin da nante Mōosō desukara!!: Komatta 'Junjapa' tono Tatakai no Hibi [Hafu Is Beautiful Is a Fantasy! My Daily Battle with the 'Pure Japanese']."* Tokyo: Chūō Kōron Shinsha.

Horiguchi, Sachiko and Yuki Imoto. 2014. "Mixed Race wa Dōkatararete kitaka: Hafu ni itaru made no Gensetsu wo Tadotte [How Has Mixed Race Been Represented in Modern Japan?: Tracing the Pre-'hafu' Discourses]," in *Hafu towa Dareka: Jinshu Konkō, Media Hyōshō, Kōshō-jissen [Who are Hafu?: Mixed Race, Media Representations, Negotiation Practices]*, edited by Koichi Iwabuchi, 55–77. Tokyo: Seikyūsha.

Ishihara, Fusao and Hifumi Sato. 1941. "Nikka Konketsu Jidō no Igaku-teki Chōsa [Medical Survey of Japanese-Chinese Mixed-race Children]." *Minzoku Eisei [Racial Hygiene]*, 9(3): 162–65.

Iwabuchi, Koichi, (ed.). 2014a. *Hafu towa Dareka: Jinshu Konkō, Media Hyōshō, Kōshō-jissen [Who are Hafu?: Mixed Race, Media Representations, Negotiation Practices]*. Tokyo: Seikyūsha.

Iwabuchi, Koichi. 2014b. "Introduction." *Journal of Intercultural Studies*, 35(6): 621–26.

Jie, Shi. 2005. "The Awareness and Development of Multiple Identities in a Multilingual Child Living in Japan." *Japan Journal of Multilingualism and Multiculturalism*, 11(1): 42–52.

Kamada, Laurel. 2005. "Celebration of Multi-ethnic Cultural Capital among Adolescent Girls in Japan: A Post-structuralist Discourse Analysis of Japanese-Caucasian Identity." *Japan Journal of Multilingualism and Multiculturalism*, 11(1): 19–41.

Kamada, Laurel D. 2010. *Hybrid Identities and Adolescent Girls: Being "Half" in Japan*. Bristol: Multilingual Matters.

Kawai, Yuko. 2015. "Deracialised Race, Obscured Racism: Japaneseness, Western and Japanese Concepts of Race, and Modalities of Racism." *Japanese Studies*, 35(1): 23–47.

Kinsella, Sharon. 1995. "Cuties in Japan," in *Women, Media and Consumption in Japan*, edited by Brian Moeran and Lisa Skov, 220–55. Honolulu: University of Hawaii Press.

Ko, Mika. 2014. "Representations of 'Mixed-Race' Children in Japanese Cinema from the 1950s to the 1970s." *Journal of Intercultural Studies*, 35(6): 627–45.

Koshiro, Yukiko. 1999. *Trans-Pacific Racisms and the U.S. Occupation of Japan*. New York: Columbia University Press.

Koshiro, Yukiko. 2003. "Race as International Identity? 'Miscegenation' in the US Occupation of Japan and Beyond." *American Studies*, 48(1): 61–77.

Majima, Ayu. 2014. *Hadairo no Yūutsu: Kindai Nihon no Jinshu Taiken [Skin Color Melancholy: Racial Experiences in Modern Japan]*. Tokyo: Chūō Kōron Shinsha.

Mori Want, Kaori. 2013. "Intermarried Couples and Multiculturalism in Japan," *CLCWeb: Comparative Literature and Culture* 15(2). Accessed December 6th, 2015. http://dx.doi.org/10.7771/1481–4374.2216.

Murphy-Shigematsu, Stephen. 2000. "Identities of Multiethnic People in Japan," in *Japan and Global Migration: Foreign Workers and the Advent of a Multicultural Society*, edited by Mike Douglass and Glenda S. Roberts, 196–216. Honolulu: University of Hawaii Press.

Murphy-Shigematsu, Stephen. 2002. *Amerasian no Kodomo-tachi: Shirarezaru Minority Mondai [Amerasian Children: An Unknown Minority Problem]*, translated by Sumiko Sakai. Tokyo: Shueisha Shinsho.

Murphy-Shigematsu, Stephen. 2008. "'The Invisible Man' and Other Narratives of Living in the Borderlands of Race and Nation," in *Transcultural Japan: At the Borderlands of Race, Gender, and Identity*, edited by David Blake Willis and Stephen Murphy-Shigematsu, 282–304. London and New York: Routledge.

Murphy-Shigematsu, Stephen. 2012. *When Half is Whole: Multi-ethnic Asian American Identities*. Stanford: Stanford University Press.

Nakajima, Shin-ichiro. 2002. "Masukomi tō ni 'Konketsu-ji' wo Sabetsu-hyōgen toshite Mitomesase, Kawari ni Kokusai-ji nado wo Shiyō surukoto Motomeru Kōdō no Keika-hōkoku [A Progress Report on Making Mass Media etc Acknowledge '*Konketsu-ji*' as a Discriminatory Expression and Demanding the Use of the Word *Kokusai-ji* etc]. Accessed December 9th, 2015. http://www.geocities.jp/kumustaka85/jp.kokusaiji.html

Nakajima, Shin-ichiro. 2004. "Hōkoku: Mainichi Shinbun-sha ga Zensha toshite, 'Konketsu-ji' Hyōki wo Sabetsu-hyōgen to Mitomete, Kongo Shiyō wo Sakeru Kettei wo Okonaimashita [Report: The Mainichi Newspapers, as a Whole Company, Has Acknowledged *Konketsu-ji* Notation as a Discriminatory Expression, and Has Decided to Avoid Using the Term in the Future]." Accessed December 9th, 2015. http://www.geocities.jp/kumustaka85/20071008_asahi.html

Noiri, Naomi. 2000. "Okinawa no Amerasian [Amerasians in Okinawa]," in *Nihon no Bilingual Kyōiku [Bilingual Education in Japan]*, edited by Masayo Yamamoto, 213–52. Tokyo: Akashi Shoten.

Noiri, Naomi. 2011. "Schooling and Identity in Okinawa: Okinawans and Amerasians in Okinawa," in *Minorities and Education in Multicultural Japan: An Interactive Perspective*, edited by Ryoko Tsuneyoshi, Kaori H. Okano and Sarane Boocock, 77–99. London and New York: Routledge.

Noro, Hiroshi. 2004. "'AmerAsian School in Okinawa': *Ichi Kōsatsu* [A Study of Amerasians in Okinawa]." *Tokyo Kogei University Kogakubu Kiyo*, 27(2): 25–33.

Oguma, Eiji. 1995. *Tan'itsu Minzoku Shinwa no Kigen: "Nihon-jin" no Jigazō no Keifu [The Origin of the Myth of Ethnic Homogeneity: The Genealogy of "Japanese" Self Image]*. Tokyo: Shin'yōsha.

Okamura, Hyoue. 2007. "Hafu towa Nanika? [What is Hafu?]." Accessed February 20th, 2016. http://www.kreuzungsstelle.com/what_is_haafu.pdf

Okamura, Hyoue. 2013. "'Konketsu' wo meguru Gensetsu: Kindai Nihongo Jisho ni arawareru sono Dōigo wo Chūshin ni. [Discourse of Konketsu: An Examination of Its Synonyms in Modern Japanese Dictionaries and Literatures]." *Intercultural Studies Review*, 26: 23–47. Accessed December 6th, 2015. http://www.lib.kobe-u.ac.jp/repository/81004802.pdf

Robertson, Jennifer. 2007. "Yuseigaku-teki Shokuminchi-shugi: Nihon niokeru Chi no Ideology [Eugenic Colonialism: The Ideologies of Blood in Japan]," translated by Chieko Hori. *Shiso*, 995: 91–106. Tokyo: Iwanami Shoten.

Sakano, Tōru. 2009. "Kagaku-gensetsu no nakano Jinshu: Konketsu to Tekiō Nōryoku [Race in Scientific Discourses: Mixed-blood and Adaptability]," in *Jinshu no Hyōsho to Shakai-teki Reality [Representations of Race and Social Reality]*, edited by Yasuko Takezawa, 188–215. Tokyo: Iwanami Shoten.

Shima, Miruwo. 2012. "Rola, Tridle Rena, Haruka Christine, etc. Hafu Tarento Hassei-chu no Naze [Rola, Trindle Rena, Haruka Christine, etc. Why are Hafu Celebrities Appearing in Mass Numbers?]," *MensCyzo* February 14. http://www.menscyzo.com/2012/02/post_3583.html

Shimabuku, AnnMaria. 2010. "Petitioning Subjects: Miscegenation in Okinawa from 1945 to 1952 and the Crisis of Sovereignty." *Inter-Asia Cultural Studies*, 11(3): 355–74.

Shimabukuro, Maria. 2002. Okinawa no 'Konketsuji' to sono Hahaoya wo Kataru Seijisei [The politics of narrating the konketsuji of Okinawa and their mothers]. *Ajia Shinseiki 3: Identity (New Century Asia 2: Identity)*. Tokyo: Iwanami.

Storrs, Dianne. 1999. "Whiteness as Stigma: Essentialist Identity Work by Mixed-Race Women." *Symbolic Interaction*, 22: 187–212.

Suzuki, Kazuyo. 2002. "'Kokusai-ji' no Bunkateki Identity Keisei: Indonesia no Nikkei Kokusai-ji no Jirei wo Chūshin ni [Cultural Identity Formation of 'Intercultural Children': Focusing on a Case of Japanese-Indonesian Children Living in Indonesia]." *Ibunka-kan Kyōiku [Intercultural/Transcultural Education]*, 19: 42–45.

Takahashi, Yoshio. 1884. *Nihon Jinshu-Kairyō-ron [Japanese Racial Eugenics]*. Tokyo: Ishikawa Hanjirō.

Takezawa, Yasuko. 2015. "Translating and Transforming 'Race': Early Meiji Period Textbooks." *Japanese Studies*, 35(1): 5–21.

Uehara Carter, Mitzi. 2014. "Mixed Race Okinawans and Their Obscure In-Betweeness." *Journal of Intercultural Studies*, 35(6): 646–61.

Yamashiro, Jane. 2008. "Hafu," in *Encyclopedia of Race, Ethnicity and Society*, edited by Richard T. Schaefer, 569–71. Thousand Oaks, CA: Sage Publications.

Yamashita, Maya. 2009. *Hafu wa Naze Sainō wo Hakki suru noka: Tabunka Tajinshu Jidai Nippon no Mirai [Why Hafu Exhibit Their Talent: The Future of a Multicultural Multiracial Japan]*. Tokyo: PHP.

Section 4

MULTICULTURALISM AND LONG-EXISTING ETHNIC MINORITIES

Chapter 11

Hwagyo under the Multiculturalism in South Korea

Residual Chinese or Emerging Transcultural Subject?

Hyunjoon Shin

INTRODUCTION: RETURN OF THE REPRESSED?

Let me begin this chapter by introducing a recent South Korean (hereafter "Korean") movie, the *New World*, which was released in 2013. The movie is about the long-term rivalry between police and mobsters in Korea. It is a film noir known as homage to the Hong Kong film *Internal Affairs* (2002). However, it is notable that the movie's protagonist, Yi Jaseong (played by Lee Jung-jae), is a Hwagyo, an ethnic Chinese in Korea. He acts as an undercover cop following his boss's order to demolish the company that is run by mobsters. Yi directly serves Jeong Cheong (played by Hwang Jung-min), a leader of one sector in the company. He and the majority of his subordinates are Hwagyo as well.

Jeong's sector partners with the Triads to monopolize the trade and traffic in Hong Kong, making his sector the biggest one in the company. For that reason, he is called the "Shanghai Big Brother" and goes back and forth from Seoul to Shanghai as if he commutes to home. Top-tier Korean actors are playing these Hwagyo roles, and they sparsely use Chinese in their dialogues. Although actors' Chinese pronunciations are not like native speakers, it shows actual linguistic habits of Hwagyo well. They usually speak Korean, but they speak Chinese when they need to deliver important messages accurately, or if it pops out spontaneously when expressing strong emotions.

Another interesting point is that not only the Hwagyo, but also the Joseonjok (ethnic Korean in China) appear in the movie. Hwagyo refer to them as the beggars of Yanbian (*Yanbiande laobangzi*). Successful Hwagyo get off the plane in suits at the Incheon International Airport, while on the other hand, Joseonjok get off the boat at the Incheon seaport in shabby clothes. These Joseonjok are hired by the Hwagyo to kill. Korean actors play the Joseonjok as well, but they are extras.

It is not necessary to go into detail about the whole movie. What we need to pay attention to is the way "others" like Hwagyo and Joseonjok are portrayed in Korean popular culture. Unfortunately, both ethnic minorities are portrayed as criminals. The Hwagyo and Joseonjok in other movies are no different. For instance, the Joseonjok protagonist in *the Yellow Sea* (2010) and Hwagyo in *Coin Locker Girl* (2015) are similar. The way the identity of the minority connects to the identity of cruel and cold-hearted criminals is controversial. It can be discredited as only existing within fictional boundaries, but it is problematic in that there is almost no movie that does not depict them as criminals.

We find some peculiarity in the *New World*. First, both minority groups appear in the movie. Furthermore, both groups act as active transnational agency and are connected to Korean society in different ways. As previously explained, Hwagyo are portrayed as people who are settled into Korean culture and have economic base despite being ethnically Chinese (different race), while on the other hand, Joseonjok are portrayed as underclass although they are compatriots (ethnic Korean). The hierarchy between two groups reflects different social positions that they occupy in Korea.

It is not necessary to argue whether a movie mirrors society here. Instead, let me raise one basic question regarding the movie. Why does Korean society suddenly pay attention to Hwagyo and Joseonjok as much as they are depicted in movies? I have written about Joseonjok elsewhere (Lu and Shin 2014), so I will focus on Hwagyo in this chapter. From the movie, we see Hwagyo, who speak Korean fluently and adapt Korean culture perfectly. Then, what is their nationality or citizenship? Is it still possible to become a policeman or a company official although their nationality is not that of the Republic of Korea? If their business basis is in Shanghai and Hong Kong, then should we consider those places their hometowns? Whether it is in the movies or not, we need to investigate where the Hwagyo came from in the past, where they are now, and where they would go in the future to locate their position in Korean society.

RECONCEPTUALIZING OF HWAGYO

It is not easy to define the term "Hwagyo" or "Korean Hwagyo." It is even more difficult to interpret it into English. It is often translated as "overseas Chinese" that refers to *Huaqiao*—the Mandarin pronunciation of Hwagyo. It might be intentional, but in any case, Korean is the only language that calls "overseas Chinese" as Hwagyo. For that reason, I will just Romanize it as *Hwagyo* for this text. This term can be understood as "ethnic Chinese in Korea" or "Chinese minority in Korea." Although Hwagyo sometimes call themselves as *Hanhwa* (韓華), abbreviation of Korean Hwagyo, it will not be used in this chapter.

The twentieth-century Korean academy did not pay much attention to Hwagyo. There were few scholarship on its ethnicity in the 1980s and 1990s (cf. Park 1986), but it did not have significant implications for other fields of research. Thus, it is interesting to witness a sudden increase of scholarship on Hwagyo since the 2000s. One trend is that the (re)conceptualization of Hwagyo as a "social minority" focuses on discrimination against them and practical implications for Hwagyo's human rights (Park and Jang 2003). It can be understood as an affective regime that self-reflects the attitude of Koreans toward Hwagyo. Whether it is evincive discourse on multiculturalism or not, it can be viewed as a theorization to carry out multicultural politics or the politics of recognition. Hwagyo is subjectified as a new aspect in relation to discourses on human rights, minority, and discrimination (Park 2008, Yuk 2014, Kim 2012).

Another trend is a bit different from the previous one. *A Country without Chinatown: Today and Tomorrow of Korean Hwagyo's Economy* (Yang and Yi 2004) is symbolic in this sense. The implication of the book is that Chinatown should be created if there is none. Actually the scholarship on Hwagyo came into close relation with Chinatown creation policy. A work in similar context was focused on the economic power of Hwagyo in the globe (Jeong 2004). The context lies within the hosting 8th World Chinese Entrepreneurs Convention in Seoul, Korea, in October 2005. It implies that Hwagyo began to be reconceptualized as an agency of global economy network and tied with national agenda.

More recent studies are relatively free from the agenda of human rights and economic development. On the one hand, the history of Hwagyo is extended as a part of East Asian modern history (Wang and Song 2013). On the other hand, ethnographical approach on the daily life of Hwagyo in specific places like Incheon, Busan, and Seoul opens up new horizons (Lee 2011; Koo 2011; Chung 2013a; Chung 2013b).

However, the term "multicultural" seldom appears in Korean scholarship on Hwagyo, because the official multiculturalism in Korea mainly referred to marriage migrants since 1990s. Because Hwagyo are long-term residents, they are distant from the center of multiculturalism discourse and practice. For that reason, it is interesting to see few scholars' works on Hwagyo in relation to multiculturalism directly and indirectly. Kim (2011), taking an architect's view, studied Chinatown in Busan and argued that this area has a multicultural landscape rather than Chinese only. Although she does not deepen the research to focus on communal relationships between people and place beyond the analysis of landscape, it is still interesting to see multiculturality appear in relation to change of space. Chung (2013b), an anthropologist, studied ethnography on the place of Hwagyo investigating the Chinese ethnic enclave in Seoul. As her research does not specify multiculturality of the place, it provides room for further research.

This chapter departs from Kim's and Chung's studies and tries to connect both. It means that place-specific/cross-ethnic scale rather than ethnic-specific/transnational scale (Parreñas and Siu 2007: 3) is chosen in this chapter. It will address how Hwagyo intersect and negotiate with other ethnic groups in the place where they have already taken over, in hopes that it would be the most effective way to call out (or not) multiculturalism. The main body of this chapter is based on participatory observation and in-depth interviews in Yeonhui-dong and Yeonnam-dong, arguably the only neighborhoods that can be called as Hwagyo enclave. The fieldwork was performed for the past three years, while the structured interviews were conducted during 2015. While the names of the interviewees are anonymous, the initial letters of theirs surnames in *pinyin* were used. Before moving on the result of the fieldwork, it is inevitable to take a look at the history and geography of Hwagyo.

THE ROOTS AND ROUTES OF HWAGYO

In the narratives of Hwagyo history, the Soldiers' Uprising in 1882 (*Imo gullan*) is always mentioned. The Qing navy was sent to Korea to aid the Korean government (Joseon dynasty) against the soldiers who revolted against the poor policy by the government. Chinese merchants who followed the Qing nave and ended up residing in Korea are considered the beginning of the Hwagyo. It is therefore argued that the history of Korean Hwagyo is much more than 100 years. Hwagyo's locality is also unique. While overseas Chinese in Japan and Southeast Asia are from the southern part of China (mostly Guangdong and Fujian areas), Korean Hwagyo are from the northern part of China, particularly from Shandong province. The roots of Shandong left its traces in language (dialect) and food, and determined the direction of remigration after 1990s.[1]

However, the identity of Hwagyo needs to be redefined through the series of events that took place in the Korean Peninsula. After going through Japanese colonial rule (1910–1945), national division was cemented after the Korea War (1950–1953). It means that Hwagyo was produced via overdetermined ideological-cum-political events. Hwagyo was further influenced by historical events of the establishment of the People's Republic of China in mainland and the retreat of Republic of China to Taiwan after the Chinese Civil War in 1949. It explains that Korea Hwagyo is a historical subject constructed by political turmoil in the East Asia region and Korean Peninsula that experienced the colonization and the Cold War in the twentieth century. The historical experience plays a significant role in terms of performative identity in Hwagyo.[2] Put simply, Hwagyo became citizens of Taiwan although their ancestors had ties with Mainland China.

Korean Hwagyo has another peculiarity compared to other overseas Chinese in Asia. This uniqueness comes from the different processes of nation-building and state formation in Northeast Asia and Southeast Asia. Wang (2015) distinguishes policies between these two. Southeast Asia adopts a "jus soli" policy that accepts Hwagyo as citizens, while Northeast Asia adopts "jus sanguinis" policy defining Hwagyo as foreigners and excluding them from the frame of citizenship. In other words, Hwagyo in Southeast Asia converted into Chinese descendent (*Huayi*), but Hwagyo in Northeast Asia still remained as overseas Chinese (*Huaqiao*).

Based on Wang's argument, we can see why the Overseas Chinese Association in Seoul officially claimed that "Still, most [of Hwagyo] are Shandong people, and more than 90% hold citizenship of the Republic of China. [Hwagyo] is overseas Chinese holding single nationality that is the Republic of China (Taiwan)."[3] Beyond this rather simplified statement, one can argue that the identity of the Hwagyo has been constructed, or even invented, through the process of a constructed matrix that has been weaved via historical origin, geographic locality (Shandong root), political experiences (colonialism and the Cold War), ideological affiliation (anticommunism), nation-state building, and state formation in South Korea and Taiwan.

This "troubled history" did not end after the 1950s. Especially from the 1960s to 1970s, the Korean government heavily ostracized them, and these memories left deep scar on their body and mind. As Hwagyo was perceived as the sole non-Korean group, they were recognized as "representative other" in the name of nationalism and experienced hardship such as many regulations on property and business. The most significant factor is that the enclave of Hwagyo, which was located in central Seoul, was displaced in the name of inner-city redevelopment, resulting in the destruction of the long-term social relations and communication network. We can witness such history in the change of the Hwagyo population. Due to the Korean War and the division, its population decreased from more than 80,000 in the 1940s to 20,000 in the 1950s. Though it gradually increased afterward and reached 40,000, it began to decrease again starting from 1973 and rapidly continued to decrease until the end of the 1980s. As a consequence, the population of the Hwagyo in 1990 was about 70% of 1972 (Yang and Lee 2002: 91). Due to the mass remigration to Taiwan, the United States, and Australia, the number of Korean Hwagyo outside Korea became greater than the number of Hwagyo inside Korea.[4]

The national and international political changes in 1990s left a great impact on the Hwagyo. One is that Korea established the diplomatic relations with the People's Republic of China (China) and broke with the Republic of China (Taiwan). As a result, the Hwagyo had to live in a country that did not have diplomatic relations with the country that they held citizenship. The other is that the Korean government gradually repealed the regulations on foreigners including Hwagyo since the 1997 IMF crisis. In 1998, the limitation of foreigners' land ownership was abolished. In 1999, Hwagyo schools were recognized as a "miscellaneous school," and the government adopted permanent residence policy in 2001. By 2005, permanent residents were allowed to vote in case of local elections.

All in all, there have emerged profound changes in sojourn qualification and legal status of Hwagyo not only in Korea but also in China and Taiwan. Hwagyo switched their cultural citizenship and sense of belonging that had been consolidated through close ties with Taiwan during the Cold War era. They began to negotiate their identity under the changes, adjusting themselves under a then-new regime of mobility.[5]

As mentioned previously, there are currently more or less 20,000 Hwagyo, but even the Overseas Chinese Association did not keep the record since 2000s.[6] The number is not negligible. However, according to the official statistics (http://www.immigration.go.kr/), the foreign resident population in Korea was 1 million in 2007, and it reached 1.5 millions in 2013 and 1.8 millions in 2014, meaning that the Hwagyo take only 1%. Among foreign residents, the Chinese population is about 899,000, which is more than 50% of total foreign resident population, and among them the Joseonjok (Korean-Chinese) are 591,000. Considering this, the Chinese, mostly Han-Chinese, in Korea excluding the Joseonjok are about 308,000, and within this framework, the Hwagyo take 2%.

If there is any official record on Hwagyo, the record of foreigners with Taiwan nationality might be useful that indicated there were 31,000 in 2014. It is smaller than China, United States, Vietnam, Japan, Thailand, Philippines, Indonesia, and Uzbekistan and little bit more than Mongol and Cambodia. However, there are Taiwanese people who come to Korea and reside, so we cannot say all of them are Hwagyo.[7] The exact number of Hwagyo became obscure, since not all the Taiwanese citizens in Korea are Hwagyo since the 1990s.

But the existence of the Hwagyo is asymmetric not only temporally but also spatially. I will focus on Seoul and its two districts Seodaemun-gu and Mapo-gu. According to the official statistics (http://stat.seoul.go.kr/), Joseonjok, Chinese, and Taiwanese (mostly Hwagyo) are 143,702, 50,161 and 8,950, respectively, in Seoul.[8] The number of Joseonjok is overwhelming, while the Chinese and Taiwanese populations follow. But if we look at the two districts only, the situation is different. Combining the two districts, the population of Joseonjok, Hwagyo, and Chinese is 3,564, 3,822, and 5,152, respectively. In Seoul as a whole, it is Joseonjok > Chinese > Taiwanese, but in two districts, it is Chinese > Taiwanese > Joseonjok. That is why the ethnographic study in this chapter focuses on two districts, especially two neighborhoods, Yeonhui-dong and Yeonnam-dong, that were mentioned before. The area is converted into a "transcultural city" (Hou 2013), where not only different types of Chinese but also other migrants and ex-pats share and contest with different territorial claims.

LIVING THROUGH SOUTH KOREAN MULTICULTURALISM BY HWAGYO

Even few years ago, young people [Hwagyo] didn't have many jobs to do. [But] Hwagyo are treated well in Korea now, because they speak English, Chinese and Korean. In my generation, running restaurants was the only choice, but young Hwagyo run tax free shops, trade companies, travel agencies.

Q, who is in his 60s, operates a restaurant for a long period of time, and he acknowledges the status of Hwagyo has been improved. "I'm probably the only one who has lived in Yeonnam-dong for 50 years," he said. His statement shows us that an immigrant has been transformed into an old-timer. He is like a "village elder" and has detailed local knowledge. He also clearly recognizes that the investment to open up cafes and guesthouses flow into this area as well. Those Hwagyo who have lived this area for long time have their own houses, and some of them own 4–5-story buildings.

Based on his statement, can we conclude that the Hwagyo obtained the social right of residence and economic citizenship through policy changes since the later 1990s? Many Hwagyo who own private business stably feel the same as Q. As many young Koreans visited and moved into this area, he realized this by saying, "There used to be only farmland before [in the 1960s]. Now this town has been developed a lot." He also mentioned that many Hwagyo who left Korea and own small business in overseas are planning to come back to Korea after they retire.

However, new types of business are different from restaurants. S is running a travel agency with Korean employee. He said, "Now, [travel agencies] are facing unlimited competition now. It's really difficult to run the business." He further explained that it was because of the Joseonjok who are involved in this business deploy cheap price policy that makes the industry over-competitive. He senses the difference between Hwagyo and Joseonjok in terms of business style on practical level rather than a cultural identity on an abstract level. Therefore, he operates the business for the "rich (ethnic) Chinese from Singapore and Malaysia," avoiding the "(mainland) Chinese coming on low price tour package."

Both Q and S received a college education in Taiwan and support KMT. Q was a member of KMT, and he even went to Taiwan to vote a few years ago. S firmly stated, "I'm not a citizen of the People's Republic of China. I'm a citizen of the Republic of China." W (40s, female) lives in Yeonnam-dong and owns a small shop in Myeong-dong. She also stated that she supports KMT saying, "Chinese and Taiwanese have different ethno-national characteristics." These show us that Hwagyo feel not only political difference but also cultural difference with Mainland Chinese.

However, this does not mean that they do not recognize the power of China. KMT member Q also reluctantly acknowledged "the status of ethnic Chinese has been improved because of the People's Republic of China, since the normalization of diplomatic relation between Korea and China." S also realized international dynamics toward domestic policy changes, saying, "Korean government adopted permanent residence system for Hwagyo, because of pressure from China. Taiwan has no such power."

Their lived experiences in Taiwan affected their thoughts on Taiwan realistically. Except old Q, the rest of them did not have pleasant experiences. W said, "Taiwanese didn't know what Hwagyo is." She was considered as a Korean with a Taiwanese passport, or as a mainland Chinese due to her accent. S went to Taiwan to settle in there, but he explicitly said, "I didn't like Taiwan. I didn't like Taiwanese people and the environment there." They studied abroad in the 1990s, which was the time of political transition of Taiwan. For that reason, they experienced the moment when the cultural and political conflicts between the islanders (本省人) and the mainlanders (外省人) were intense. Saying again, their ancestors were from Shandong, which is part of the mainland. Though their political orientation is sided with KMT, they were treated as the mainlanders in Taiwan, where islanders were the majority in school.

We cannot simplify the reason why they still hold onto Taiwanese passport as a political affiliation or an ideological allegiance. They already have experienced a political mechanism, so that the reason must be more of a practical choice rather than political one. According to Z (woman in 50s), the reason she still keeps Taiwanese passport is that it is "easier to go abroad." She had a chance to obtain a Chinese passport, but she has not considered to get it since "it is more difficult" to go abroad with a Chinese passport. In other words, if she can easily travel with a Chinese passport, she will not need a Taiwanese passport then. Actually it is an open secret that many Hwagyo have changed their citizenship to China. This is an example of the so-called flexible citizenship (Ong 1999). Y (50s male), who travels back and forth to Yantai in China, claims that he does not disclose his nationality "unless they asked," when he does business with Mainland Chinese. His case reveals the social condition that disclosing residence or nationality is not beneficial.

In this sense, W's definition of Hwagyo as those "who were born here [Korea] and have resided here with the Republic of China nationality" has subtle differences with mine. She emphasized more on "residence" than "nationality," and the Republic of China meant the political entity that was established in 1911 rather than the geographical entity such as Taiwan. The memory of *minguo* (民國), which is fading away among Taiwanese, distinctively exists in diasporic Hwagyo's memory. Thus, the imagined community for Hwagyo is becoming less associated with the real existing nation called Republic of China (i.e., Taiwan).

However, Hwagyo aged over 40 insist that the identity that their generation and their predecessors have had is now under serious change. According to them, many Hwagyo in their 20s think they are "Korean." Does this mean that the place one where has life experiences is more important than his or her formal nationality? But we need to be reminded that Korea here does not mean the political entity of Republic of Korea. In order to clarify, now we will take a look at C1, who is considering obtaining a Korean citizenship, and C2, who already obtained the Korean citizenship. Both of them are male in their early 30s.

While C1 and C2 spent their youth in other districts in Seoul or in another city outside Seoul, both entered Seoul Hwagyo Middle and High School. C1 graduated from a university in Seoul majoring in science, while C2 graduated from one of the top universities in Taiwan studying management. Most of the interviewees I have presented in this chapter are doing business and are socially connected in the place where the biggest Hwagyo community exists. But C1 and C2 work at Korean companies, and the latter moved to other town in Seoul. I was able to contact them via an Internet-based community, Human Rights Forum of Ethnic Chinese in Korea. On this Internet community, C1 once posted a statement saying, "Basically, Korean Hwagyo are refugee[s]."

These two have quite different personalities, but both sensitively acknowledge micro-history of Hwagyo via experiences of their family members. C1 told me a hidden historical incident regarding his grandfather. C1's grandfather was a famous chef, but he was "kidnapped as he was sitting on a chair and thrown onto a small desert island in Taiwan," because he contested the expropriation of land during the Park Chung Hee's era. "It took [a] very long time for him to get back to Korea," C1 added. When C2 traveled with family overseas (except China and Taiwan), he had to go to Taiwan to get visa of the country they wanted to go to. They were told when they visited the embassy of the country in Korea that if they were Taiwanese, they needed to go to that country's consulate in Taiwan.

So it is understandable that younger generation of Hwagyo have formed a political stance, which is different from that of older generation. When I cautiously asked their political orientation, which is a delicate issue in Korea, C1 responded "progressive" while C2 replied "left." As C1 pointed out, they are "not much different from Korean young generation," indicating that generational consciousness overwhelms national consciousness for them. They also concluded that they are "neither pro-KMT nor pro-DPP" toward Taiwanese politics (C2).

They became adults after some conflict issues resolved, so it is important to closely investigate how they acknowledged and experienced these conflicts. Both of them experienced hidden inequality in the company. When colleagues at work do not know they are Hwagyo, or if they speak Chinese involving China-related work, they are surprised and think "he can even speak Chinese." But if they find out they are Hwagyo, they think it is only natural for them to speak Chinese (C1). It is not easy to speak two languages simultaneously, but such ability has been easily ignored since they do not have any certificate of languages skills. C2 pointed out the unfairness of this issue. It is an example of how bilingual or trilingual (including English) ability is abused. The visible discrimination in the past still continues as an invisible inequality in everyday life.

Regarding the issues of multiculturalism in Korea, about half of the interviewees, especially those from the older generations, never heard of multiculturalism. The most amicable answer was from W saying, "If your children go to kindergarten, there is subsidy." However, this means Korean multiculturalism only supports international families including Korean spouses. For that reason, in the case of a Hwagyo man with Taiwan nationality like S, who marries a Singaporean woman, it is not considered a multicultural family. He said, "It becomes multicultural if Hwagyo marries Korean. If Hwagyo marries non-Koreans like Singaporean, then that's a different story."

Considering the fact that many Hwagyo families consist of a Hwagyo man and Korean woman, the arrival of multiculturalism is too late for the Hwagyo. For Hwagyo families with all foreign (mostly Taiwanese) nationalities are still considered a foreign family instead of a multicultural family. These Hwagyo families do not get any benefit from the government though they are facing new types of inequality. For instance, C1 mentioned that they have to pay high prices for childcare centers, and the hospital does not provide free wheelchairs for elders over 60. He further explained, "Criteria of multicultural policy in Korea are too narrow. That's because it's for international marriage rather than for [the] whole." For that reason, they can only feel the effect of multiculturalism within their "mind." Some mentioned, "Since the word multicultural emerges, Koreans became something like nicer to foreigners or more acceptable of foreigners." As C1 stated, the change is like there was a sense that "Hwagyo hid the fact that [they were Hwagyo] in 1980s. But now people with less [previously bad] experience do not hide it."

However, not every interviewee agrees with "nicer Korean" and "no hiding" parts. S said, "I heard we're overlapped with Joseonjok a lot, so the image of Hwagyo is becoming bad again." His point marks Korean's prejudice against the Joseonjok that extends to the Hwagyo, not about the Hwagyo's prejudice against the Joseonjok. He now wants to negotiate the new situation on a daily basis where he became a part of the "men from China" whether it was intentional or not. What do young Hwagyo practice a new identity of Hwagyo in this condition? Now let's go back to C1 and C2.

The biggest reason C1 wanted to obtain Korean nationality was to avoid uncomfortable issues he would face in economic activities. The experience of studying at a Korean university and having a Korean mother affected his preference as well. He never visited Taiwan, and he did not have any affinity to the formal Hwagyo community or to Taiwan. He visited the Hwagyo Association "just once to receive the scholarship" when he was in college. To him, Hwagyo School is a corrupted place where "the principal has ruled for a few decades." After he graduated from school, he realized that "Chiang Kai-shek is not a hero." Furthermore, he thinks "Taiwan did not do anything for Hwagyo," and he "does not have any interest in" Taiwanese politics. He even thought that "it would not matter whether Taiwan becomes independent or not." He also mentioned that some friends felt differences about the Chinese regime and its ideology, though they want to "make a lot of money in the place where language is comfortable, and price is right and live like a lumpen."

His point reflects the young generation's sentiment of "we are neither Chinese nor Taiwanese. We are Hwagyo." As international mobility becomes more common, they fall into a complicated identity game from being Chinese in Korea, Korean in Taiwan, and Taiwanese in China, and eventually they became "neither this nor that." Thus, his conclusion was that it would be rather better that he became either Sinified or Koreanized. He sensed that the era that an individual body could embody both "China" and "Korea" is passing. As for himself, he gradually integrates into Korean society. For that reason, he suggested that I meet C2 if my interest was in the identity issue of the Hwagyo.

C2 can be categorized as a cultural elite in that he is from a family of Hwagyo schoolteachers. He is actually known as "hardcore." His acquaintance thought that he is "the one who will never give up his nationality (of the Republic of China)," so that it was a great "shock" to people around him that he was naturalized to Korea. What is the reason that he became Korean citizen? What does nationality mean to him? He stated:

I thought about the importance of nationality a lot. Now many people have dual nationality. . . . I have travelled around every corner of the world and met overseas Chinese of that area. I realized that they have different values and perspectives. My thoughts have been changed after I met overseas Chinese from Southeast Asia and Europe while I was in Taiwan. This cannot be done by reading books. It will take time to have changes in thoughts and awareness after experience in daily life and communicate. [with others]

Interestingly, C2 felt a strong sense of belonging to the transnational Hwagyo community rather than strengthening his own political affiliation to Taiwan. When I asked him about cultural affiliation, he replied, "I conclude that I'm a global person after I have lived here and there." To the question of nationality, his conclusion was that it is not "absolute," and to the question of nation, it is "meaningless." His family and relatives are geographically spread out around China, Taiwan, Southeast Asia, the United States, and Costa Rica. His thoughts and practices can be seen as transculturalism[9] rather than multiculturalism, and perhaps we can say that he is close to the ideal model of future Hwagyo. Though the possibility of Hwagyo to be transcultural-cum-transnational seems to be limited to the well-educated elite, it cannot be denied that it is an unprecedented one.

What should be noted is that younger generation of Hwagyo like C1 and C2 have a strong attachment to Yeonhui-dong and Yeonnam-dong. The place attachment by Hwagyo might be stronger than the Korean residences in the area. Even after they moved out, they chose this place "whenever they have reunions or gatherings" (C2). To them, this area is the actual Chinatown and they believe that the Chinatowns in Incheon and Busan and the Chinatown under construction in a suburb of Seoul are mere artificial ones. In the 2000s, there were two attempts to create Chinatown there, but to no avail. In the second attempt in 2008, the Hwagyo did not welcome this project because they did not want to have Chinese newcomers in the old Hwagyo neighborhood. Rather than intermingling with the newcomers with the same ethnicity, they have been (per)forming a distinct place-specific identity based on their unique version of transnational imagination.

Does it mean that Hwagyo, though a minority, are not multiculturalistic and egalitarian enough? (About this, see Hsia's chapter in this volume.) Actually, the attitude of Hwagyo to newcomer migrants does not seem to be so different from that of the ordinary Koreans. However, it is not because Hwagyo is against the ideal of cultural diversity and mutual tolerance, but because the new ideology of Korean multiculturalism is as useless as the old ideology of Korean ethnonationalism. What is worse is that the gaze of majority to Hwagyo by Koreans is not changing that much. I will deal with this issue in the conclusion.

OUTRO: BACKLASH OR RESENTMENT

In the summer of 2014, Hwagyo became an issue. It can be illustrated by the provocative titles of newspapers such as "Chinese Big Players [Taking] Hongdae area bit by bit: Hwagyo capital added . . . Surge of land purchasing 3 times in 1 year" (*Koomin ilbo* 1 Aug 2014) and "Invading Seoul real estate by Chinese big players has begun: Rental price of Yeonnam-dong area increases by 10% every year, 'beyond control'" (*Financial Today*, September 24, 2014). Here, the Hwagyo are represented as brokers of Chinese investors who try to purchase Korean properties. As I am not an expert on real estate economy, I was not able to do an in-depth research on this topic. However, my impression is that the Hwagyo's roles in those newspapers are exaggerated. While Korean media kept silent when the Hwagyo faced hardship for a long time due to the limitation of property rights, they speak out loudly about Hwagyo owning real estate. It is an antinomy for sure. While they are absolutely generous about Korean's investment on real estate, they are showing sensitive reactions toward foreigner's investment on real estate. Although the significant issue is to the effect on residences in this area due to the real estate investment whether it is done by Koreans or non-Koreans, the focus is usually on Hwagyo's involvement in the investment.

The aggressive voice onto the Hwagyo started previously by certain groups of Koreans. In April 2008, at the time of the relaying of the Olympic torch for the Beijing Olympics in Seoul, some Chinese used violence against Korean civic groups who protested against the repatriation of North Korean defectors by China and supported the independence of Tibet from China. Unexpectedly, Hwagyo became the backlash victim due to this incident. On discussion boards on the Internet, comments like "Park Chung Hee's Hwagyo exclusion policy was prescience" and "we should kick out all Hwagyo in Korea now" were noticed.

The aggression against the Hwagyo gradually formed into some kind of political stance. A comment posted on the notorious Internet extreme right community, *Ilbe* (short form for *Ilgan-best* that translates into "Daily Best"), in 2013 is a perfect example of the aggression against the Hwagyo.[10] It begins with "the discrimination of Hwagyo is a lie. They are rather privileged." Touching upon the "'[university] entrance exam hell' and 'compulsory military service' that are very sensitive in Korea, this group insisted the Hwagyo keep Taiwanese citizenship (instead of Korean one) in order to avoid the hardship by young, mostly male, Koreans." The side effect of the exclusion from being a proper citizen is misinterpreted as "privilege." In their words, Hwagyo is perceived as one of "multicultural," even though they don't actually get any benefit from the multicultural policy. It is no doubt that the view is nonsense from the young extreme rightist's insistence. The socio-psychological conditions behind the reasons why this kind of insistence becomes influential need to be under serious examination that is beyond the scope of this chapter. To put it simply, it is supported by the difficulties of getting proper jobs by young Koreans under neoliberal restructuring of the economy and society. It is expected that these neo-nationalists will continue to attack the ethnic minority via discourse of "youth frustration," if the economic depression persists for long period (see Kohei's chapter in this volume for the comparison with Zainichi in Japan).

Let's returning to the movie *New World* mentioned in the introduction. In the middle of the movie, the boss finds out that the protagonist is an undercover cop, but he does nothing to him. Later when internal struggle erupts within the organization, the boss gets a severe wound. As he is dying, he leaves a dying message to the protagonist saying, "You now choose . . . you stay strong." The protagonist then gets rid of the Korean policeman boss and becomes the boss of the organization. It is a twist. At the end of the movie, we see flashbacks of the protagonist and the boss who used to be a gangster in Yeosu (a port city in southern part of Korea) when they were young, and the policeman boss puts him in this plan because of his Hwagyo identity. One can suspect the protagonist becomes a boss of the organization based on the well previously planned scenario. Although it is not the case, one can see that it is true that the Hwagyo have been exploited in Korean society, and they developed a strong bond among them because of it. It is clear that the protagonist betrays the selfish police boss and chooses the mob boss who trusted him to the end even though the boss knew that he was an undercover cop.

A movie is a movie. However, it seems this movie portrays the "China Fear" that lies within Koreans' subconscious whether the director intended to or not. The history of repression of the Hwagyo in Korea paradoxically shows that this fear is not new, but rather it has been around for a long time. Furthermore, ressentiment against them emerges in 2008 after the 10 years (1998–2007) of redemption policy toward the Hwagyo. A short response from a Hwagyo on an Internet forum says, "Do not touch the odd nerve (of Korean)," depicting ressentiment clearly.

However, is the Hwagyo an "answer" instead of a "problem" from the standpoint of official policy? They developed a dual cultural identity by themselves without getting any benefits from the multiculturalism policy so far. They never contested the system, and they never carried out group activities for minority rights. They even feel uncomfortable with the gaze that does not differentiate them from the newcomer Chinese. In that sense, Hwagyo need to be reconceptualized not as residual Chinese diaspora after the rise of China (Ang 2013), but as hybrid and transcultural subject who are neither Chinese nor Korean. It has the implication that the multicultural policy in South Korea needs to go beyond the essentialist notion of ethno-national culture, be it Chinese or Korean.

NOTES

1. Overseas Chinese in Northeast Asia including Korea are not dealt with in the edited volume on Chinese transnationalism by Aihwa Ong and David Nonini (1997). That is partly because overseas Chinese in Northeast Asia is much smaller compared those in Southeast Asia. But it is true that the former is a missing link in overseas Chinese scholarship.

2. More than half of Hwagyo before 1945 resided in the northern part of the Korean Peninsula (today's North Korea), and there are still large number of Hwagyo in North Korea, so that Hwagyo in this chapter is limited to Hwagyo in South Korea. The Cold War in Korean Peninsula caused separation among not only Koreans, but Hwagyo as well.

3. http://www.craskhc.com/htm/sub03.htm

4. An interesting point is that Hwagyo's destinations overlap those of overseas Koreans. For instance, there are about 8,000 Hwagyo in Los Angeles. It tells us that the connection in previous location continue even after the (re)migration. Furthermore, Shandong origins of Hwagyo could not capitalizes among the dominant overseas Chinese community. As I mentioned earlier, most of overseas Chinese have Guangdong and Fujian origins that have different linguistic culture from Korean Hwagyo.

5. One important aspect of the mobility is that Hwagyo could travel to ancestral homeland since 1987, thanks to the policy change of Taiwan. Furthermore, some Hwagyo business people played an intermediary role in the early investment from Korea to China, see Chen (2005), especially pp. 127–132.

6. In Incheon Chinatown homepage, it says, "We do not know exact number Hwagyo now in 2010, but based on the statistics, it was about 22,917 in May 2001" (http://www.ichinatown.or.kr/introduction/overseas_chinese/present.asp). According to the Overseas Chinese Association, it says, "21,806 are registered," without indication of the date (http://www.craskhc.com/htm/sub03.htm).

7. I need to mention about gender issue of Hwagyo. The record "female Hwagyo is about 26%," (http://www.ichinatown.or.kr/introduction/overseas_chinese/drift.asp) indicates that male Hwagyo population has overwhelmed female one. For that reason, the number of marriage between Hwagyo men and Korean women has dominated the opposite case after 1945. In these cases, Korean women generally changed their nationality to Taiwan, and this was the way to make Hwagyo although they were not pure-blood. This implies that the paternal jus sanguine in both Korea and Taiwan made possible to increasing, or avoiding rapid decrease of Hwagyo. Now Hwagyo are in the 5th generation, and pure Chinese line is about 6.25%. They self-mockingly refer themselves as "625 generation." About more in detail, see *Chosun Ilbo*, 4 August 2011.

8. This criteria is problematic since not every Taiwanese is Hwagyo as I pointed out. Furthermore, Joseonjok are officially belonging to Chinese. We can separate them into "Korean-Chinese" and "Han-Chinese," but not every Non-Korean-Chinese is Han-Chinese. This chapter focuses on qualitative difference on cultural identities of three groups keeping inaccurate numerical value and criteria in mind. Recently, the

existing Hwagyo is referred to old Hwagyo (*laohuaqiao*, or *laoqiao* in short form), and new comers to new Hwagyo (*xinhuaqiao*, or *xinqiao*), but these terms have not been theorized properly yet. It is a controversial whether to see Joseonjok as new Hwagyo. As an introductory study on this issue can be found in Rhee's article (Rhee 2009).

9. Ulrike Meinhoff and Anna Triandafyllidou suggested transculturalism to criticize the multiculturalism and its crisis in Europe. It requires derivative concept of transcultural capital to explain it. It is defined as "the strategic use of knowledge, skills, and networks acquired by migrants through connections with their country and cultures of origin which are made active at their new places of residence" (Triandafyllidou 2009: 94). The concept is useful because it suggests ethnic culture of minority, which has been seen as stagnant in classical multiculturalism, has been formed and transformed through constant process. The point is that one should not conclude by confirming the presence of transcultural capital. One should further discuss through specific examples of how it operates and deploys within certain circumstance and condition.

10. http://www.ilbe.com/1034567515. This posting has been removed now.

REFERENCES

Ang, Ien. 2013. "No longer Chinese? Residual Chineseness after the Rise of China," in *Diasporic Chineseness after the Rise of China: Communities and Cultural Production*, edited by Julia Kuehn, Kam Louie, and David M. Pomfret, 17–31. Vancouver: University of British Columbia Press.

Chen, Xiangming. 2005. *As Borders Bend: Transnational Spaces on the Pacific Rim*. Lanham, MD: Rowman & Littlefield Publishers.

Chung, Eun-ju. 2013a. "Chainataun anin junggugin jipgeoji: Geunhyeondae dongasia yeoghag soge jujodoen seoul Hwagyo jipdangeojujiui jihyeong [Chinese streets without being a 'Chinatown': Topography of the Chinese Ethnic Enclave in Seoul Shaped in the Modern East-Asian Dynamics]." *Seoulhagyeongu*, 53: 129–75.

Chung, Eun-ju. 2013b. "Diaseuporawa minjokgyoyugui sinhwa: Hangugui junggugin diaseupora gyoyuksilcheone daehan minjokjijeog yeongu [Diaspora and the Myth of Ethnic Education: An Ethnographic Study on the Education Pratices of the Chinese Diaspora in Korea]." *Hangungmunhwaillyuhak*, 46(1): 135–90.

Chung, Eun-Ju. 2012. "Learning to be Chinese: The Cultural Politics of Chinese Ethnic Schooling and Diaspora Construction in Contemporary Korea." PhD thesis, Harvard University.

Hou, Jeffrey. 2013. *Transcultural Cities: Border-Crossing and Placemaking*. New York: Routeledge.

Jeong, Seong-ho. 2004. *Hwagyo [Overseas Chinese]*. Seoul: Sallim.

Hwang, Inho and Jongseon, Lee. 2014. "Jung keunsondeul jeju ieo hongdae apt ttangdo yageumnyageum: Hwagyo jabon gase . . . toji chwideuk ilnyeon sae baeisang geupjeung [Chinese Big Players taking Hongdae area bit by bit: Hwagyo capital added. . . . Surge of land purchasing 3 times in 1 year]." *Kookmin Ilbo*, 1 August, 2014.

Heo, Yunhee and Yujin, Lee. 2011. "Junggukpi 6.25% hangukpi 93.75%: i aineun jungguginimnikka hanguginimnikka [Chinese blood 6.25%, Korean blood 93.75%: Is this kid a Chinese or a Korean?]." *Chosun Ilbo*, 4 August, 2011.

Shin, Hyeonho. 2014. "Jungguk 'keunson'deurui seoul budongsan gongseubi sijakdwaetda!: Yeonnam- dong ildae imdaeryo maenyeon 10% sangseung, 'gamdanghagi himdeulda' [Invading Seoul real estates by Chinese big players has begun: Rental price of Yeonnam-dong area increases by 10% every year, 'beyond control']." *Financial Today*, 24 September, 2014.

Kim, Hyun Jin. 2012. "Politics of Race in East Asia: The Case of Korea and the Chinese Community in South Korea." *Provincial China*, 4(1): 101–15.

Kim, Na-young. 2011. "Busan chainataunui garoeseo natananeun damunhwas eonggwa gukgajuui ganui gilhang [Antagonism between Multi-culturalism of China Town's Streetscape and the Nationalism in Busan]." *Yeoksawa gyeonggye*, 78: 35–63.

Koo, Jiyoung. 2011. "Dongasia haehangdosiui imunhwa gonggan hyeongseonggwa byeonhyeong: Busan Choryangdong 'chainataun'eul saryero [A study on the Creation and Transition of Cross-cultural space in an East Asian city: A case study on the 'China Town' in Choryang-dong, Busan]." *Seokdangnonchong*, 50: 613–53.

Lee, Chang-ho. 2011. "Hwagyosahoeui jeongchijeog jojikgwa yeokdongseong: Incheon chainatauneul jungsimeuro [Political Organizations and Dynamics of Overseas Chinese Society in Korea: Focusing on Incheon Chinatown]." *Jungangsaron*, 33: 41–85.

Lu, Melody Chia-wen and Shin, Hyujoon. 2014. "Ethnicizing, Capitalizing and Nationalizing: South Korea and the Returning," in *Return: Nationalizing Transnational Mobility in Asia*, edited by Xiang Biao, Brenda S. A. Yeoh, and Mika Toyota, 162–77. Durham: Duke University Press.

Ong, Aihwa and Nonini, David (eds.). 1997. *Ungrounded Empires the Cultural Politics of Modern Chinese Transnationalism*. New York: Routledge.

Ong, Aihwa. 1999. *Flexible Citizenship: The Cultural Logics of Transnationality*. Durham: Duke University Press.

Park, Eun-gyeong. 1986. *HangukHwagyoui jongjokseong [The Ethnicity of Chinese in Korea]*. Seoul: Hangungyeonguwon.

Park, Kyung-tae and Jang, Soo Hyun. 2003. *Gugnaegeoju Hwagyo ingwonsiltae josa [Research on the Reality of Human Rights of Hwagyo in Korea]*. National Human Rights Commission of Korea.

Park, Kyung-tae. 2008. *Sosujawa hangug sahoe: iju nodongja, Hwagyo, honhyeorin [Minority and Korean Society: Ethnic Chinese, Migrant Worker and Amerasian]*. Seoul: Humanitas.

Rhacel S. Parreñas and Siu, Lok C. D. (eds.). 2007. *Asian Diasporas: New Formations, New Conceptions*. Stanford: Stanford University Press.

Rhee, Youngju. 2009. "Diversity within Chinese Diaspora—Old and New Huaqiao Residents in South Korea," in *Diasporas: Critical and Interdisciplinary Perspectives*, edited by Jane Fernandez, 111–26. Oxford, United Kingdom: Inter-Disciplinary Press.

Triandafyllidou, Anna. 2009. "Sub-Saharan African Immigrant Activists in Europe. Transcultural Capital and Transcultural Community Building." *Ethnic and Racial Studies*, 32(1): 93–116.

Wang, En-mei. 2015. "Haebang 70nyeongwa hangukwagyoui sam: hangukwagyoege jinjeonghan haebangeun chajawanneunga? [The 70 Years' Anniversary of Liberation and the Life of Ethnic Chinese in Korea: Is the Genuine Liberation coming to ethnic Chinese in Korea]." *Rokeollitiui inmunhag*, 44(1).

Yang, Pil-seung and Yi, Jung-hee. 2004. *"Chainataun eobsneun nara: Hangug Hwagyo gyeongjeui eojewa oneul [A country without a Chinatown: The yesterday and today of Hwagyo economy in Korea]."* Seoul: Samsung Center for Economic Research.

Yuk, Joowon. 2014. "Talking Culture, Silencing 'Race,' Enriching the Nation: The Politics of Multiculturalism in South Korea." PhD thesis, University of Warwick.

Chapter 12

Multiculturalism and Indigenous Peoples

A Critical Review of the Experience in Taiwan

Daya Dakasi Da-Wei Kuan

INTRODUCTION

Indigenous movements played an important role in the institutionalization of multiculturalism in Taiwan (Zhang 2002, Wang 2016). However, it is sometimes questioned whether the institutionalization of multiculturalism can ensure the achievement of justice (Zhang 2008, Wang 2016). Such a question is especially applicable to the highly tensioned indigenous land issues in this settler country. Therefore, indigenous peoples' experience in relation to the practice of multiculturalism cannot just provide the insight of its limitations but also inspire to seek for the realization of justice.

Austronesian languages speaking peoples lived autonomously in Taiwan for thousands of years before their encounters with colonial powers. Dutch and Spanish landed and built their colonies in the western plain area during the seventeenth century. In 1662, the Jieng, a rebel army claiming itself as the successor of the Ming Dynasty in China defeated the Dutch and took over west plain area. After the rebel army surrendered in 1683, the Ching Dynasty from China controlled the plain area for 212 years, during which the Han-Chinese settlers gradually became the dominant population through waves of immigration. In the late years of its control over the plain area, the Ching Dynasty tried to invade the mountain area but was repelled by indigenous peoples in highland battles. The Ching government named the Austronesian language–speaking peoples living in the mountain area as "raw barbarians"[1] and named their living space, where the dynasty was unable to exert its control, "barbarian land." Japanese took over Taiwan in 1895 and subordinated the "barbarian land" under the colonial control with a series of military "pacification."

After World War II, the ethnic discourse in Taiwan shifted rapidly along with changing social political context. The transition can be divided into three periods: (1) under the postwar state-led developmentalism and political authoritarianism, the dominating One Chinese Nation discourse deems all the ethnic minorities as part of Chinese nation. KMT[2] government succeeded the colonial control named the previous "raw barbarians" as "mountain compatriots." The main policy toward "mountain compatriots" is assimilation; (2) intensive social movements that burst out in the 1980s led to political democratization in Taiwan. Economic de-regularization initiated the neo-liberal regime. At the same time, the ethnic discourse turned to respect and appreciate indigenous cultures. The "mountain compatriots" are recognized as "indigenous people" in the 1994 constitutional amendment; (3) the constitutional amendment in 1997 further rectified the term "indigenous people" into "indigenous peoples," which recognizes each indigenous people as an entity. Later, the Indigenous Peoples' Basic Law passed in 2005 legalizes indigenous peoples' collective rights. The ethnic discourse shifted to the multiculturalistic approach.

Multiculturalism is the concept and practice upholding the recognition and appreciation of difference. Drawing on Mead's (1934) work that "conceptualized the development of self as a process of seeing oneself through the perspectives of the others" (Howarth and Andreouli 2012: 3), multiculturalism believes the protection of cultural minorities will not just benefit the minorities, but enrich the whole society (Taylor 1992). Since the achievement of real justice requires the efforts to redistribute resources and rectify the structural inequality, the government is responsible for institutional support and affirmative action (Young 1990). Furthermore, realizing the collective rights of ethnic groups is fulfilling the human rights of individuals in the groups, as completed human dignity includes fully respected group identity (Kymlicka 1995). Nevertheless, multiculturalism is not without its critics. Some critics argue that multiculturalistic policy usually essentializes culture and stagnates difference (Benhabib 2002, Sen 2006). Otherscriticize its ignorance of class and gender inequality (Phillips 2007). Regarding indigenous issues, it is pointed out that superficial multiculturalistic education cannot really diminish the discrimination toward indigenous ways of living, for example, hunting and whaling (Marker 2008). Cases of backlash against indigenous land claims in the United States and Canada unearth that the settler nationalist narratives legitimizing the appropriation of indigenous land is still central to the ideology of nationhood (Mackey 2005).

Aiming to scrutinize the insufficiency of multiculturalism in discoursing indigenous rights, this chapter takes the land issues as an example to: (1) retrace the social context under which multiculturalism turned into a mainstream ethnic discourse and became institutionalized in Taiwan;

(2) elaborate how multiculturalism was adopted in government's policies and implemented in the indigenous society; (3) point out the phenomena such as re-stereotyping indigenous cultures and continuously ignoring indigenous peoples' demand of self-determination; (4) analyze the power relations reflected in these phenomena. Furthermore, based upon the experience and analysis, this chapter argues that multiculturalistic discourse in Taiwan over-simplified indigenous cultures as a static status and overlooked the historical injustice. In the end, this chapter makes suggestions to further inquire about social dynamic and colonial process, so that the shortcomings of multicultur-alism can be rectified, and the real justice can be achieved.

INDIGENOUS MOVEMENTS AND THE INSTITUTIONALIZATION OF MULTICULTURALISM

1. Indigenous Peoples and Indigenous Lands

The census made by the Japanese colonial government in 1905 shows that the "barbarians" comprise about 2% to 3% of the total population in Taiwan. However, the "barbarian land" occupied more than 40% of the total area of the island with abundant resources. After the land survey and law declaration

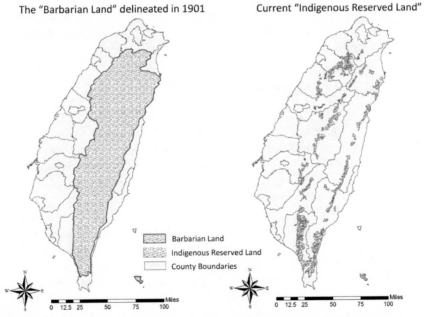

Figure 12.1 From the "Barbarian Land" to "Indigenous Reserved Land." *Source:* courtesy of the author.

along with the military pacification, the Japanese colonial government nation-alized most of the mountain and forest into state property. Only very small and fragmentary land parcels were reserved to the indigenous communities (see Figure 12.1). At the same time, many communities were forced to real-locate to low mountainous areas and shift from traditional hunting and gather-ing to fixed-location agricultural production.

After World War II, succeeding KMT government continued the Reserved Land system. Indigenous intellectuals who received modern education tried to dialog with the state and express their wish to return the land but failed. For example, in 1947, *Losin Watan*, a *Tayal* physician who received Western medical training during the colonial era, made a petition in the Provincial Legislative Assembly, with more than 100 signatures from previous residents of the settlement that were reallocated by the colonial government. However, the KMT government rejected their petition. In 1949, a group of *Tayal* high school students studying in Taipei organized an alliance and made a state-ment of "self-awareness," "self-governance," and "self-defense." The KMT government soon repressed these political expressions. *Losin Watan* and other five indigenous intellectuals were arrested and executed in 1954. The *Tayal* students were arrested and sent to jail. Under the coercion, the govern-ment implemented a series of assimilation policies including the prohibition of speaking indigenous languages in the schools. In 1960s, the government began to privatize Indigenous Reserved Land by surveying, dividing, and entitling the lands to individuals. It was part of the assimilation policies that transformed indigenous societies. There was no political opposition recorded until early 1980s, while Taiwan began its democratic reform.

2. The Indigenous Movements

Marches and protests in the urban areas organized by different social move-ments rose prosperously to challenge KMT government and its governance in 1980s, The movement striving for indigenous people's rights was one of them. Along with the enlarging gap of economic incomes between mountain and plain area, indigenous labor forces began to move to urban in 1970s. They encountered ethnic/class discriminations and human right problems because of their "Mountain Compatriot" identity, as well as their disadvantaged social-economic status. The indigenous movement in the 1980s began with accusing of racial discriminations, inhuman exploitation to indigenous labor, and the human trafficking that slaved indigenous adolescent girls in the sex industry.

The movement gradually turned to seek for an institutional solution for the problems it sees in the late 1980s. Protests rose to strive for the land rights and political autonomy. A series of "Return My Land" protests were held in 1988, 1989, and 1993. During five years, the discourse of "Return My

Land" moved from the request for additional pieces of Reserved Land to the request for a total adjustment of the relation between indigenous peoples and the state. Indigenous activists claimed indigenous sovereignty over the "traditional territories" in their statement. Another significant progress during 1990s was that the National Assembly passed the official appellation of "indigenous people" in the constitutional amendment in 1994. In 1996, the central government established the Council for Indigenous Affairs. It was a response to indigenous movement's long-term request to promote the highest office in charge of indigenous affairs from previous provincial level to the national level in the administrative body.

3. The Institutionalization of Multiculturalism and Its Influences

In the 1997 constitutional amendment, the term "indigenous people" was changed to "indigenous peoples." Furthermore, the amendment states: "The state affirms the multi-cultures. The state must take aggressive measures to conserve and develop indigenous languages and cultures." It also addresses the state's responsibility to "protect the status of indigenous peoples and their political participation according to their collective wiliness" and to "support the development of their education, communication, health, economy, land, and social welfare." This constitutional amendment is a breakthrough of the institutionalization of multiculturalism in Taiwan.

The achievement is accomplished with many reasons. The deliberation of the concept of multiculturalism can be traced back to the academic discussion of social differentiation and pluralism in 1970s. Later, it was adopted by the political opposition activists against the KMT government's political authoritarianism. The democratization from 1980s to 1990s was highly propelled by identity politics (Zhang 2006). The discourse of Taiwan as a multiethnic state legitimized the demand to modify the constitution carried on by the KMT government from China. Even though indigenous people comprise only 2% of the total population, they are significant to prove the uniqueness of Taiwanese ethnicities. As China claims Taiwan is a part of China with the consanguinity-based One Chinese Nation discourse and keeps suppressing Taiwan in the international arena, highlighting the Austronesian component of Taiwan is a way to disprove China's claim. The institutional recognition of the special status of the indigenous peoples therefore involves the Taiwan independence movement and geo-politics in a broader context.

It is not fair to oversimplify such institutional recognition as tokenism. The governmental resources redistribution underpins the destigmatization and revitalization of indigenous cultures in many aspects. For example, the Legislative Yuan passed the "Indigenous Education Act" in 1998 according to the 1997 constitutional amendment. It requires all schools must adapt multicultural perspectives and introduce indigenous histories/cultures in their curriculums. Since 2002, the Council of Indigenous Peoples[3] investigates to edit indigenous language teaching textbooks every year. By the end of 2006, 360 textbooks of 40 indigenous dialects for grade 1–9 curriculums were published and applied in the nine-year compulsory education schools (Lee 2013). Following the experience of "Integrated Community Development" projects emphasizing participatory process that the government promoted in the plain rural societies in 1990s, the Council of Indigenous Peoples launched a series of projects in 2003 to guide indigenous communities to elaborate their own development plans and provide financial funding to support these plans. These plans range from recovering traditional ceremonies, to rebuilding the vernacular architecture, to initiating local ethnic/ecological tourism business (Sun and Zhou 2009). Even though the titles of projects changed from time to time, this community-based development policy is continued. Besides, the Indigenous TV established in 2004 plays an important role for indigenous people to access media and interpret indigenous cultures. It also provides an arena for indigenous media workers to express their concerns from the indigenous perspectives (Lin 2010).

Nevertheless, there are some critiques toward the phenomena that appeared after the institutionalization. First, even though the discriminative image of indigenous peoples has been removed from the textbooks,[4] and the image of indigenous peoples seems to be more positive than before, the textbooks tend to present the stagnated cultural features of the indigenous peoples recorded in the colonial ethnographical studies[5] rather than their current struggles under the current state regime (Liao 2007). Second, the government-funded community development projects very often superficially applied the iconic cultural symbols to decorate the visible infrastructures, but ignored to empower the community to engage modern challenges (Hwang 2013). Therefore, when the governmental financial supports ended, the projects stopped as well. Third, when indigenous cultures turned to be appropriated as an important national symbol to show the cultural diversity of Taiwan to the foreigners in many occasions, indigenous peoples are still disadvantaged in the power relations of domestic politics (Mata Taiwan 2015). An obvious example is that indigenous peoples' wish to return to their traditional territories has rarely been fulfilled.

CURRENT SITUATION OF INDIGENOUS LAND RIGHTS

1. The Legal Regime

Land is essential to indigenous development, but it also has the potential to create conflicts of interest between indigenous peoples and the state.

Therefore, even though "Return My Land" was an important motivation for the indigenous movement during 1980s and 1990s, the KMT's policy toward indigenous peoples was largely devoid of recognition of indigenous land rights (Lin et al. 2008). The turning point appeared in 2000, when the presidential candidate Chen Shui-Bian of DPP[6] assumed the presidency and announced a "New Partnership Policy" as his major indigenous policy. This policy committed the government to recognizing indigenous peoples' claims of traditional territories. Consequently, it is codified in the Indigenous Peoples' Basic Law (which is another achievement of the institutionalization of multiculturalism) passed by the Legislative Yuan in 2005.

The Indigenous Peoples' Basic Law clearly defines that Indigenous Lands include current Indigenous Reserved Land and indigenous traditional territories (§2). It affirms that the government recognizes indigenous peoples' rights over the Indigenous Lands (§20). Any land development, resources utilization, ecological conservation, or academic research project over indigenous land must consult with indigenous peoples, get their prior consent or participation. In addition, the regulation limiting indigenous land and resource use must consult with indigenous peoples and get their prior consent as well (§21).

Even though the subtle processes for the claim, restoration, and management of indigenous land require further legislation (§20), many scholars and policy advocates suggested the rights over their traditional territory must be collectively owned by the indigenous communities or peoples. Different to the private ownership promoted in the indigenous societies during the privatization of Indigenous Reserved Lands during 1960s, the collective ownership emphasizes the recognition of community and people as the subject of rights. Furthermore, the rights refer to the access to utilize and manage the resources in the traditional territories but not necessary the exclusive possession (Lin 2007, Ji and Yang 2010, Yen and Chen 2011, Kuan 2014).

2. The Governmental Projects

Before the Legislative Yuan passed the Indigenous Peoples' Basic Law in 2005, the Council of Indigenous Peoples in the Executive Yuan launched an Indigenous Traditional Territory Survey Project in 2002 to fulfill the commitment of "New Partnership Policy." Through open tender, the Council of Indigenous Peoples contracted a research team of mainly geographers from different universities to conduct this nationwide project. The three-year survey integrated community maps, community participation, and computer-based GIS to identify the territories of indigenous communities.[7] Consequently, a supplementary project to confirm and enrich the results of previous survey was conducted from 2007 to 2009.

As the first large-scale community mapping action initiated by the government that tries to figure out the geographical boundaries of indigenous traditional territories, this survey accumulated precious practice experiences but also gave rise to the self-criticism from the academic participants based on these experiences. They acknowledged the uneven power relations between the government, research team, and the community members; they also noticed that modern mapping tools might misinterpret and even undermine indigenous concept of territory (Ishigaki Naoki 2005, Tsai et al. 2006, Lin et al. 2008, Kuan and Lin 2008). However, clear geographical boundaries seem to be needed for the realization of indigenous territorial rights in the modern administrative logic. The effort to bridge the gap between indigenous concept and the state regime is therefore especially important.

The Beech Event in the *Smangus* settlement of *Tayal* people that happened in 2006 showed the importance. Following a settlement meeting, three young men from the *Smangus* settlement brought back a wind-fallen beech tree lying on the road to their village. Soon afterward they were interrogated by the forest police and accused of stealing state property according to the Forest Law. These three young men refused to admit their guilt in stealing state property with strong support from the whole *Smangus* settlement, even though the judge intended to settle the case on the lenient side at the first trial. The defendants insisted they were realizing the territorial right according to the Indigenous Peoples' Basic Law passed in 2005. After a long process of lawsuit, the high court revised its judgment and announced these three young men not guilty. This is a groundbreaking case because it was the first time that indigenous territorial rights were recognized by the judicial system. Such a success was achieved by subjective efforts from the *Smangus* settlement, the support from indigenous NGOs, environmental groups, and also the testimony from the academic workers. In the court, one geographer who participated in the Indigenous Traditional Territory Survey Project was subpoenaed as a professional witness. He proved that, according to the *Tayal* tradition, *Smangus* settlement actually has the rights over the region where the wind-fallen beech was located (Lin 2010).

Ever since, the result of the territorial survey and the knowledge learned in the survey process were no longer simply academic data, but possible interface for the dialog between the state and the indigenous communities. Indigenous societies urged the government to publish all the results of the survey conducted in the past few years so that the government's resource management bureaus, such as the Forest Bureau, can recognize indigenous peoples' traditional territories according to it (Zhong and Hwang 2010). Eventually, the result is published in an exhibition held by the Council of Indigenous Peoples in 2011.

3. The Unsettled Conflicts

The publication nevertheless did not work as it was expected. Table 12.1 demonstrate examples of significant land conflicts between the state and indigenous peoples. These events relate to different indigenous peoples, but they all happened over indigenous traditional territories. Some conflicts began prior to 2005, when the Indigenous Peoples' Basic Law was passed. The others occurred after it. Notably, conflicts still happened after the publication of survey result in 2011. Most of the conflicts are unsettled because the government bureaus refuse to consult indigenous communities about the governmental development projects, or deny indigenous people's rights to access the resources.

How could this happen after the institutionalization of indigenous territorial rights in the Indigenous Peoples' Basic Law? There are mainly three aspects of debate, and these debates reveal the reasons.

The first aspect of debate focuses on the incomplete legislation. The government bureaus usually didn't deny indigenous peoples rights over traditional territories since the rights are affirmed in the articles of the law.

Table 12.1   Examples of Land Conflict between the State and Indigenous Peoples

No.	Indigenous Peoples Involved in	Event	Year
1	Truku	Anti-Asia Cement Company	1973
2	Paiwan	JinLun Hot Springs BOT case	1999
3	Amis, Tayal, Kavalan	Mt. Fortress Scenic Area	2002
4	Tsou	Community Leader honey events	2004
5	Amis	Beautiful Bay Resort	2004
6	Truku	Tianxiang Recreation Area development project	2004
7	Tsou	Alishan BOT case	2005
8	Tayal	Smangus Beech Wood event	2005
9	Amis	Hualien Fenglin leisure resort park development project	2005
10	Thao	Ita-ThauTourism Culture Park BOT case	2006
11	Thao	Sun Moon Lake Xiangshan Hotels BOT case	2009
12	Amis	Taitung Sanxiantai Hotels district case	2009
13	Amis	Forest Recreation Park event	2011
14	Amis	Baosheng Aquatic Recreation Area development project	2011
15	Amis	Dulan Nose Recreation Area BOT case	2011
16	Tayal	Anti-Tkatay Dam case	2012
17	Amis,Puyuma	Taitung City sixth, tenth Cemetery Re-interment	2012
18	Sediq	Mei-Fengnong Farm case	2013
19	Bunun	NTU Experimental Forest cases	2014
20	Tayal	Stacis Water Rights dispute	2014
21	Truku	Tongmen Community closing off the road	2014

However, these bureaus often argued that they are not sure about where indigenous traditional territories are. According to the Indigenous Peoples' Basic Law, the branch law for the claim, restoration, and management of indigenous land should be legislated in three years.[8] But the legislation of this branch law is not yet completed at the time of writing this chapter. For those who assert immediate realization of indigenous territorial rights, the delay of consequent legislation should not be an excuse to violate the rights already affirmed. However, it is actually often used an excuse by the administrative system.

The second aspect of the debate is in relation to the departmentalism. The forest lands administered by the Forest Bureau highly overlap indigenous traditional territories, because most "national forests" were in fact indigenous peoples' living spaces nationalized by the colonizers and succeeded by the postwar government. If the exact obstacle for the realization of indigenous territorial rights is the incomplete legislation as many government bureaus, including the Forest Bureau, claimed, then accelerating the legislative process should be the solution of the problem. However, the Forest Bureau is very reluctant and self-defensive to the discussion of the branch law during negotiations in the administrative system. More than once, the officers of Forest Bureau expressed their concern of losing control over the forests that will decrease the necessity of the existence of Forest Bureau.

The third aspect of the debate explains the underlying reason of the reluctance. Considering itself as the guardian of national property, the Forest Bureau very often expresses its worry about the forest degradation once the indigenous traditional territories are returned to indigenous peoples (Shi and Wu 2008). Such a discourse implies that indigenous people will over-exploit the forest without the state regulation, and it further situates indigenous people against public interest. It seems very outdated and controversial to the multiculturalistic thinking. But the distrust of indigenous peoples' ability for ecological conservation and the highlighting of indigenous peoples' traditional ecological knowledge are very often two sides of one coin.

A relevant discussion over the legitimization of indigenous people's hunting activities began in 2004 explicates the relation between these two seemly opposite points of view. Hunting is continually practiced in the indigenous societies, even though the Forest Law set severe regulations for indigenous people to enter the national forest lands. In the 1980s, Taiwan established the national park system and started to ban the hunting and gathering activities in the parks.[9] Meanwhile, the legislation of the Wildlife Conservation Act set up further prohibitions. It became one of the laws most frequently violated by indigenous people (Wang 2007). In 2004, an experimental project was implemented to open a certain area to *Bunun* indigenous people in a certain period of time for their hunting activities, after the revises of the Wildlife Conservation Act earlier in the same year. This project soon caused fierce disputes. The supporters believed it is a progress to respect indigenous traditional cultures (Chen 2005, Wu 2005, Liou 2005). The opponents argued that indigenous peoples' traditional hunting cultures might be ecological friendly, but market economy and modern hunting tools have undermined the traditional hunting cultures. It will be an ecological disaster once the bans are removed (Life Conservationist Association 2004, Lai 2015, Shi 2005). The disputes brought up further delicate discussion of the possibility for community-based conservation (Lu 2005, Yen and Kuan 2005). However, the controversy is not ceased. In 2013, a media conference held by animal protection groups accusing some indigenous ceremonies of animal abuse once again caused the disputes (Yang 2013). Furthermore, indigenous hunters constantly get arrested and convicted in the courts as their shotguns are too "modern." Legitimizing the resource rights by highlighting the ecological superiority of traditional cultures indeed provides indigenous peoples a position in the conservation politics, but it also very often re-stereotypes indigenous cultures and gets challenged when indigenous people appear not so "traditional" anymore.

From the indigenous perspectives, improving the tools for hunting does not mean unlimited slaughter. The ethics of hunting are tied to the management of hunting fields embedded with lineage or other social relations, but not the tools people use. Stereotyped and fragmental understanding of indigenous cultures, however, lead to the focus on tools superficially. Thus, there is still a huge gap between the institutionalization of indigenous rights and the mainstream society's trust. This is exactly the profound factor that makes the congress unable to reach the consensus to pass the branch law 10 years after the Indigenous Peoples' Basic Law was passed.

ANALYSIS AND DISCUSSION

1. Utilitarianism and Cultural Diversity

As Marker (2008) pointed out in his study of racist backlash against the Makah tribe in North American for their whale hunting, superficial multiculturalism education sustains the persistence of injustice. In Taiwan, comparing to previous assimilation policy, the multiculturalism education in school is relatively a progress. However, in the history text books, indigenous peoples appear in the precolonial history and disappear from the construction of contemporary society. Their festivals are celebrated, but their struggles are invisible. It is criticized for both fragmentizing indigenous cultures, and avoiding the presentation of historical conflicts (Leu 2000, Chen 2006, Tsai 2006, Zhang 2008, Shu 2008, Wei 2012).

The fragmental understanding of indigenous cultures is also reflected in mainstream society's utilitarian thinking of cultural diversity. Under the multiculturalistic discourse that emphasizes benefit and harmony, indigenous peoples in Taiwan constantly have to prove the beauty, wisdom, and usefulness of their cultures. In other words, the cultures that seem "useless" are then unworthy of conservation or even need to be removed. The debate over hunting right is a significant example. Similar to the Makah whaling case, Taiwan indigenous peoples' hunting activities are stigmatized as brutal and outdated, since they are not in accordance with mainstream expectation. The returning of traditional territory is even more difficult, as it might conflict the interests of current land use. Therefore, to compare with the government's increasing investment in the representation of indigenous music, dance, language, and art, the progress of indigenous territorial rights is almost stagnated. The stagnancy reflects the seesaw battle for the readjustment of power relations in the legal and political institutions, as well as the space for self-interpretation.

2. Public Interest and Historical Justice

The utilitarian approach of multiculturalism in Taiwan makes the mainstream society ask "Will the realization of indigenous rights reduce public interest?" or "How can it benefit the whole society?," but forget to ask "What have been taken away from the indigenous peoples?" The discussion of public interest turns out to be superficial without looking into the historical injustice. Like many other settler countries in the world, the acquirement of the Taiwanese national territory that sustains the nationhood is based on the colonial invasion. Indigenous land claims therefore challenge the settler narratives that selectively erase indigenous peoples from the history. The fundamental tension behind it is similar to what Mackey (2005) revealed in her study of US and Canadian cases. The argument of violation of public interest implicitly excludes indigenous peoples from the "public."

Therefore, the clue to reconcile such tension is not to ignore the history of conflict, but to conceptualize a more inclusive "public." What already happened in the history can't be started over. However, the way a state faces its history decides its future. The realization of indigenous land rights is the core of the restoration of historical justice. It should not be seen as a violation to public interest. Instead, it is enhancing the public interest by carrying out the value of justice.

3. Dynamic Transition and Heterogeneity

Representing the positive image and praising the beauty of indigenous cultures are necessary steps for destigmatization, as indigenous cultures were depreciated as inferior and backward in the mono-ethnic nationalism discourse. The institutional investment to revitalize indigenous cultures is necessary as well, since the state is responsible for the harm it did to these cultures. However, as criticized, the top-down approach will easily re-stereotype indigenous cultures into a static status. In the example of indigenous land issue, the debates surrounding whether indigenous peoples have lost their traditions to maintain the ecological balance is ideologically freezing indigenous cultures in certain space and time.

It is undeniable that indigenous societies in Taiwan are largely integrated with the market economy and state politics. The real world situations in the indigenous societies are therefore far more complicated than what have been recorded in the colonial ethnography. Facing the fact that indigenous cultures are changing does not undermine the legitimacy for indigenous peoples' to return to their traditional territories. Since culture is dynamic and the ecological knowledge is adaptively evolving in the interaction between human and their environment, it is more than reasonable for indigenous peoples to re-engage the environment and develop their ways of sustainable living based on contemporary conditions. Prohibiting indigenous peoples from accessing the resources over their traditional territories with the argument that indigenous peoples have lost their abilities to take care of the environment is a tautological mistake. If the argument sustains, it ignores the fact that loss of such abilities begins with the loss of access to the resources.

On the other hand, the ways indigenous communities integrate with the market economy and state politics differ from place to place. The *Smangus* settlement of *Tayal* people established a cooperative system, according to their interpretation of tradition, to share the labors and distribute the benefits from the eco-tourism business they run collectively. The *Rukai* people in Wu-Tai organized a forest patrolling troop to contribute their understandings of the forest and work with scientists to monitor the environment change. The Hunter School created in the *Lalaulan* settlement of *Paiwan* people plays the role to pass on the old hunters' knowledge to younger generations and also educate the visitors. These cases show different strategies but they are all subjective efforts to adapt to the changes. The real world situations in the indigenous societies are far more complicated than simply loss their traditions.

CONCLUSION

Taiwan indigenous peoples' inferior status under the assimilation policy underpinned by the mono-ethnic nationalism has been changed since the rise of multiculturalism in the society. The institutionalization of indigenous rights in 1990s was a landmark of the transition. The consequent policies to invest in the positive representation of indigenous cultures are needed to rectify previous mistakes of assimilation, but also very often over-simplified indigenous cultures as a static status. The utilitarian approach without looking into the historical injustice will wrongly place indigenous peoples in opposition to the public interest, especially in dealing with the land issues. These experiences in Taiwan are calling more attentions to the inquiry of social dynamic and colonial process. They are also calling more attentions to avoid re-stereotyping indigenous cultures.

Furthermore, though the struggles of new immigrants (especially those who migrated to Taiwan through marriage after 1980s) seem irrelevant to indigenous rights, the lessons learned from the indigenous issue can actually provide inspiration to advance the discussion. As the power of state can redistribute resources to sustain indigenous cultures but also re-stereotype them, the immigration policy needs to be aware of same effect. It requires further empowerment for new immigrants to interpret their cultures beneath the formal legal arrangement. In so doing, the new immigrants will gradually be able to redefine the meaning of law and turns out redefining their own life, as Liao in this volume expects.

Most importantly, the concern of justice with a long-term perspectives looking into injustice past and seeking for a more inclusive future should also be applied to the newest comers of this island. Shin and Kawabata in this volume reveal the complicated historical contexts of Zainechi in Japan and Hwagyo in Korea. Both of them are reminding the importance to review the history that forms the structural reasons of present injustice.

In general, pointing out the shortcomings of multiculturalism does not mean to underestimate its overall contributions. After all, the diversity recognized and the forces released are just the motivation of continual seeking for further progress. In this sense, the unsettle conflicts raised in this chapter do not refer to the failure of multiculturalism. Instead, they represent the opportunity to deepen the discourse, strengthen the practice and realize the justice.

NOTES

1. There was another group of Austronesian languages–speaking peoples lived in the plain area categorized as "cooked barbarians" as they had been administrated by and paid tax to the Ching Dynasty. These "cooked barbarians" were registered during the Japanese colonial era, but lost their special status in the official registration system after World War II.

2. Kuomintang, the Chinese Nationalist Party.

3. The previous "Council for Indigenous Affairs" renamed to distinguish the recognition of indigenous "Peoples'" status in 2002.

4. For example, a story of a heroic Han-Chinese settler Wu-Fong who sacrificed himself to be killed by the "barbarian" Tso people and eventually stopped Tso people's barbarian head hunting practice was told in the textbooks of elementary school.

However, According to Tso people's oral history, Wu-Fong was a trader killed by Tso people because of his cheating to the Tso people. This fabricated heroic story is therefore a Chauvinistic interpretation of history upholding the superior Han-Chinese in contrast to the backward indigenous people who need to be civilized. This story was removed from the textbook after a series of protests against it in 1980s.

5. As the earliest and most systematic records, the ethnography of indigenous societies surveyed in Japanese colonial era is very often deemed as the authentic features of indigenous cultures.

6. The Democratic Progressive Party.

7. By the end of the third year survey, approximately 464 indigenous communities belonging to 12 different tribes located in 55 villages were mapped. About 3,700 native place names in indigenous languages were recorded along with folk stories, myths, and oral tales attached (Zhang et al. 2004).

8. It means the branch law need to be legislated by 2009, since the Indigenous Peoples' Basic Law is passed in 2005.

9. The Legislative Yuan passed the National Park Act in 1972. So far, there are nine national parks in Taiwan. Within the nine national parks, three are located in the indigenous peoples' traditional territories. The area of these three parks covers more than 80% of the total land area of the nine national parks.

REFERENCES

Chen, S. C. 2006. "Duo yuan wen hua lun zai guo zhong she hui xue xi ling yu li shi jiao xue shang de ying yong—yi tai wan shi jiao ke shu zhong you guan yuan zhu min de lun shu wei li [Apply pluralism in the field of social learning and historical teaching of secondary education—a case study of Indigenous-People-relevant discourses in textbook of Taiwan history]." Master's thesis, National Taiwan Normal University.

Chen, Y. L. 2015. "Qu chu shou lie wen hua pian jian cai shi zun zhong sheng ming [Dispelling prejudices of hunting culture is showing the real respect for life]," Accessed April 12. http://e-info.org.tw/node/1256

Howarth, C. and Andreouli, E. 2012. "'Has Multiculturalism Failed?' The Importance of Lay Knowledge and Everyday Practice." Accessed April 6, 2016. https://lse.academia.edu/CarolineHowarth/Papers.

Hsu, Y. C. 2008. "Zhan hou tai wan guo (chu) zhong li shi jiao ke shu de yan bian (1948–2007)—yi tai wan shi jiao cai wei zhong xin [The Development of Postwar History Textbook in Junior High School in Taiwan, 1948~2007—Focused on Taiwan History]." Master's thesis, National Chung Hsing University.

Huang, Y. H. 2013. "Duo chong bian jie de mo chu chong xie: tai wan yuan zhu min zu chuan tong ling yu quan di jing de bian dong [Multiple Boundaries as Palimpsests: The Shifting Landscapes of Native Land Rights in Taiwan]." PhD diss., National Dong Hwa University.

Ishigaki, N. 2005. "'Bu luo di tu' diao cha zhi xing si: yi bu nong zu zhi nei ben lu diao cha wei li [Reflections on Community Mapping Researches: A Case of the Laipunuk Research by the Bunun]." *Journal of Eastern Taiwan Studies*, 10: 37–62.

Ji, J. J. and Yang, M. H. 2010. "Yuan zhu min zu chuan tong ling yu wen ti fen xi yu jian yi [The Analyses and Suggestions toward the issue of Indigenous Traditional Territory]," in *Tai wan yuan zhu min zheng ce bian qian yu she hui fa zhan [Government Policy and Social Development among Taiwanese Indigenous Peoples]*, edited by Huang, S. M. and Zhang, Y. H., 461–93. Taipei: Institute of Ethnology Academia Sinica Press.

Kuan, D. W. and Lin. Y. R. 2008. "Shen me chuan tong? Shei de ling yu?: cong tai ya zu ma li guang liu yu de chuan tong ling yu jing yan tan kong jian zhi shi de zhuan yi [What Tradition? Whose Territory?: A Critical Review to the Indigenous Traditional Territory Survey and the Translation of Spatial Knowledge in Marqwang Case, Taiwan]." *Journal of Archaeology and Anthropology*, 69: 109–42.

Kuan, D. W. 2014. "Yuan zhu min zu tu di quan de tiao zhan: cong yi ge dang dai bao liu di jiao yi de qu yu yan jiu tan qi [Challenges for the Realization of Indigenous Land Rights in Contemporary Taiwan: A Regional Study of Indigenous Reserved Land Trade between Indigenous and Non-indigenous People]." *Journal of Archaeology and Anthropology*, 80: 7–52.

Kymlicka, Will. 1995. *Multicultural Citizenship: A Liberal Theory of Minority Rights*. Oxford: Oxford University Press.

Lai, B. Z. 2015. "Wo dui lin wu ju ping gu kai fang dan da zuo wei shou lie qu de kan fa [My Personal Perspectives about the Forest Bureau evaluates to open Dan-Da as a hunting area]." Accessed April 6, 2016. http://e-info.org.tw/node/2299.

Leu, J. Y. 2000. "Guo xiao she hui ke jiao ke shu zhong yuan zhu min nei han zhi fen xi yan jiu [The Study of Analyzing the Aboriginal Content in the Elementary Social Studies Textbooks]." Master's thesis, National Taiwan Normal University, 2000.

Li, T. Y. 2013. "Tai wan yuan zhu min zu yu yan de shu mian hua li cheng [The Literation of Taiwanese Aboriginal Languages]." PhD diss., National Cheng Chi University.

Liao, M. J. 2007. "Guo min xiao xue she hui ke jiao ke shu zhong de yuan zhu min zu xing xiang yan jiu [The Study of Images of Indigenous Peoples in Elementary School Social Studies Textbooks]." Master's thesis, National Taipei University of Education.

Life Conservationist Association. 2015. "Can bao bu ren jie ze er yu fan dui 'kai fang dan da shou lie' [Such a Brutal Behavior and Eventually Leads to Resource Exhaustion—Oppose Against Opening Dan-Da as a Hunting Area]." Accessed April 6, 2016. http://www.lca.org.tw/column/node/25.

Lin, F. Y. 2010. "You 'ta zhe' zhuan xiang 'wo qun' – yuan zhu min dian shi tai chuan bo zhu ti xing shi jian zhi tan tao [Changes 'We Group' by 'the Others': The Practice of the Indigenous Peoples' Subjectivity in Taiwan Indigenous Television]." *Taiwan Journal of Indigenous Studies*, 3(2): 131–62.

Lin, S. Y. 2007. "Jie/ Chong gou tai wan yuan zhu min zu tu di zheng ce [De-/Reconstructing the Land Policies for Indigenous Peoples in Taiwan]." PhD diss., National Taiwan University.

Lin. Y. R. 2015. "Smangus wu zui pan jue de chi shi [The revelation of the not guilty verdict in the Smangus Beech Tree Incident]." Accessed April 6, 2016. http://blog.yam.com/smangus/article/27068759.

Lin, Y. R., Icyeh, L., and Kuan, T. W. 2007. "Indigenous Language Informed Participatory Policy in Taiwan: A Socio-Political Perspective," in *Documenting and Revitalizing Austronesian Languages*, edited by D. V. Rau and M. Florey, 134–61. Hawai'i: University of Hawai'i Press.

Liu, J. X. 2005. "Guo xin nian da lie ji [Indigenous People's Traditional New Year-the Mangayau Ceremony of Puyuma People]." *United Daily News*, January 17.

Lu, D. J. 2005. "Zong jiao tuan ti yu bao yu tuan ti yi yi duo yuan kai fang de tai du lai tao lun yuan zhu min de shou lie [Religious and Conservation Groups Should Adopt a Diverse and Open Attitude to Discuss Indigenous Hunting]." Accessed April 6, 2016. http://e-info.org.tw/node/1219.

Lu, D. J., Que, H. J., Huang, S. J., Lin, H. Z., and Wang, Z. R. 2011. "She qu pei li yu zi yuan bao yu: wo guo she qu lin ye zheng ce ping xi [Community Empowerment and Resource Conservation: Reviewing the Community Forestry Policy in Taiwan]." *The Taiwanese Political Science Review*, 15(1): 137–204.

Mackey, Eva. 2005. "Universal Rights in Conflict: 'Backlash' and 'Benevolent Resistance' to Indigenous Land Rights." *Anthropology Today*, 21(2): 14–20.

Mead, George Herbert. 1934. *Mind, Self, and Society from the Standpoint of a Social Behaviourist*. Chicago: University of Chicago Press.

Parod, I., (eds.). 2008. *Tai wan yuan zhu min zu yun dong shi liao hui bian [Documentary Collection on the Indigenous in Taiwan]*. Taipei: Academia Historica Press.

Shi Z. F. and Wu, P. Y. 2008. "Yuan zhu min zu yu zi ran zi yuan de gong guan [Indigenous Peoples and Co-management of Natural Resources]." *Taiwan Journal of Indigenous Studies*, 1(1): 1–38.

Shi, Z. H. 2005. "Shao le 'ai jin wu xi' zhi qing [Lost the Sense of Empathy]." *Liberty Times*, January 20.

Snayian. 2005. "Tong xue a, ni men ji zhe guo ji jiao liu qian, you mei you xian yong xin zuo hao 'guo nei jiao liu' [Students, Please Remember to Communicate with Domestic Ethnic Groups before Rush to International Exchange and Cooperation]." Accessed April 4, 2016. http://www.pure-taiwan.info/2015/03/19/dont-consume-indigenous-cultures/

Sun, D. C. and Zhou, H. M. 2009. *"Yuan zhu min bu luo yong xu fa zhan ji hua' ping gu yan xi [The Research and Analysis toward Indigenous people Sustainable Development Plan]."* Taipei: Research, Development and Evaluation Commission, Executive Yuan.

Taylor, Charles. 1992. *Multiculturalism and "the Politics of Recognition."* New Jersey: Princeton University Press.

Tsai, Y. C. 2006. "Cong duo yuan wen hua jiao yu guan dian lun guo zhong she hui xue xi ling yu jiao ke shu zhong zhi yuan zhu min zu qun ne rong [The study of analyzing the aboriginal context in junior high school social studies textbooks]." Master's Thesis, National Taiwan Normal University.

Wang, H. Y. 2007. "Wen hua chong tu yu tai wan yuan zhu min fan zui kun jing zhi tan tao [The Cultural Conflicts and the Criminal Dilemma of Taiwanese Indigenous People]." *National Taiwan University Law Review*, 36(3): 255–304.

Wei, W. R. 2012. "Yi duo yuan wen hua jiao yu guan tan tao guo zhong she hui xue xi ling yu jiao ke shu zhong guan yu yuan zhu min zu zhi nei rong

[Indigenous-People- relevant discourses in the textbooks of social learning field of secondary education –a study on from pluralism Perspective]." *E-Soc Journal*, 103. Accessed April 5, 2016. http://society.nhu.edu.tw/e-j/103/a2.htm.

Wu, P. C. 2005. "Zhi shi xie xing yu ye man? Yuan zhu min shou lie de she hui sheng huo yi han [Beyond Cruelty and Savage-The Social and Cultural Context of Indigenous hunting]." Accessed April 15, 2016. http://e-info.org.tw/node/1499.

Yang, S. M. 2013. *"Shou lie bian diao cheng ling nüe dong wu da shang guan guang [Hunting Turns to the abuse of animals, hurts tourism as well]."* *CNA News*, May 12. Accessed April 15, 2016. http://www.cna.com.tw/news/first-news/201305020025–1.aspx.

Yen, A. C. and Chen, T. Y. 2011 "Yuan zhu min chuan tong ling yu gong tong guan li zhi yan jiu: yi xin zhu xian jian shi xiang tai ya zu bu luo wei li [The Study on Co-management of Indigenous Traditional Territory: Cases Study of Atayal Communities in Jianshin Township, Hsinchu County, Taiwan]." *Journal of Geographical Science*, 61: 1–30.

Yen, A. C. and Kuan, D. W. 2005. "'Fan dui' yu 'kai fang' shou lie zhi jian de di san tiao lu [Te Third Path between Opening and Forbidding Hunting]." Accessed April 5, 2016. http://e-info.org.tw/node/1511.

Young, Iris Marion. 1990. *Justice and the Politics of Difference*. New Jersey: Princeton University Press.

Zhang, C. Y., Cai, B. W., Liu, J. X., Wang, M. H., Lin, Y. R., and Ni, J. C., et al. 2004. *"Yuan zhu min zu chuan tong ling yu tu di diao cha yan jiu bao gao [The Survey Report of Indigenous Traditional Territory]."* Taipei: Council of Indigenous Peoples, Executive Yuan.

Zhang, E. M. 2008. "Xian xing guo min xiao xue she hui xue xi ling yu jiao ke shu zhong guan yu yuan zhu min nei rong zhi yan jiu [A case study of Indigenous-People- relevant discourses in the textbooks of social learning field in present primary education]." Master's thesis, National Taiwan Normal University.

Zhang, M. G. 2002. "Duo yuan zhu yi, duo yuan wen hua lun shu zai tai wan de xing cheng yu nan ti [The Formation and Problems of Pluralism and Multiculturalism Discourse in Taiwan]," in *Tai wan de wei lai [Taiwan's Future]*, edited by Xue, T. D., 223–73. Taipei: Hwa Tai Publishing Co. Ltd.

Zhang, M. G. 2006. "Tai wan zu qun he jie de kan ke lu [The Dilemma of Taiwan Ethnic Groups' Reconciliation]," in *The Cultural Discourse of National Identity*, edited by Shi, Z. F., 43–82. Taipei: Taiwan International Studies Association.

Zhang, M. G. 2008. "Duo yuan wen hua zhu yi zai tai wan yu qi kun jing [Multiculturalism and It's Dilemma in Taiwan]," in *zhi shi fen zi de xing si yu dui hua [Intellectuals' Introspections and Dialogues among them]*, edited by Shen, X. Q., 310–25. Taipei: China Times Culture and Education Foundation.

Zhong, L. H. and Huang, W. Z. 2010. "Yuan min yao gong gao chuan tong ling yu [Indigenous people proclaims their Indigenous Traditional Territory]." *Liberty Times*, January 21. Accessed April 5, 2016. http://news.ltn.com.tw/news/life/paper/367926.

Chapter 13

Living in Love and Hate

Transforming Representations and Identities
of Zainichi Koreans in Contemporary Japan

Kohei Kawabata

MULTICULTURAL POLITICS IN JAPAN
AND ZAINICHI KOREANS

Civil movements by Zainichi Koreans (Korean residents in Japan) against discrimination in urban ethnic communities established the foundation of the multicultural politics in Japan by the early 1990s. Zainichi Koreans were the largest ethnic group in Japan until 2007, and they are the permanent ethnic Korean residents of Japan who trace their roots to Korean peninsula during Japanese imperial rule, distinguishing them from those who came to Japan after the 1980s. The official multicultural policy of *Tabunka Kyosei* (multicultural co-living) has been promoted at both national and local administrative levels since the mid-2000s. However, it is critically argued that the official policy tends to focus on issues of newly arrived immigrants, and issues concerning the "old-comers" including Zainichi Koreans are mostly forgotten.

Meanwhile, the 2002 Japan-Korea World Cup and the subsequent Korean Wave have presented Zainichi Koreans from a rather "cosmetic" angle, and Korean ethnic images and identities have become much more visible in consuming space and discourse. Yet, on the reverse side of the same coin, the former prime minister Koizumi's visit to North Korea and its confession of involvement in the kidnapping of Japanese citizens in 2002 invoked bashing against North Korean Zainichi communities in Japan, and the Anti-Korean Wave and street and cyberspace hate demonstrations by the Citizens against Zainichi Special Privileges reveals continuing racist perceptions of Zainichi Koreans.

Under these conditions, their former ethnic enclaves are breaking down. Many of them acquire Japanese nationality and most of them marry Japanese. Indeed, they are literally becoming invisible in the statistical sense, even though they are still living everyday lives between the official multicultural policy and philiac/phobic public images. Therefore, based on a critical analysis of the implications of transforming representations of Zainichi Koreans at the political and public levels, this chapter attempts to clarify such invisible yet transforming hybrid identities through examining their everyday practices. To do this, I analyze interview data relating to Zainichi Koreans who grew up in suburban areas under individualized conditions.

First, this chapter gives an overview of the historical transition of multicultural activities from the grassroots activities in the urban ethnic communities to official multicultural policy led by the Japanese government, focusing on the discontinuity between these two phenomena. Second, it discusses transformations in and discontinuities between the identities of young Zainichi Koreans in the media, focusing on positive representations after the Korean Wave of the 2000s. Third, it critically examines the backlash and hate speech against Zainichi Koreans, which was the reverse side of the same wave. Fourth, it examines the transformation of their identities and such positive/negative representations by focusing on the identities of young Zainichi Koreans in their everyday practices, lived as they are becoming invisible in a double sense in the context of declining identity politics and the rise of neoliberalism. In order for us to reimagine multicultural realties in contemporary Japan and its hybrid natures, this chapter examines hybrid identities of "daburu," or double Zainichi Koreans, who have both Japanese and Korean backgrounds. Overall, this chapter proposes the necessity of reconsidering the official multicultural policy in Japan by critically looking at the scene from the perspective of the everyday multicultural practices.

GRASSROOTS PRACTICES TO THE OFFICIAL MULTICULTURAL POLICY

The term *Tabunka Kyosei* spread to society and local governments all over Japan in 2006 as a result of the implementation of the Multicultural Coexistence Promotion Plan by the Ministry of Internal Affairs and Communications. In order to deal with an increase in the number of foreign residents,[1] or so-called "newcomers," the multicultural policy stated that "the people whose nationality and ethnicity are different shall respect each other's differences through establishing equal relationships, and living together as a member of local communities." In particular, it focused on support for communication, living, and building multicultural communities.

However, the program is mostly oriented toward the initial settlement of newly arriving residents through language and residential support, and it almost ignores the foreign residents from the colonial era, or so-called "old-comers," including Zainichi Koreans. Therefore, it lacks the perspective of cultural hybridity and the evolving multicultural conditions of Japan as a host society for more than one hundred years. Such perceptions also reveal a lack of recognition of the fact that the discourse and practice of *Tabunka Kyosei* has been embraced through grassroots activities by Zainichi Koreans.

The term is the mixture of two different concepts *Tabunka* (multicultural) and *Kyosei* (co-living). According to Takezawa, *Tabunka* is derived from *Tabunka Shugi*, the translation of multiculturalism. The other term *Kyosei* or co-living has been used since the 1970s with reflexive implications toward modernity, especially referencing environmental issues and human rights issues. The term originally appeared in the Mainichi Shimbun on January 12, 1993, in an article about an international forum on development education held in Kawasaki city, which is known as an area with a high concentration of Zainichi Koreans. It was the establishment of the nonprofit organization group *Tabunka Kyosei Sentaa* (Center for Multicultural Information and Assistance) that entrenched this term. This organization was established to support foreign residents right after the Great Hanshin-Awaji Earthquake in 1995, which caused severe damage to the area where large Zainichi Koreans and Vietnamese communities were located (Takezawa 2011: 3). In order to understand the overall scheme of *Tabunka Kyosei* in Japan, we must first examine the concept of *Kyosei*, which had been embraced through the practices of identity politics by citizens after the 1970s.

The term *Kyosei* was originally used in the field of natural science and applied to social and human relations after the 1970s. It is important to note that the term implies a reflexive attitude toward the unintended results of rapid economic growth and modernity after World War II. For example, Hanazaki Kohei, a philosopher and activist who has written books and articles on Ainu issues, reflects about how he started to use the term *Kyosei* in 1978 in the context of identity politics claims by Ainu people in Hokkaido as follows.

> I recalled the Ainu fishermen who fought against the construction of the Date thermal power plant at Usu beach in Date city along the Funkawan bay, and the philosophy of the Ainu people carried on by Shigeru Kayano, who represented the Ainu people as a member of the House of Councilors, inspired by walking the sites of citizen's movements in Sanrizuka, Shibushiwan bay, Amami-Ooshima islands, and Kinwan bay in Okinawa as follows. "It seems to be that we have passed the point of no return regarding how our lives today are saddled with a civilization heavily dependent on oil. Meanwhile, by finding ourselves stricken by the sense of a lack of peace in our souls, we may gradually realize that we are attracted to a way of living that does 'not worship material civilization and indulgence.'" (Hanazaki 2002: 128–29)

Hanazaki's idea of "co-living with nature" in the late 1970s later developed into the "ethics of co-living." In his book titled *Identitii to kyosei no tetsugaku*

(Identity and the Philosophy of co-living), he pointed out how the ethics of *Kyosei* had been embraced through the identity politics practices of various actors, including Buraku people, handicapped people, women, Zainichi Koreans, and so on after the 1970s (Hanazaki 1993, 2002: 130).

As Hanazaki mentioned, the grassroots activities by Zainichi Koreans in urban ethnic communities led to cooperation with local governments by 1970, when Japan's high economic growth period almost ended. Indeed, this era of cooperation between Zainichi Koreans and local governments can be regarded as the formative period of Japanese multiculturalism. For example, Kawasaki city in Kanagawa prefecture started their early multicultural attempts based around the Sakuramoto area, where Zainichi Koreans had organized an ethnic education group for their children. Sakuramoto Preschool was established by the Korean Christian church in 1969 and *Seikyusha*, a social welfare corporation recognized by the Japanese government was set up in 1973. During the 1970s, particularly after Park Jong-seok's court case against Hitachi Corporation's discriminatory employment practices, Zainichi Koreans around the Kawasaki area started to negotiate with local government regarding the ethnic discrimination against them. Eventually, they succeeded in the establishment of the "Policy for Education of Foreign Residents in Kawasaki," which was primarily aimed at the education of Zainichi Koreans in 1986. Furthermore, the community hall *Fureaikan* was established to be a center for ethnic education for Zainichi Korean children by Kawasaki city, and it has been managed by Seikyusha (Shiobara 2011: 68–69).

Meanwhile, an organization for Zainichi Korean children's education was also established at the Takatsuki 6th Junior High School in Osaka prefecture by 1970. Some Zainichi Korean youth (14–18 years old) who had previously been receiving ethnic education became involved in the establishment of the *Takatsuki Mukugeno kai* (Takatsuki Rose of Sharon Group). The teachers of the Takatsuki 6th Junior High School and the Takatsuki City Teachers' Union supported the formation of this group, which was able to receive a grant from the Takatsuki board of education in 1972 and 1973. In 1985, the local board of education decided to recognize the group's activities as one of its official projects. Furthermore, this group negotiated with Takatsuki city to scrap the Japanese nationality requirement to be a Takatsuki civil servant, and succeeded in its abolition in 1980 (Kim 1999: 137–39).

Multicultural practices based on identity politics since the 1970s in the urban ethnic communities conducted by associations such as *Fureaikan* and *Takatsuki Mukugeno Kai* established the foundation for today's multicultural environments in Japan. However, it must be noted that the strategic essentialism that the identity politics of Zainichi Koreans were based on also involved a dilemma. On the one hand, the erosion of urban ethnic communities, the diversification of identities among the younger generations, the increasing numbers of Zainichi Koreans who acquired Japanese nationality and who were born between Japanese and Zainichi Koreans, all enhanced the diversification of Zainichi Korean identities. This made it difficult to maintain a homogeneous ethnic identity shared among community members. Furthermore, multicultural practices did not succeed in changing Japanese society's essentialized as well as binominal host/guest perception of such diversified multicultural realities.

Yet, the concept of *Kyosei* spread and was welcomed by the mainstream Japanese society. According to Hanazaki, "The term *Kyosei* as a catch-phrase overflowed" in the discourses of journalism and advertising by the mid-1980s. He criticized this tendency as follows. "The trend involved the circulation of the image of *Kyosei* to give an aesthetic nuance to commodities, and therefore it was disconnected from the bitter side of *Kyosei* such as contradictions in reality and the struggles of people on the sites of everyday life" (Hanazaki 2002: 132). Furthermore, Kim Tae-young pointed out that the term *Kyosei* was used in responding to the demands of industry and financial circles, due to globalization, to increase the numbers of foreign laborers from the late 1980s, and also that it had become disconnected from "nature" in the process. The term *Kyosei*, detached from its original inspirations concerning respect for nature and reflexive modernization, became a key component of official multicultural policy by the mid-2000s.

THE KOREAN WAVE AND "NEW ZAINICHI"

Under the conditions of globalization, social movements and collaborations between the people and government are forced to transform from welfare state-oriented redistribution politics to a neoliberal market-oriented politics. While the term *Kyosei* spread through society as a result of the official multicultural policy, Zainichi Korean ethnic communities in urban areas are eroding, and the identities of the younger generations are more diversified than ever. In particular, soft power strategies in the post–Cold War era in the Northeast Asian region have had a great impact on the identities of young Zainichi Koreans, as well as on mainstream Japanese society's perceptions of them, through ethnic imagery in consumer culture.

Under Kim Dae-jung's Sunshine policy and changes in South Korean policy toward Japan, the Hollywood-styled blockbuster movie *Shuri* was screened at 150 movie theaters all over Japan in 1998 (Kwon 2010: 71–72). The popularity of this film in Japan also had positive impacts on Zainichi Koreans in Japan. For example, Emi Kaneda, a third-generation Zainichi Korean born in 1974, who uses her Japanese name *Tsumei*[2] rather than her real ethnic name in everyday life, mentioned that she was not interested in

Korea and did not have a positive image of it. I interviewed her amid the Korean Wave in the autumn of 2003. According to her, having watched the film at a movie theater, she started to become interested in Korea, and later traveled to South Korea for the first time. For people like her, or most of the Zainichi Korean young generations who were brought up in suburbs and with few Zainichi Korean acquaintances except for relatives, the film provided an encounter with some ethnic background.

Around the same time, in 2002, South Korea and Japan cohosted the Football World Cup, and the Korean TV drama series *Winter Sonata* enjoyed tremendous popularity in Japan in 2003. A Korean Wave changed the landscapes of urban ethnic consuming cultures. Korean towns such as Tsuruhashi and Shin-Okubo became thronged with fans of Korean dramas and cultures. The regional city Okayama, where I have engaged in fieldwork for more than 10 years, was no exception. Restaurants owned by Zainichi Koreans who used to hide or hesitate to reveal ethnic imagery in public started to display ethnic imagery by, for example, using roman lettering to say "Korean BBQ" in their advertising displays, and Korean ethnic images were openly and proudly shown. This trend also made Japanese people into Korea-lovers. I met several Japanese women in their 30s and 40s who started to attend Korean language classes held at Zainichi Korean ethnic organizations such as *Mindan* (an association of Korean Residents in Japan, affiliated with the South Korean government). They often traveled to South Korea, went to bars and restaurants owned by Zainichi Koreans, and become close friends with them.

The Korean Wave provided a sense of coevalness among Zainichi Koreans and Japanese fans through consumption, and it led to the perception that the "time lag" between the two countries was resolved and had engendered an "equal" relationship between them. This kind of perception also influenced the representations of young Zainichi Koreans in the Japanese media. For example, one Australian female journalist depicted the younger generations of Zainichi Koreans in a Japanese magazine as follows.

> New Zainichi Koreans are wealthy and have not experienced so much discrimination. On the other hand, young generations of Japanese people have started to think being different from others is rather cool. New Zainichi Koreans maintain their ethnic names, learning Korean languages, and revive disappearing Zainichi Korean cultures even though they acquired Japanese nationality and are married to Japanese. (*Newsweek Japan* 2003: 18–25)

This chapter represents young Zainichi Koreans as cool youth who have not experienced collective discriminatory practices against the Zainichi communities created after World War II and who are economically independent. Furthermore, they are not fettered by any essentialized homogeneous identity created through identity politics by the old generations, and so they have flexible and diversified ethnic identities.

Indeed, most of her argument seems not to be very different from the realities of young Zainichi Koreans whom I had interviewed. One answer in my interviews with young Zainichi Koreans that shocked me was, "I don't have much experience of being discriminated against." Some of them started to confront their ethnic backgrounds after they began to study at universities and language schools in South Korea, and I got the impression that they are helping to support the sense of coevalness between Japan and Korea. In fact, through interacting with them, I felt very positive regarding the future of multicultural environments of Japanese society. While they were brought up in very individualized conditions and with no Zainichi Korean acquaintances except their relatives, unlike their parents' generation, they fluently speak Korean.

However, I also had an uncomfortable feeling regarding this sense of coevalness, for these representations of young Zainichi Koreans identities are so individualized. There also seems to be some sort of discontinuity between their representations of identity, which doesn't clearly intersect with the civil multicultural practices of Zainichi Koreans, which led to the development of official multicultural policy. This is because of the fact that young Zainichi Koreans are relatively economically independent, and have not experienced severe racial discrimination heavily, owing to the very identity politics conducted by earlier generations after the 1970s. Thus, the individualized and cool representations of Zainichi Korean identities are disconnected from the former ethnic identities. Furthermore, they also conceal the fact that racial discrimination against Zainichi Koreans continues to exist in different forms. The representations of individualized Zainichi Korean identities imply that the discriminatory practices against them continues on an individual basis in invisible manner, and that such discriminatory practices are considered individual problems rather than social problems. In fact, once I interviewed them in detail, it turned out that those young Zainichi Koreans whom I have interviewed and answered that they have no experience of being discriminated against, have actually experienced discrimination such as in the process of job hunting and marriages with Japanese. My sense of discomfort concerning this sense of coevalness that became gradually visible through the media and consumer society by the mid-2000s, strengthened, as extremely Zainichi-phobic discourse and imagery spread to both streets and cyberspaces.

BACKLASH AND HATE SPEECH

At the same time that *Shuri* was being screened at movie theaters all over Japan, there were controversies over historical perceptions of East Asia and World War II, including Japan-Korea relations, especially as they were described in history textbooks. The collapse of the Cold War structure and globalization accelerated the sense of crisis of Japanese society, stuck in what was described as a "lost decade." The Japanese Society for History Textbook Reform[3] claimed that historical narratives concerning comfort women and the Nanjing massacre constituted a masochistic view of history that needed to be overcome, by creating a history textbook that Japanese could be proud of. Among members of that society, besides academic researchers and critics, there was a popular cartoon artist named Kobayashi Yoshinori, who played an important role in spreading such nationalistic discourse to a wider audience. Furthermore, the former Japanese prime minister Koizumi's visit to North Korea and their confession that they had engaged in kidnapping Japanese citizens led to North Korea bashing in the media. The bashing also targeted Zainichi Koreans who are assumed to be associated with the North Korean government, such as the North Korean–affiliated ethnic association *Chosen Soren* (General Association of Korean Residents in Japan), credit unions, and students at Korean ethnic schools (Wakate Bengoshi no Kai 2003). Somewhat parallel to the case of *hwagyo* in South Korea that Shin discusses in Chapter 10, these phobic sentiments developed further by linking up with a backlash against ethnic minority groups and majority fears were directed against North Korea and associated bodies.

A cartoon titled *Manga Ken Kanryu* (Manga Anti-Korean Wave) by Yamano Sharin[4] published in 2005 directed these phobic sentiments against entire bodies of Zainichi Koreans in Japan. Yamano was very much influenced by Kobayashi Yoshinori. As well as making a clear phobic statement against the Korean Wave as indicated by the title, the message and logic of this comic book is the "pop" version of conventional conservative discourse. Since the mid-2000s, the images and discourses propagated by Kobayashi and Yamano spread to cyberspace, in particular through bulletin boards, and created cultures of so-called *Netto Uyoku* (Internet Right-Wingers).[5] Eventually, the phobic cultures on the cyberspace developed into hate speech and demonstrations by grassroots conservative groups on the streets.

The most influential group among these grassroots conservative groups is *Zainichi tokken o yurusanai shimin no kai* (Association of Citizens against the Zainichi Special Privileges) or *Zaitokukai* established in 2007. This group is rather different in nature from conventional civic groups, and it is more like an offline community in its nature. The group is led by Sakurai Makoto (Kimura Makoto) born in 1972, and there are 34 branches all over Japan with 11,181 members and 270 overseas members (Yasuda 2012). The core claim of this group is that Zainichi Koreans have more privileges than ordinary Japanese and other foreign residents, and therefore this is unfair. They practice phobic demonstrations in urban ethnic communities such as Tsuruhashi and Shin-Okubo, and Korean ethnic schools as well as advertising their performances on YouTube and other media. One member is a 14-year-old junior high school student. She demonstrated at Tsuruhashi and shouted as follows. "We will commence the massacre of Tsuruhashi, just like the Massacre of Nanjing before it." These phobic expressions are identical to the ones spread on conservative web bulletin boards. Violent and phobic phrases which they repeatedly use are mixtures of colonial discriminatory words and phobic words such as *Futei Senjin* (Criminal Koreans), *Gokiburi* (Cockroach), *Korosu* (We'll kill you), and so forth.

Yasuda Koichi, a journalist who intensively interviewed members of this group including the leader Sakurai, explains that the factors of their expressions of hatred are deeply related to the increasing sense of fear in Japanese society (Yasuda 2002). As Ghassan Hage once mentioned in the Australian context, they are "refugees of the interior" who cannot adjust to the globalizing and neoliberal world, and who express their resulting anxiety against ethnic minorities in a phobic manner (Hage 2003). However, minority phobia cannot be simply explained as a phenomenon involving only the 'losers' of the globalizing era. For example, Higuchi Nato, who also interviewed members of *Zaitokukai* for his sociological survey, argues that many of members of the group work full-time and hold university diplomas (Higuchi 2014). All the same, as Yasuda states, the members of this group tend to feel isolated from society and that they are "not doing well" in many ways.

It is symbolic that these exclusive practices and phenomena spread in Japanese society simultaneously with the official multicultural policy after the mid-2000s. It is also important to note that the spread of phobic discourse against Zainichi Koreans from cyberspaces to the streets is related to the globalized designs of urban security. Order-keeping in most Japanese urban areas began to draw on broken windows theory after the 2000s, and 'zero-tolerance' environments were created. This theory was firstly advocated by psychologist Philip Zimbardo in 1970 and reshaped into a theoretical framework for criminal sociology by Wilson and Kelling in 1982. With the reputed success of a 'zero-tolerance' policy in New York City in the 1990s, this theory was advertised by the American think-tank, the Manhattans Institute by the mid-1990s and spread to Europe, South America, and Japan (Wacquant 1999).

The point here is that broken window theory intensively focuses on creating an environment, which would not allow any crimes to occur, in particular minor crimes. It shows little concern in the social and historical backgrounds of potential criminals. Its rise meant the decline of the welfare state-oriented ideas about rehabilitating criminals, as environments became managed so as not to allow crimes to occur. As a result, demonized outsiders in urban spaces, from *Yakuza* to homeless people, were excluded from the public. It is this 'zero-tolerance' space that enables *Zaitokukai* to perform their phobic demonstrations (Kawabata 2016). Thus, while the local branding of cities and places become prevalent in global urban spaces, including most Northeast Asian cities, the diversifications of people's social and historical implications are becoming more invisible in public. In fact, the majority of Zainichi Koreans today have left the target areas of *Zaitokukai*, the former ethnic enclaves and community of Zainichi Koreans such as Korean towns and ethnic schools, and many of them are brought up in suburban areas under the individualized conditions. In order for us to reimagine these diversified as well as hybrid multicultural realities of contemporary Japan, this chapter next focuses on multicultural practices of Zainichi Koreans in their everyday lives, which are not targeted by the official multicultural policy nor represented in the philiac/ phobic representations of young generations.

MULTICULTURAL PRACTICES IN EVERYDAY LIFE

The urban ethnic communities of Zainichi Koreans are breaking down, and many of the young generations live under individualized conditions in suburbia (Kawabata 2013). Furthermore, most Zainichi Koreans today marry with Japanese, and those who get married to Japanese became a majority by the 1980s. It has been 30 years since then. From this perspective, those young generations born after the 1980s naturally have dual ethnic identities, both Japanese and Korean. A majority of them acquired Japanese nationality, in particular after the reform of Nationality Act in 1985.[6] In addition, more than 10,000 Zainichi Koreans acquired Japanese nationality annually by the mid-2000s. Given these trends, the numerically largest minority group of postwar Japan has been clearly shrinking in a statistical sense. This trend leads us to the question of where those invisible Zainichi Koreans went. To answer this question would illuminate the 'ordinary' as well as hybrid multicultural practices in everyday life, which are hidden by cosmetic multiculturalism (Morris-Suzuki 2002), and the awkward combination of official multicultural policy and ethnic consumption.

Unlike 'new' Zainichi Koreans "who maintain their ethnic names, learn Korean languages, and revive disappearing Zainichi Korean cultures even though they acquired Japanese nationality and married to Japanese," most Zainichi Koreans still use their Japanese adopted names rather their ethnic names. For example, Yamamoto Harue (South Korean nationality, born in 1974) is a third-generation Zainichi Korean, and she says that she is Zainichi Korean only to "a person that I can trust." In particular, she became very careful about informing others of her ethnic background after her early 20s, when her boyfriend's parents opposed their marriage. Since then, she did not tell her nationality to any new boyfriends if she felt "it would not last too long." Like Harue, many Zainichi Koreans brought up in the individualized environment maintain their ethnic identity in various strategic ways.

As mentioned above, the majority of young Zainichi Koreans are born between Japanese and Korean parents. In fact, I have met many of them through interviews. Based on 2010 statistical data from the Ministry of Health, Labor, and Welfare, 4,631 children were born from Japanese and Korean couples, while 1,194 were born from solely Korean couples. Some of them identify themselves as *"daburu"* or double, instead of using stigmatized term *"half."* As Horiguchi and Imoto argue, while this term has been "a platform for raising the voices of the parents" and "has not been used by the children themselves as a self-identifying label" such as in the case of Amerasian (see Horiguchi and Imoto's chapter), the term is strategically used to reveal ethnic identities for some *daburu* Zainichi Koreans in order to differentiate themselves from other Zainichi Koreans in their everyday lives. For example, Takanori (South Korean nationality, born in 1983) was born of a father who is a second-generation Zainichi Korean from Osaka and a Japanese mother born in Hiroshima. His case is rather unusual in terms of nationality, as most children in his position usually choose Japanese nationality. Having graduated from junior high school in Takarazuka, Hyogo Prefecture, Takanori decided to study in South Korea. He received a high school and college education in South Korea. After graduation from college, he decided to go back to Japan, since he had to do military service if he remained in Korea. Having returned to Japan, he started to be actively involved in Zainichi Korean youth organizations, and he became an executive member of the Korean Youth Association affiliated with Mindan. Since then, he started to identify himself as *daburu* in order to reveal his difference from a monolithic understanding of ethnic identity. While he is discriminated against as "a Korean" in the Japanese community, he is often discriminated against as "a Japanese" in the Zainichi Korean community. One member of the Korean Youth Association one day told him "I hate *daburu*." Takanori stopped using his last name when he became 20. Only his given name is printed on the business card that he gave me. Using a Korean name makes him feel that "I have to give up my Japanese identity." By not using his last name in public, he maintain his hybrid identities, and avoids binominal essentialism between Japanese and Korean.

When we focus on multicultural practices in the everyday lives of Zainichi Koreans like Takanori and Harue, the realities and identities of young Zainichi Koreans are more diversified and hybrid, and less sensational than and even 'banal' compared to the images created through the media. Perhaps, it is even less sensational or banal compared to the former ethnic identities constructed by identity politics, activists, academic researchers and so forth. When we critically look at globalized cosmetic multiculturalism and its associated governmental policies, including Japanese multicultural policy, those banal everyday practices are starting points to reimagine what is seriously multicultural.

REIMAGINING WHAT IS MULTICULTURAL SERIOUSLY

This chapter has critically examined discontinuities between official multi-cultural policy under globalization and the rise of neoliberalism and multi-cultural practices embraced in the urban ethnic communities at the grassroots level. Due to historical discontinuities, official policy ended up ignoring Zainichi Koreans who actually played crucial roles in forging multicultural conditions in postwar Japan. Such perceptions embedded in historical discontinuities are also reflected in the representations of young Zainichi Koreans in Japanese society.

While the urban ethnic communities are breaking down, more Zainichi Koreans today marry with Japanese and acquire Japanese nationality, so that their ethnic identities are diversified more than ever, as well as becoming invisible, in particular in the statistical sense. Under these individualized conditions, ahistorical representations of Zainichi Koreans such as 'new' Zainichi are spread by and consumed through the media. The positive flows of the Korean Wave invoke a positive and strong subjectivity of the young generation, while the colonial discriminatory discourses are reproduced in very violent form such as by the hate demonstrations on both streets and cyberspaces.

However, these philiac/phobic representations of Zainichi Koreans are dissociated from the diversified and hybrid identities of young generations today. As I have pointed out, these media representations actually make their identities invisible. Being brought up in urban suburbs under individualized conditions, young Zainichi Koreans maintain their ethnic identities through banal yet hybrid everyday practices. Their ethnic identities would not disappear even if they acquired Japanese nationality. As *daburu* Zainichi Koreans like Takanori maintain, their ethnic identities lie between Japaneseness and Koreanness, and their existences embody the diversified multicultural conditions of contemporary Japanese society, where more than two ethnicities and cultures intersect with each other. While the official multicultural policy essentializes binominal confrontations and harmonization of host and guest, the everyday practice of *daburu* Zainichi Koreans illuminates the development of multicultural conditions through the intersections of host and guest. In this sense, their everyday practices are the frontier of multicultural society in Japan, which has been obscured in governmental and media images of multiculturalism.

To end, I would like to repeat and summarize two crucial problems regarding official multicultural policy in Japan. First, it is discontinuous with history as well as with local communities. Second, it is dissociated from the very realities at the frontiers of multicultural conditions in Japan. I would argue that the official policy is based on the national ideology of social assimilation aimed at adjusting to the globalizing world, rather than on any attempt to respect and appreciate differences between and within societies. Despite the governmental attempts of multicultural society, the fact that the hate demonstrations are allowed in Japanese society clearly shows that these two seemingly confronting ideologies and practices are partially complementary to each other. In order to reimagine what is seriously multicultural in Japanese society today, we must critically question the national time and space of multicultural policy by articulating it with the hybrid everyday practices of people living in both love and hate. In that sense, it would be civil groups to inherit assets from forerunners of multicultural practices on grassroots level, and constantly question and alter official multicultural policies in Japan.

NOTES

1. The number of foreign residents in Japan has doubled in the past two decades, from 984,455 in 1990 to 2,066,445 in 2013.
2. *Tsumei* is a legacy of Japan's colonialism and its policy of assimilating Koreans through *Soshi Kaimei* and the enforced adoption of Japanese surnames and forenames toward the end of World War II. Having formally not been allowed to use their ethnic names in public, many young Zainichi Koreans today still strategically use Japanese names in order to not stand out at schools, workplaces, residential areas, and on public occasions.
3. The Japanese Society for History Textbook Reform was established in 1997, led by Fujioka Nobukatsu, Nishio Kanji, and other conservative scholars, critiques, and celebrities.
4. Yamano Sharin is a Japanese male manga artist born in 1971. According to Yasuda Koichi, who interviewed Yamano, he was very much influenced by Kobayashi Yoshinori and confessed to him that he created the manga because he had strong anxiety about and fear of Zainichi Koreans.
5. Netto Uyoku refers to Japanese online right-wingers. They use the Internet as a medium to express nationalistic and often racist views on modern Japanese identity and history.
6. The most important change of this act in 1985 was the replacement of two principles, one of matrilineality for the offspring of unmarried Japanese women and the other of patrilineality for all offspring of Japanese men and of married Japanese women, with the single principle of ambilineality for all offspring of Japanese nationals. As a result, most children born between Japanese and Zainichi Koreans who intend to live in Japan permanently decided to choose Japanese nationality.

REFERENCES

Hage, Ghassan. 2003. *Against Paranoid Nationalism: Searching for Hope in a Shrinking Society*. London: Pluto Press.
Hanazaki, Kohei. 1993. *Identitii to kyōsei no tetsugaku [Identity and the philosophy of co-living]*. Tokyo: Misuzu Shobo.
Hanazaki, Kohei. 2002. *Kyōsei e no shokuhatsu: Datsu shokuminichi, tabunka, rinri wo megutte [Inspirations for co-living: On decolonization, multicultures, and ethics]*. Tokyo: Mizuzu Shobo.

Higuchi, Naoto. 2014. *Nihon gata haigai shugi: Zaitokukai, Gaikokujin sanseiken, Higashi Azia chiseigaku [Japanese-style xenophobia: Citizens against the Special Zainichi Privileges, the foreign residents' franchise, and Geopolitics in East Asia].* Nagoya: Nagoya University Press.

Kawabata, Kohei. 2013. *Jimoto o aruku: Mijikana sekai no esunogurafii [Walking my hometown: Ethnography of everyday life].* Tokyo: Ochanomizu Shobo.

Kawabata, Kohei. 2016. "Hamā taun no yaroudomo wa doko he ittanoka? [Where did the boys of Hammer Town go?]," in *Dekigoto kara manabu karuchuraru sutadizu [Learning cultural studies from case studies],* edited by Yamamoto, Atsuhisa. Kyoto: Nakanishiya Shuppan.

Kim, Tae-young. 1999. *Aidentiti poritikusu wo koete: Zainichi chōsenjin no esunishitii [Beyond identity politics: the Ethnicity of Zainichi Koreans].* Kyoto: Sekai Shisosha.

Kōsei roudōshō daijin kanbou toukei jōhōbu [Ministry of Health, Labor, and Welfare]. 2010. *Jinkō dōtai toukei* [Population trends statistics].

Kwon, Yongseok. 2010. *Hanryū to nichiryū: Bunka kara yomitoku nikkan shinjidai [Korean wave and Japan wave: Understanding the new Japan-South Korea relations from culture].* Tokyo: NHK Shuppan.

Morris-Suzuki, Tessa. 2002. *Hihanteki sōzōryoku no tameni [For a critical imagination],* Tokyo: Heibonsha.

Newsweek Japan, Nov. 26th 2003, Hankyu Communication.

Shiobara, Yoshikazu. 2010. "Rentai to shiteno tabunka kyōsei wa kanouka? [Is a multicultural policy of solidarity possible?]," in *Tabunka shakai no bunka o tou: Kyōsei, comyunitii, media, [Inquiring into the 'culture' of multicultural society: Coexistence, community, and media],* edited by Iwabuchi, Koichi. Tokyo: Seikyusha.

Takezawa, Yasuko. 2011. "Imin kenkyū kara tabunka kyōsei o kangaeru [Regarding the multiculturalism from the migration studies]," in *Imin kenkyū to tabunka kyōsei [Migration Studies and Multiculturalism],* edited by Japan Association for Migration Policy Studies, 1–17. Tokyo: Ochanomizu Shobo.

Waquant, Loïc. 1999. *Les Prisons de la Misère,* Paris: Éditions Raisons d'Agir.

Wilson, James, Q. and Kelling, George, 1982. "Broken Windows: The Police and Neighborhood Safety," in *Atlantic Monthly,* March 1982, pp. 29–37.

Yamano, Sharin. 2005. *Manga Ken kanryū [Manga Anti-Korean Wave].* Tokyo: Fuyusha.

Yasuda, Koichi. 2012. *Netto to aikoku: Zaitokukai no yami o oikakete [Internet and Patriotism: Illuminating the Darkness of the 'Citizens against Zainichi Special Privileges'].* Tokyo: Kodansha.

Zainichi korian no kodomotachi ni taisuru iyagarase o yurusanai wakate bengoshi no kai eds., [The young lawyers' association against the discrimination toward children of Zainichi Koreans]. 2003. *Zainichi korian no kodomotachi ni taisuru iyagarasejitsutai chōsa houkokusho [Survey report on actual discrimination against Zainichi Korean children].*

Zimbardo, Phillip, G. 1970. "The Human Choice: Individuation, Reason, and other versus Deindividuation, Impulse and Chaos," in *1969 Nebraska Symposium on Motivation,* edited by W. J. Arnold and D. Levine, 237–307. Lincoln: University of Nebraska Press.

Index

Act on the Treatment of Foreigners in
    Korea, 23, 29
aging population in East Asia, 1, 3, 5,
    24, 56, 129
Amerasian, 173–75
Anti-Korean Wave, 227–30
Association of Citizens against the
    Zainchi Special Privileges,
    228–29
Association of Korean Residents in
    Japan (*Mindan*), 113, 226, 231
Austronesian, 203, 207, 216

backlash, 15, 22, 197, 204, 213, 222,
    227–30
Broken windows theory, 229

citizenship:
    cultural, 39, 66, 190, 191;
    economic, 191;
    and localities in Japan, 60, 62;
    and military service, 131;
    mono-ethnic notion of, *jus sanguinis*,
        3, 6, 7–8, 13, 30, 62, 64–65,
        128, 135, 141, 142, 189;
    multicultural, 7–10, 49, 142–44, 146;
    national, 7, 10, 12, 33, 38, 42, 60, 61,
        62, 63, 65, 88, 95, 96, 99, 171,
        173, 186.

See also politics of representation
    postnational, 7;
    second-class, 96–97;
    urban, 64.
    See also politics of presence
Cold War, the, 189
comfort women, 228
Constitution of the Republic of China
        (Taiwan), 85, 87, 92, 95, 96,
        99, 101;
    constitutional court, 92, 96, 97, 99;
    Due Process, 85, 89, 91, 92, 99, 101
Council of Cultural Affair (CCA or the
        Ministry of Culture), 40, 45
Council of Indigenous People (CIP), 37,
        40, 42, 208, 209, 210
Council of Labor Affairs (CLA), 40
Cross-Strait Relations Act, 88

declining birthrate in East Asia, 1, 3, 6,
        26, 56, 58, 128, 133
Democratic Progressive Party (DPP), 39
deportation, 89–92, 100
detention, 89, 91, 99, 101
discrimination:
    institutional, 134;
    against marital immigrants, 96;
    national origin, 96, 97;
    racial, 87, 96, 99;

About the Contributors

Ji-Hyun Ahn is an Assistant Professor of Global Media Studies at University of Washington Tacoma where she teaches courses on media globalization, global TV format, and Asian media culture. Her research interests include racialized desire in East Asian popular culture and Asian multiculturalism, and her most recent works have been published in Media, Culture & Society, Cultural Studies, and Asian Ethnicity. She is currently working on a book project that examines mixed-race politics in contemporary South Korean TV.

Sachiko Horiguchi is an Assistant Professor of Anthropology at Temple University, Japan Campus in Tokyo. She is a social/ medical anthropologist with a D.Phil. in Social Anthropology from the University of Oxford (2006). Her research interests lie in mental health and diversity in Japan, and her major publications include *Foreign Language Education in Japan: Exploring Qualitative Approaches* (Sense Publishers 2015, co-edited with Yuki Imoto and Gregory S. Poole).

Hsiao-Chuan Hsia is Professor and Director at the Graduate Institute for Social Transformation Studies, Shih Hsin University, Taiwan. Her publications analyze issues of marriage migrants, migrant workers, citizenship, empowerment and social movement. Hsia is also an activist striving for the empowerment of immigrant women and the making of im/migrant movement in Taiwan. She also serves as officers of various regional and international network and alliance for the rights of immigrants and migrants.

Yuki Imoto is an Assistant Professor at Keio University where she teaches anthropology, sociology and academic English. Her main research interests are in education, transnational identity and Japanese Studies. Her book publications include: *A Sociology of Japanese Youth: From Returnees to NEETs* (2011) co-edited with Roger Goodman and Tuukka Toivonen, and *Foreign Language Education in Japan: Exploring Qualitative Approaches* (2015) co-edited with Sachiko Horiguchi and Gregory Poole.

Koichi Iwabuchi is Professor of Media and Cultural Studies at Monash University and Director of the Monash Asia Institute. His main research concern is cultural globalization and transnationalism, trans-Asian cultural flows and connections and multiculturalism and cultural diversity in East Asia. He is the author of *Recentering Globalization: Popular Culture and Japanese Transnationalism* and *Resilient Borders and Cultural Diversity: Internationalism, Brand Nationalism and Multiculturalism in Japan.*

Hyesil Jung is currently a PhD candidate of Cultural Anthropology, Hanyang University, South Korea. Her research interests include gender, racism and multiculturalism. She has been NGO activist working for migrant human rights issues for long years. She is currently the president of Transnational Asia Women's Network, and the co-president of Dreaming Tree of Multicultural Community. She also serves as the co-president of Migrant World TV which makes a radio and television program and hosts annual Migrant Film Festival in South Korea.

Kohei Kawabata, BA (UCLA), MA (IUJ), PhD (ANU), is an Associate Professor of Faculty of Administration and Social Sciences at Fukushima University, Japan. His research is based on fieldworks and interviews, and has written ethnographies about minority groups in Japan. His current research project is about Zainichi Koreans and their families in Fukushima living under the radioactive contamination after 2011 earthquake disaster.

Yuko Kawai is Professor of Communication in the Department of Intercultural Communication, Rikkyo University, Japan. Her research interests include Japanese cultural nationalism, racism, and multiculturalism. She is particularly interested in critically examining and transforming the dominant idea of Japaneseness. Her most recent work is "Using Diaspora: Orientalism, Japanese Nationalism, and the Japanese Brazilian Diaspora," in *Intercultural Masquerade: New Orientalism, New Occidentalism, Old Exoticism* (Springer: 2016). She is currently editing a book on multiculturalism and intersectionality in Japan.

Hyun Mee Kim is Professor at the Department of Cultural Anthropology and Graduate Program in Culture and Gender Studies, Yonsei University, South Korea. Her research interests include gender and migration, feminist cultural theories, city and human ecology and globalization and labor. She is the author of *Cultural Translation in a Global Era* (2005) and *We Always Leave Home: Becoming Migrants in South Korea* (2014), and co-editor of *Intimate Enemy: How Neoliberalism Has Become Our Everyday Lives* (2010), and We Are All People with Differences: Towards Multiculturalism for Co-existence (2013). She was a Committee Member of the Division of Human Rights for Foreigners, National Human Rights Commission of Korea (2008–2010) and is a member of the Forum on Human Rights for Migrant Women in South Korea.

Daya Dakasi Da-Wei Kuan, a member of the Tayal indigenous group in Taiwan, PhD in geography from the University of Hawaii at Manoa, is currently an Associate Professor in the Department of Ethnology at NCCU, Taiwan. Daya's research interests include: development geography, indigenous land policy, indigenous community mapping, and community-based resource management. He devotes to integrate academic research, teaching and social practice over the indigenous issues. He collaborates with indigenous communities in many traditional territory mapping and community development projects.

Bruce Yuan-Hao Liao is an Associate Professor at National Chengchi University College of Law. His expertise includes constitutional law, administrative law, multiculturalism and law, immigration law and policy, and comparative law. In addition to publishing a great number of influential articles and newspaper articles, he also takes part in various sorts of social movements aiming at the rights of marital immigrants, migrant workers, and other marginalized groups in Taiwan. Professor Liao has been invited to participate in several advisory committees of government body, including the ROC Presidential Office Human Rights Consultative Committee.

Hyunjoon Shin is an Associate Professor in the Institute for East Asian Studies (IEAS) of Sunkonghoe University, South Korea. Having received his PhD from the Department of Economics of Seoul National University with the thesis on the transformation of the Korean music industry in a globalized age, he has carried out researches on popular culture, international migration and urban space in East Asia and beyond.

Li-Jung Wang is Professor in Department of Hakka Language and Social Sciences, National Central University, Taiwan. Dr. Wang's academic interests are ethnic cultural policy, Hakka studies, cultural identity, cultural citizenship, sociology of consumption, transnational community and media uses. Her recent works include: *The Development of Hakka Ethnicity and Cultural Policy in Taiwan* (2012, in Chinese); and *Cultural Rights and Citizenship in Cultural Policy: Taiwan and China*, International Journal of Cultural Policy (AHCI) (2014), *Towards Cultural Citizenship? Cultural Rights and Cultural Policy in Taiwan*, Citizenship Studies (SSCI) (2013).